CW01023963

Ambitious

AND

Anxious

HOW CHINESE COLLEGE STUDENTS
SUCCEED AND STRUGGLE IN
AMERICAN HIGHER EDUCATION

YINGYI MA

Columbia University Press

New York

Columbia University Press
Publishers Since 1893
New York   Chichester, West Sussex
cup.columbia.edu

Copyright © 2020 Columbia University Press
All rights reserved

Library of Congress Cataloging-in-Publication Data
Names: Ma, Yingyi, author.
Title: Ambitious and anxious : how Chinese college students succeed
and struggle in American higher education / Yingyi Ma.
Description: New York : Columbia University Press, [2020] |
Includes bibliographical references and index. |
Identifiers: LCCN 2019032360 (print) | LCCN 2019032361 (ebook) |
ISBN 9780231184588 (cloth) | ISBN 9780231545563 (ebook)
Subjects: LCSH: Chinese students—United States. | Chinese
students—Education (Higher)—United States. | Chinese
students—Education (Secondary)—China. | Foreign study—Social
aspects—United States.
Classification: LCC LB2376.5.C6 M3 2020 (print) | LCC LB2376.5.C6 (ebook) |
DDC 378.1/982691—dc23
LC record available at https://lccn.loc.gov/2019032360
LC ebook record available at https://lccn.loc.gov/2019032361

Columbia University Press books are printed on permanent
and durable acid-free paper.
Printed in the United States of America

Cover image: Jonathan D. Goforth/Getty Images
Cover design: Lisa Hamm

To my parents—
Ningsheng Ma and Fenghua Wang
Whose love is the backbone of my life

Contents

Acknowledgments

I first set foot in the United States almost twenty years ago, right after attaining my bachelor's degree in China. At that time, the only way that I knew for students like me to come to America was through graduate school, fully funded by American higher education.

I started teaching in a private research university around 2006, nestled in a quiet and almost never-changing town in upstate New York. Over time there has been a noticeable influx of Chinese undergraduate students, adding to the town's vitality and sparking a boom in Asian restaurants and grocery stores that cater to them. These students are almost all self-funded. Now, nationwide, the Chinese undergraduate population studying in the United States has exceeded their graduate peers. What accounts for this change is, in no small way, rooted in the rise of China over the past two decades.

This change is what motivated this book: Chinese international students embody a new China, and their experiences in the United States are inextricably linked to their social, cultural, and educational backgrounds in rapidly transforming China.

When I started this project in 2012, American media covered this phenomenon with a strong focus on the wealth of this new generation of Chinese students studying abroad, as if they were uniformly rich. Since the Trump administration came into power, Chinese international students are now under suspicion, often labeled as potential spies. As a result, these students' voices have been silenced and their experiences obscured. The scrutiny has dehumanized them.

It is my hope that this book will provide a more balanced and nuanced portrait of this new wave of Chinese students. They are not the inhabitants of an elite academic preserve, as they used to be; nor are they just failing in or fleeing from the ultra-competitive Chinese education system. They are as diverse academically as they are socioeconomically. They are the sons and daughters of entrepreneurs and engineers, doctors and drivers, professors and programmers. They are the children of a new China, one characterized by a duality of phenomenal ambition and anxiety, and they embody this duality.

This project is my post-tenure labor of love. I owe tremendous gratitude to all the people who helped bring it to fruition. First and foremost, I thank all of the study participants—students in colleges and high schools harboring the aspiration to study in America—and all of the educators involved in international education who devote their careers to the still nascent international education sector in China. I am truly grateful for their generosity and their tremendous trust in this project, as well as their commitment to education.

I am also indebted to the Maxwell School Dean's Office at Syracuse University for naming me the inaugural O'Hanley Faculty Scholar from 2014 to 2017, which provided me with three years of extra research funding. Research projects such as this one are rarely considered a funding priority by American funding agencies, so this financial support was both timely and immensely helpful.

I want to thank my dear colleagues and friends Amy Lutz, Madonna Harrington Meyer, Terry Lautz, and Jerry Miner at Syracuse University's Maxwell School. Our many coffees and lunches not only stimulated my mind, but also spiced up an otherwise bland academic routine. My mentors Lingxin Hao, Karl Alexander, and Andrew Cherlin at Johns Hopkins University not only invited me to return to my alma mater to give a talk about this project in the early stages of research and writing, but also read multiple chapters of the manuscript. Their feedback was both pithy and profound. Dear friends Vivian Louis at Hunter College and Hua-Yu Sebastian Cherng at New York University took precious time to read chapters of this book and give me comments that have significantly improved it as a whole.

Several research assistants along the way were involved in this project. My former graduate student Yue Zhang, who is now blazing her own academic path in child and family studies, was involved in the project from conception to finish. I have no doubt that she will have a stellar academic career ahead. Undergraduate research assistants Ashley Han, Alex You, and others helped update the study's statistics and recruit diverse participants. Their passion and support helped sustain me through the countless hours of work on this book.

Eric Schwartz, the executive editor at Columbia University Press, took the plunge to sign this project when it was not quite yet in shape. The trust and confidence he bestowed on it shines through the final text here. I want to thank associate editor Lowell Frye, production editor Kathryn Jorge, and Cenveo project manager Ben Kolstad for their kind professionalism in the final stages of this project to bring it to completion. I also want to thank my personal editor, Henry Jankiewicz. Henry taught me how to treat writing as a craft and approach it with patience and precision.

I am highly appreciative to anonymous reviewers of the book proposal and the book manuscript. Their critiques and comments have undoubtedly sharpened my focus and crystallized some key themes in the writing of the manuscript. In addition, the Columbia design team is marvelous. The book cover is nothing but amazing: it perfectly reveals the mood and theme of the book in a way that only the eye of an artist could capture.

As a former international student, I too have had a journey punctuated with ambition and anxiety. This journey has been made much easier and even enjoyable by my husband Ying Lin, my companion at every step of the way. He was also once an international student from China. Trained in the natural sciences, he is gifted with intellectual curiosity and incredible insight into social issues. His quick wit and dry humor make me laugh daily. Our many conversations inspire me and lighten our journey together.

Our son—Jayden Ma Lin, now nine years old—saw me working on this book for a majority of his life. I could hardly escape from the "working-mom syndrome" of guilt and self-doubt, since much of my time was consumed with this book rather than with him, until one day he gave me a pleasant surprise. He had also started writing a book—a little notebook comprising cartoons he drew and a few words he could spell out for the storyline. At that moment, he was just starting second grade and was poised to be a budding writer. He even seriously proposed we have a race: "Mommy, let's have a race and see who can write more books." I laughed hysterically. I am so gratified to see that the writing of this book has had some positive influence on him.

My dear parents, tens of thousands of miles away, are the ultimate anchor for me. Quite ordinary socioeconomically, they are truly among the most extraordinary parents of their generation in China. They respect my voice and choices, and rarely do they even try to make me into a person I am not. Their attitude towards life—laughing constantly and self-deprecating occasionally—grounds me both at home and in the world. Although we are far apart physically, I can feel their love each and every day. Their support is the backbone of my life. For that, I am eternally grateful and thus I dedicate this book to them.

Ambitious and Anxious

CHAPTER 1

Ambitious and Anxious

CHINESE UNDERGRADUATES
IN THE UNITED STATES

I plan to attend the no. 1 fashion school in Central Saint Martins in London for my graduate school, after completing my BA here at Parsons. Then I hope I can work for one to two years as a fashion designer for brands like Vera Wang. Then I plan to return to China to develop my own brand. But I am uncertain whether I can make it.

—Joy, a fashion design major at the Parsons School of Design in New York City

I do not even know the exact amount of money I have spent to study and live here. My parents always comforted me and said not to worry. We don't talk about it. I know that they also expect me to get a good job with high pay. So I study accounting here, hoping to get a job. I am often uncertain whether studying here is worth it.

—Samantha, an accounting major at the Indiana University at Bloomington

Joy and Samantha are both members of a new wave of undergraduate students from China who are almost all self-funded, studying at American colleges and universities. Joy, a native of Shanghai, arrived as a high school student in 2010 and spent three years in a private boarding school in the Boston area before enrolling as a fashion design major at Parsons School of Design in New York City. As one of the earliest among the fast-growing number of Chinese students in American secondary schools, she was able to escape the ultracompetitive Chinese education system and avoid its intensive, test-oriented high school education primed for the college entrance examination in China (*Gaokao* hereafter). Three years in a private boarding school plus four years in an elite private college in America costs close to half a million dollars, tuition and living expenses included. But Joy comes from a well-heeled family—both of her parents are successful entrepreneurs in Shanghai. They are college graduates who set up their own textile business and reaped the benefits of China's open market since the reforms initiated in the late 1970s.

Samantha's route to the United States was quite different; she was a sophomore in her hometown college in Guangzhou in South China, and she came as an exchange student to the University of California (UC) at Riverside in 2012. She completed the stressful Chinese Gaokao and enrolled in a highly selective, albeit a second-tier, college in China. Her journey to America was made possible under the auspices of international partnerships between higher education institutions in China and the United States, which have mushroomed in recent years.[1] Samantha transferred from UC Riverside to Indiana University Bloomington as a full-time student majoring in accounting. The cost of her education in the United States was much lower than Joy's, as she attended universities in China for her first two years at less than $1,000 per year, even though she had to pay out-of-state tuition to attend IU Bloomington.[2] Samantha's family is an ordinary one; her mother does not work and her father owns a small business. Her father works a second job driving Didi—the Chinese version of Uber—at night to supplement their income. Neither of her parents went to college, so she is a first-generation college student. She intends to begin her career right after graduation to pay her parents back for their investment in her education. As an accounting major, she can expect a higher starting salary in the United States than in China, so she wants to stay in the United States. She is, however, unsure whether she can secure a work visa in an increasingly restrictive immigration environment in the United States.

PRIVILEGED BUT DIVERSE

American colleges and universities bear witness to the staggering growth of international undergraduates from China over the past decade. These Chinese undergraduates are driving the expansion of international student enrollment in America. On the national level, from 2005 to 2015, undergraduate enrollment from China rose from 9,304 to a staggering 135,629, a more than tenfold increase (see figure 1.1). Despite the Trump administration's

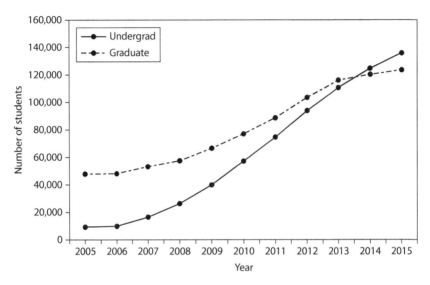

FIGURE 1.1 Number of Chinese undergraduate students versus graduate students in the United States, 2005–2015

Source: Institute of International Education

chilly immigration policy, Chinese student enrollment increased by 6.8 percent during the 2016–2017 academic year.[3] In the context of the decline of overall international student enrollments during 2017–2018, Chinese undergraduate student enrollments still grew by 4 percent, and graduate student enrollments grew by 2 percent. During the academic year 2017–2018, there were 148,593 undergraduates from China studying in the American higher education system.[4]

These developments have given rise to major headlines in the media, such as "China's Rich Kids Head West," published in the *New Yorker* in 2016.[5] Articles like this fail to capture the stories of many students like Samantha, students from ordinary families in China whose parents—and even extended family members—have scrambled to pool resources to pay for an overseas education. This book examines a diverse set of Chinese students with different family backgrounds, traveling along distinct educational trajectories. The vast majority of Chinese international undergraduates in the United States are paying full tuition; so in general they are from more well-off families than the average student in China. However, it is misguided to assume that they are uniformly rich. Some are like Joy, beginning their education in the United States as high school students; some are like Samantha, starting college in China and then transferring to the United States, substantially reducing the economic burden on their parents. Their parents' educational backgrounds and occupations also differ considerably. Some parents are self-made, small business owners who never attended college, let alone studied abroad, and may not know English at all. Other parents are college educated, or even have an advanced degree, and are members of China's economic and educated elite.

This generation of Chinese students consists almost entirely of singletons, the progeny of China's one-child policy, which was changed to allow families to have two children starting January 1, 2016.[6] As the only hope of these families, these children bear immense pressure and high expectations from their parents,[7] which often lead to a laser-like focus on investing in their child's education.[8] However, the high expectations of these parents fall short in the face of the ultracompetitive education system in China and the lack of choices among the world-class universities there. According to the *Times Higher Education* world university rankings, only two Chinese universities are among the top 100 universities in the world; almost half are located in the United States.[9] In this context, parents in China are seeking education abroad for their children as an exit strategy—to escape from the ultra-competitive Chinese schooling and to buoy their child's chances to access quality higher education in the United States. Parents with varying resources invest in their children's educations to the best of their capability. Some parents borrow money from relatives and friends, some sell their apartments, and some work multiple jobs to cover the cost of their child studying in America.

Once, during my office hours with an American student, when I told her about this book project on Chinese students, she immediately asked, her face shining with curiosity, "Can you tell me why Chinese students want to work in our dining halls? Aren't they all wealthy?" She added that she worked on-campus part-time as a dining hall supervisor, and she was perplexed by the increasing number of job applications from Chinese students. I replied: "They are not all wealthy." The student was incredulous. "Really?! But why are they all working in the dining halls?" I brought this question to Samantha. She said, "The dining hall jobs are the jobs that we can apply to. We are not allowed to work off-campus. Many on-campus jobs, such as work-study opportunities, are closed to us." Indeed, my visit to IU Bloomington, where Samantha studied, happened to be during the school's fall break. The dining hall workers were almost all Chinese students, because most of the American student workers had gone home for the break. As a matter of fact, the survey in this book shows that a third of the participants worked for pay on campus, and a quarter of them worked more than ten hours a week to defray the cost of living abroad.

The aim of this book is to present a diverse picture of Chinese international undergraduate students in the United States, paying particular attention to how their family backgrounds influence their heterogeneous educational trajectories and experiences.

AMBITIOUS AND ANXIOUS

Despite their heterogeneity, what most Chinese students studying abroad share in common is that they are both ambitious and anxious. Joy is realizing her dream of studying at Parsons, and next she aspires to study at the Saint Martin School of Art in London because, according to her, that is "the best in the world." She has set her career goal on developing her own fashion brand in China. As an exchange student at UC Riverside, Samantha likes her college education in the United States. There she feels she can make many choices, from selecting her major to transferring colleges, whereas in China it is unlikely that she could have changed majors, much less schools, due to the rigid regulation in Chinese higher education that discourages the mobility of college students.[10] At Riverside, Samantha immediately took action to apply to a higher-ranking school and got accepted to IU Bloomington. "The accounting program is ranked eighth in the nation," Samantha beamed. She had quickly moved from a second-tier Chinese university to a top-tier program in America.

While pursuing their college ambitions, both Joy and Samantha struggle academically and socially. Academically, they were excited about, but unfamiliar with, the dynamic American classroom where student-led discussions are often expected. They know they need to speak up more but are frustrated that they simply can't. They are worried that their relative reticence in class could negatively affect their grades. They are at a loss for why they are not able to speak up, because they perceive that their English is strong.

There seems to be a confluence of cultural and social barriers that inhibit them from participating as freely as their American peers. To cope with this, they try to work extra hard to compensate for the potential loss of credit due to the participation gap.

Socially, both Joy and Samantha have few close American friends, and they feel that it is hard to mingle with Americans. Prior to their study in America, both imagined Americans to be warm and gregarious—at least as perceived from American TV shows, such as *Friends* and *Sex and the City*, that they watched in China. The contrasts between their expectations and reality are glaring and hurtful: they both tried to make American friends—to no avail—and ended up hanging out with their Chinese friends. Their social and cultural marginality on the often white-dominated U.S. college campus is palpably disappointing to them.

In addition to academic and social struggles, both Joy and Samantha are indebted to their parents and uncertain about their futures: they worry whether they can be successful and make enough money so that their parents' investment in their education will pay off. As Samantha puts it, "I would feel awful and anxious if I could not pay them back." Filial piety is not necessarily lessened by access to more resources. Joy's financial burden may not be as heavy as Samantha's, but her mental burden is no less, as the pressure for her to succeed in the Western-dominated world of fashion is nerve-wracking.

Compared to the previous generation, which consisted primarily of graduate students, this new wave of Chinese students is coming to America younger, wealthier, and desirous of success in the social and cultural arenas as opposed to merely the academic. In his engaging book, *Age of Ambition*, which earned him the National Book Award in 2014, Evan Osnos gives a vivid portrayal of the rising ambition of contemporary Chinese who are chasing wealth and seeking growth within China and all over the world.[11] Accompanying this ever-growing ambition, or indeed an integral part of it, is anxiety. Ambition breeds anxiety. I argue that this new wave of Chinese international students embodies the duality of ambition and anxiety, on their own part and on behalf of their parents, their extended families, and their peer networks. In part, the duality of ambition and anxiety is rooted in the desires of emerging middle- and upper-middle class families in China to preserve their social statuses and transmit them to the next generation. French sociologist Pierre Bourdieu has long conceptualized education as "cultural capital," which serves as a mechanism for social reproduction.[12] Other scholars, such as Aihwa Ong, Rachel Brooks, and Johanna Waters, have specifically argued that the acquisition of a Western education for well-off people in East Asia and Southeast Asia has become a family strategy of accumulation.[13] During this process of accumulation and social reproduction, much of the academic and public attention has been on the motivations for education abroad, but we know very little about the lived experiences of these students once they are abroad.

This book explores and analyzes the multifaceted experiences of Chinese undergraduates in the United States, with a focus on the duality of ambition and anxiety that is manifested through Chinese students' experiences in straddling two distinct education systems and social and cultural norms in American and Chinese societies. Specifically:

(1) They are ambitious about getting into the higher-ranked institutions in the United States, but they are anxious about navigating the entirely alien and sometimes whimsical college admissions process, which requires a whole set of materials (personal statements, recommendation letters, etc.) and activities that are not part of the test-oriented Chinese system.

(2) They are ambitious about gaining a global outlook in the United States. A key mechanism is to make American friends, but they are anxious about their often unfulfilled desires to venture out of their largely Chinese peer networks (due to various internal and external barriers).

(3) They are ambitious about choosing the right college major to fulfill their personal interests and professional goals; yet they are anxious about the tensions between their pragmatic values instilled in China, which prioritize STEM and business fields over humanities and social sciences, and the expressive values privileged by American society.

(4) They are ambitious about combining the best parts of American and Chinese education; but they are anxious about the new expectations of American classrooms, such as public speaking, as the value of speaking itself was often cast into doubt by their prior socialization in China. They also share their views about academic integrity violations, which drive up their anxiety and concerns that the reputation of the whole Chinese student community is at risk.

(5) They are ambitious about putting their education to good use in either China or the United States, but they are anxious about increasing

competition in China and the current anti-immigrant environment in the United States. The ultimate question that drives their anxiety is whether studying in the United States is really worth it.

DEFICIT DISCOURSE IN MEDIA AND ACADEMY

As the enrollment of Chinese students has spiked, media coverage has escalated as well, and the drumbeat of critical views has gathered force, as has their negative tone. Negative media headlines of Chinese students are pervasive in the United States and other Western societies.[14] Anthropologists Nancy Abelmann and Jiyeon Kang have analyzed American media discourse on Chinese international undergraduate students and identified a struggle in media coverage between the images of "the excellent Chinese students" and "the ethically suspect and inassimilable Chinese students."[15] They trace this contradiction to the long-standing American social imaginaries of an alluring Chinese market and the Yellow Peril. The alluring Chinese market promises a large-scale enrollment of Chinese students paying full tuition, who nonetheless could pose a threat to American higher education, ranging from crowding out American students to academic integrity violations. Abelmann and Kang did note that the term *Yellow Peril*, which became popular around the turn of the twentieth century,[16] has not appeared in recent media. However, the notion of threat and mistrust is not gone and has been on the rise recently, particularly given the Trump administration's inflammatory rhetoric about China.

In other words, the media coverage of Chinese international students has much to do with American perceptions of Chinese society—its past and its present. Due to the rise of the Chinese economy, American media coverage has fixated on the new wealth and the nouveau riche in China. Chinese students overseas wearing Louis Vuitton fashions and driving Lamborghinis have caught much attention. This focus on the wealth of Chinese students feeds into the threat narrative. However, the coverage suffers from a lack of diversity, particularly socioeconomic diversity, in representing the Chinese student body. In other words, students such as Samantha, who come from ordinary families, are often absent from the articles; but students such as Joy, who come from wealthy families, are often featured and covered in sensational terms. Articles in high-profile media outlets have catchy headlines such as "A Lust for Speed: Young Wealthy Chinese in Rural America."[17] Such articles focus on wealth and flashy lifestyles while glossing over students' academic and social challenges. The lives of students from average families, the sacrifices their parents have made for them, and their ambitions and anxieties go largely unrecognized. A few media articles have captured the socioeconomic diversity, but the catchy title belies the content of the article containing more complexity. For example, an article published in *Foreign Policy* was titled "China's Nouveau Riche Have Landed on America's Campuses." Among the stories on the wealthy families, the article did include a story of a taxi driver who sold his house and plowed all of his annual $12,885 salary into sending his son abroad.[18] His story is one of the ordinary Chinese, who have little in common with the nouveau riche.

Even though the media coverage of Chinese international students has much to do with fast-changing China, few articles include any in-depth analysis of the context of Chinese society. The lack of contextual analysis and investigative reporting is especially salient concerning the pervasive coverage on cheating by Chinese international students in America. There are real cases of violations of academic integrity, and the media has covered these individual cases.[19] But the coverage sometimes portrays this as if cheating were a norm among Chinese students. For example, the 2015 article "In China, No Choice But to Cheat," published in *Inside Higher Ed*, describes issues of fraud in some Chinese applications to American schools. The title suggests a pervasive culture of cheating in China. In this article of more than 1,000 words, there is only one short paragraph with a little over fifty words about the complex American admission system with its requirements for personal essays and recommendation letters, which are foreign concepts in China. Instead of talking about differences in college admissions that may push students to turn to third-party agents, whose qualities vary a great deal, the article abruptly ends. Articles like this stoke a widespread mistrust of Chinese students in American schools.

Academic research in this area, although not as sensational as media headlines, falls into a similar trap of deficit discourse on international students. A majority of extant studies on Chinese students in American universities focus on their lack of linguistic, academic, social, and cultural attributes amenable to success in American schools. These studies tend to conceptualize within the traditional paradigm of international students seeking to adjust and assimilate to the host society.[20] For example, research shows that American students considered Chinese internationals as bad at English, loud, and uninterested in making American friends.[21] American faculty members saw Chinese international students as obedient, lacking participatory spirit, and dependent.[22] Recently, some scholars have argued for a paradigm shift, contending that this perspective pathologizes international students and emphasizes their unidirectional adjustment while ignoring their agency and multidimensional experiences.[23] Education scholar Simon Marginson, for example, argues for shifting the paradigm from "understanding international education as a process of 'adjustment' of foreign students to local requirements . . . to understanding international education as self-formation."[24] This is indeed a call for a paradigm shift that has the potential to truly understand the experiences of international students and what international education brings to them.

While the focus on agency of international students effectively moves beyond the deficit discourse, this book aims to contextualize that agency and argues that the process of self-formation while abroad needs to take into account the educational, social, and cultural backgrounds of international students. In the case of Chinese students, I argue that a deep understanding of them must be situated in the context of the vast and profound social changes that have happened, and are happening, in China and around the world over the past few decades. The current wave of Chinese international students may have fresh and unique characteristics that may not fall within the realm of the expectations of Americans, who are likely to base their understanding of Chinese society on an older generation.

Without understanding the new context from which these Chinese students come, we run the risk of misconstruing their agentic experiences. American universities may not provide the right amount or type of support that these students need, nor may American universities reap desirable social and cultural benefits from their Chinese international student bodies apart from their significant financial contributions. In sum, this project will shift the focus from expecting international students to adapt to the United States to bringing China, and in particular, the transformative context of social change in China, into the picture to better understand the multifaceted experiences of Chinese students. Such investigations need to begin by listening to the voices and experiences of Chinese students themselves.

RESEARCH QUESTIONS

This study spans three key stages: Chinese student experiences before their arrival in the United States, their lived experiences during their study in America, and then looking ahead and thinking about their futures. Drawing from interdisciplinary scholarship, this book poses the following questions about these interrelated stages:

(1) Before arrival: Why and how did these students choose to study in the United States? How did they prepare their American college applications while in China? How did social class influence their college applications and placements?

(2) After arrival: As they straddle both Chinese and American education systems, in what respects do they think their prior schooling in China helped or hurt them in their education in the United States? How are their college major choices similar to or distinct from those of their peers in China and in the United States? Do they have close American friends? If not, what are the barriers? How do social class and institutional characteristics affect their academic and social experiences in the United States?

(3) Looking back and ahead: What do Chinese students think about their experiences in the United States, and in particular, how do these experiences change them? Transnational student migration is often linked to the issue of immigration—how do these students deliberate about their future place of living after getting a degree?

TRANSFORMATIVE SOCIAL CHANGE IN CHINA

The above questions cannot be addressed sufficiently without taking into account the broader social changes in China, which have been nothing less than transformative since the initiation of the reform and opening up national policy in 1978. This policy has sustained the fastest-growing economy in the world, averaging double-digit growth for most of the past four decades.[25] In 2010, China surpassed Japan to become the second-largest economy in the world based on gross domestic product (GDP), and China is poised to surpass the United States with the largest economy, although the per capita GDP ranked only seventy-first as of 2017. In 2016, China topped the United States in its number of billionaires.[26]

Although the economy has slowed down in recent years, and 2018 in particular witnessed the slowest GDP growth over the past twenty-eight years,[27] decades of fast and sustained growth have given rise to the well-heeled and the burgeoning middle class sector, which has grown to 430 million as of 2018.[28] According to the prominent Chinese sociologist Lu Xueyi, the largest change in social strata in postreform China has occurred in the growth of white-collar jobs, such as private business owners, civil servants, corporate professionals, managers, etc. They constitute the bulk of the burgeoning middle class in China,[29] and education abroad has increasingly become an integral part of their consumption in urban areas. China is the leader in sending the most students to traditional destinations for international study, like the United States, the UK, and Australia. To illustrate, one in three international students in both the United States and Australia is from China.[30]

To a lesser extent, Chinese students with working-class backgrounds—whose parents are factory workers, supermarket cashiers, and drivers—join the league of those ambitious and anxious youth that seek better education abroad. Their primary means to afford overseas higher education is not their parents' meager income but wealth appreciation of their homes. In almost every major city and town, housing prices are surging. For young people who want to achieve homeownership, this is a curse; however, people who already have property, including native residents from such megacities as Beijing and Shanghai, are riding this surge and benefiting from astronomical appreciation.[31] Many have converted their assets into an educational investment in their children. Jack and Peter from Shanghai, covered in chapter 2, are from such families. Their parents, and many like them, sold their apartments or moved from downtown to the margins of the city to realize the profit so that they can afford the high price tag of American higher education.

This book is framed against the backdrop of these sweeping social changes in China. International student migration from China has itself become a prominent aspect of social change. Since the opening up policies implemented in 1978, there have been 5.19 million Chinese with study abroad experience; and in 2017 alone, there were 1.45 million Chinese studying overseas, with 350,755 of them studying in the United States—the top destination country.[32] As Vanessa Fong discussed in her book *Paradise Rede-fined*, the earlier generation of international students from China often studied abroad through scholarships, but now students increasingly use family funds for their studies.[33] Fong's work focuses on adolescent and late adolescent students in the 1990s from Dalian, a port city located in Northeast China adjacent to Japan and South Korea, and she followed them overseas as some went abroad to study. Japan was the number one destination country for her study participants. Only 8 percent of her sample studied in the United States. The economic development in China since then has brought studying in the United States within reach of many rising middle-class families. Now the United States hosts the largest number of Chinese international students who are lured by a great number of high-quality colleges and universities, which they would otherwise have had no access to in China.

The Chinese students featured in this book were born in the 1990s and came of age in the first decade of the twenty-first century, so they are of a more recent cohort than those in Fong's book. These two cohorts are at least a decade apart, during which period a significant number of Chinese families have risen into the middle class, while a smaller number have grown immensely wealthy.[34] In other words, the China my subjects lived in is far more developed than the China of Fong's subjects, and this has impacted our respective research findings. For example, while the students in Fong's book often talked about poverty and *lack of development* in China, despite their love for their motherland, the students in this book are concerned about the *costs of development* in China, such as pollution, corruption, over-work, and negligence of family. While the students in Fong's book were often afraid to be stuck in China if they returned, the students in my book have not shown such concerns. Many choose to return voluntarily, driven by the lure of family and booming opportunities; and others feel that they are not really bound by their decisions and they can still travel to the United States and leverage opportunities in both countries, primarily due to the increasing interconnectedness of the world.

However, transformative social changes have given rise to increasing social inequality, and the gap between the rich and the poor in China is ever-widening.[35] Regional differences are marked by urban prosperity and rural poverty. The study abroad phenomenon is largely urban in China. Scholars have long pointed out that transnational student mobility has the potential to exacerbate social inequality.[36] Upper- and middle-class families in China's cities are willing and able to finance an American undergraduate education for their children to escape the cutthroat Chinese education system and gain a competitive advantage through overseas education credentials. This is vastly different from just a decade ago, when Chinese students were often doctoral students, funded by the Chinese government or by American graduate programs, and subjected to a highly competitive screening process. In recent years, the growth rate of undergraduates from China has quickly outpaced that of graduate students, and the overall enrollment of undergraduates now surpasses that of graduates. Figure 1.1 shows that undergraduate enrollment has exceeded graduate enrollment among Chinese international students since 2014.

THE INTERNATIONALIZATION
OF AMERICAN UNIVERSITIES

It takes two to tango. While Chinese students desire an American education, American universities need Chinese students in an era of declining financial support, particularly in the aftermath of the 2008 financial crisis. Although the financial crisis may have exacerbated the need for full-pay students, the advent of the large-scale increase in Chinese undergraduate enrollment came *before* the financial crisis kicked in. As shown in figure 1.2, which covers the ten-year period from 2005 to 2015, the turning point occurred during the 2006–2007 academic year. The enrollment rate of Chinese undergraduates in the United States increased by over 60 percent during the 2006–2007 academic year, while the rate of increase in the previous year had been less than 10 percent. In other words, before the financial crisis kicked in, self-funded Chinese undergraduates had already made significant inroads into American higher education as a result of the emerging middle class and their ever-increasing capacity to afford American education, greenlighted by the student visa policies during the later term of the George W. Bush administration.

After the 2001 attacks on the World Trade Center in New York City, the number of student visas being granted plummeted, as heightened security needs led to increased visa denials. In subsequent years, American higher education and the high-tech sector have taken the hit, as decreasing international students put their research and innovation productivity at risk.

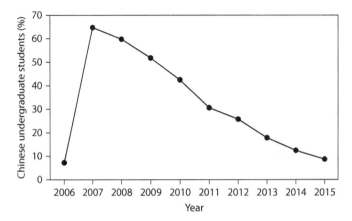

FIGURE 1.2 The growth rates of Chinese undergraduate students in America, 2005-2015
Source: Institute of International Education, https://www.iie.org/en/Research-and-Insights/Open-Doors/Data/International-Students/Enrollment

They persuaded the State Department to correct the course and improve the visa process.[37] In 2005, the U.S. authorities extended the terms of student visas from six-months to allow for multiple-entry twelve-month visas.[38] By 2006, Secretary of State Condoleezza Rice considered student visas a "top priority" and instituted a series of policies to expedite student visa applications, including increasing the number of consular officers, more active outreach in foreign schools, and expediting the interview process.[39] Moreover, policy changes under the Obama administration, such as the launching of a ten-year visa for tourists and business people, have enabled the Chinese to travel between China and the United States more easily. The Trump administration has already embarked on the platform to restrict and reverse some of the Obama era visa policies, which has created serious repercussions on the internationalization of American universities.[40] New international student enrollment in the United States has been in decline since 2016 (before Trump was elected into office) for the first time since the attacks of September 11, 2001.[41] Nevertheless, Chinese student enrollment is still increasing, albeit at a slower pace than previously.

Another factor is the appreciation of the yuan, the currency of the People's Republic of China, between 2006 and 2014. Notably, from 1998–2005, the dollar/yuan exchange rate remained constant at 8.28, but around mid-2005 the Chinese modified their currency valuation policies. By 2014, the yuan had appreciated by about 37 percent. This has augmented the rising capacity of the Chinese family to pay for American higher education. Not surprisingly, international student enrollment has a positive economic impact on American society. In 2016, international students contributed $39.4 billion to the U.S. economy.[42] The Institute of International Education Open Doors 2017 reports that about 67 percent of all international students receive the majority of their funds from non-U.S. sources.[43]

The extra tuition revenue brought by Chinese students sometimes directly subsidizes domestic American student scholarship and financial aid.[44] Research has established the link between changes in state funding and foreign enrollment in recent years. Specifically, economists have identified that a 10 percent reduction in state appropriations is associated with an increase of 12 percent in international students at public research universities.[45] State universities in the Midwest, where ethnic diversity is not as prevalent as on the coasts, nevertheless have the largest concentration of Chinese international students. A recent report from the Brookings Institution analyzing the geography of international students in American higher education found that nine out of twenty-five universities with the highest share of Chinese international students belong to the Big Ten located in the Midwest.[46]

The impact of these unprecedented levels of Chinese international students goes beyond economics and has changed the landscape of American college campuses and their adjacent communities. The number of Chinese undergraduate students at Michigan State University grew from only forty-three in the fall of 2005 to close to 4,000 by 2014. Iowa City, where the University of Iowa is located, now has more bubble tea (a popular drink that originated in Taiwan) stores than Starbucks.[47] Similar examples abound in numerous other state universities and private colleges. International students' impact on diversifying and globalizing campuses is often touted by academics and administrators as a key benefit of international education.[48] In other words, the enrollment of international students helps American universities to achieve the dual purposes of balancing their budgets and creating a diverse educational environment. But these benefits also come with challenges. Peter Briggs, former director of the International Students and Scholars Division from Michigan State University (MSU), wrote a chapter in the book *Understanding International Students from Asia in American*

Universities[49] that details the changes brought about by Chinese undergraduates at Michigan State University, rippling across college classrooms through the East Lansing community. In the context of the dramatic changes in the student body, only 24 percent of the MSU faculty think that they are prepared to teach Chinese students. Michigan State faculty is not unique in feeling unprepared.[50] The lack of preparation may lead to ill-suited advice or even deeply offensive interactions with Chinese students. Most recently, in early 2019, a scandal involving Duke University faculty admonishing Chinese students for speaking Chinese in a student lounge provoked widespread outrage and protest. This incident highlights a strong need for faculty support and training.

In addition, the social and cultural benefits brought by international students cannot be realized without organically integrating them into American campus life. This has proven to be a thorny challenge. Elisabeth Gareis, professor of communication studies, has documented distinct differences among international students' home regions in the number of American friends they have.[51] Those from East Asia are most likely to have no close American friends and least likely to report satisfaction with their friendship. Professor Gareis's sample does not disaggregate into individual countries. This book presents further evidence of the yearnings for American friendship among Chinese students who express frustrations about social integration on campus. Due to the massive enrollment of Chinese students in many American higher education institutions, it is much easier to form their conational cliques than branch out to other networks. Given the pervasive use of Chinese social media platforms such as WeChat, many Chinese students are able to connect, share information, and even decide to room with each other before their arrival to American campuses. Some Chinese students from the same city or even the same high school directly import their social cliques to American campuses. The conational networks provide comfort and support, which is positive and should be encouraged. However, Chinese international students need to feel that they have other options—access to diverse networks in addition to their affinity group. The lack of options would rob Chinese students of a truly international education they desire. Their experiences highlight the need for systematic and institutionalized support for Chinese students to access diverse networks and to better integrate within the American campus community.

RESEARCH METHODS

Study Population

This book focuses on full-time undergraduates at four-year institutions. In 2016–2017, more than 86 percent of Chinese international students were enrolled in four-year institutions in the United States, although their enrollment numbers in community colleges are also rising.[52] In addition, among a minority of students who enroll in community colleges, many treat this as a cost saving strategy and later transfer to four-year colleges.[53]

There are two reasons for this exclusive focus on undergraduates: First, Chinese graduate students used to dominate the international student population; it is a relatively new phenomenon that undergraduates from China are flocking to American campuses, and they have only recently become a majority among Chinese international students. Second, undergraduates inhabit quite different academic and social spaces than their graduate counterparts.[54] Academically, undergraduates have a much wider range of coursework than graduate students and thus have more opportunities to be exposed to, and interact with, students from diverse backgrounds. Socially, most American universities require undergraduates to live in dorms, while graduate students tend to make their own arrangements for housing, and some even bring their families with them. In other words, undergraduates from China have many more opportunities, as well as much more pressure, to integrate in American colleges and universities than their graduate peers.

Research Design and Data

There is no nationally representative data on Chinese students in the United States. Many previous studies on Chinese students are based on data collected from a single college or university.[55] The purpose of this research is to collect individual-level data from diverse institutions, while at the same time putting individual students' experiences in the macro contexts of Chinese and American society. This book draws macro-level data from the Chinese Ministry of Education and the Institute of International Education and the National Science Foundation in the United States. From the Chinese

Ministry of Education, I draw data on the number of students in China attending the Gaokao, college major distributions among students in China, and the number of overseas students returning to China. From the Institute of International Education, I draw enrollment data at the national level to show the overall trend of Chinese international student enrollment in American higher education. I also extract data from the U.S. National Science Foundation to show the college major distributions among American undergraduate students, to draw comparisons with Chinese international students in the United States.

In order to get a comprehensive and in-depth look at student experiences, mixed-method research design is employed. I describe the data sources and research methods in detail in an appendix. In sum, there are three components in the data collection effort for individual student experiences:

One is an online survey to gather quantitative data on Chinese students' demographic backgrounds, their social networks, their academic records, and their intention to stay in the United States versus return to China. Five hundred seven participants from 50 institutions completed the survey. Although not a nationally representative survey, it provides broad patterns and identifies important associations of Chinese students' backgrounds, behaviors and plans from a diverse set of institutions (See details in the appendix).

Second, I conducted one-on-one, in-depth interviews among current Chinese students at American universities to understand their college application processes, their expectations before arrival, the context of these students' friendship formation, the meaning of their academic and social challenges after arrival, and looking ahead upon graduation, the rationales behind their intentions to stay or return. The participants are those who show willingness at the end of the online survey to participate in the interview. I've conducted 65 one-on-one in-depth interviews with them, among whom sixty were in-person, and five were phone interviews.

Third, I conducted fieldwork in eight public high schools and one private high school in six cities in China. These schools offer international education to students preparing to study abroad. I made classroom observations, interviewed prospective students, high school counselors, principals, and foreign teachers. Altogether, I've conducted 43 one-on-one in-depth interviews in these high schools. The fieldwork provides insights into how

Chinese students are prepared prior to coming to the United States and identifies unique pathways transitioning from secondary education in China to higher education in the United States.

Survey Data Characteristics

Table 1.1 presents the online survey participants' characteristics. Close to 90 percent of the survey respondents were from major research universities,

TABLE 1.1
Survey Sample Characteristics (N=507)

CATEGORY	PERCENTAGES (%)
Female	50.7
Urban	94.5
Taking Gaokao	32.2
Parental education	
Less than high school	5.7
High school	11.4
College	47.1
Graduate	35.7
Arrival time in the United States	
High school	18.3
Freshman	56.6
Sophomore	8.7
Junior	16.5
Perceived English	
Poor	7.1
Fair	34
Good	42
Excellent	16.9
Finance education	
Family funds	91.7
Scholarship	6.9
Loan	1.4
Institutional types	
Selective	41.3
Major research	88.4

Note: Parental education is coded as the highest education attainment of a student's father or mother. Selective institutions are defined as the top fifty national universities and top twenty liberal arts colleges based on *U.S News and World Report*, accessed through https://www.usnews.com/best-colleges. Due to some fluctuations of rankings across years, I consider those schools selective as long as they were ranked at least once among those top institutions during the survey year of 2013 and 2014.

and more than 10 percent were from small liberal arts colleges. This is a disproportionately urban group. A bit over 5 percent of the study participants were from rural areas. The urban-rural divide concerning socioeconomic resources is salient in China.[56] Over 90 percent of the students used family funds to pay for their American education, and over 80 percent had parents with a college education and beyond. In other words, less than 20 percent of them were first-generation college students. Parental education was measured using the highest educational attainment of a student's father or mother.

Several chapters in this book show that first-generation Chinese international students are at a disadvantage concerning both academic and social outcomes compared to their peers with college-educated parents. This is a key class divide among this relatively privileged population. Another crucial factor is English proficiency. I used self-evaluations of English proficiency rather than test scores such as TOEFL results. As chapter 3 notes, many Chinese students take English tests multiple times, on top of countless test prep classes, so test scores are sometimes inflated. Self-evaluations of English proficiency reflect students' confidence and comfort with their own mastery of the language. Fifty-eight percent of the sample participants thought their English was good or excellent. A strong self-evaluation of English proficiency turns out to be a significant booster for positive academic and social outcomes.

Chinese undergraduate international students are in general a socio-economically privileged group—our sample characteristics reflect that. However, they are not at all homogeneous. In addition to parental education and English proficiency, other essential factors diversify the survey sample. For example, 18 percent came here as high school students, 32 percent took the Chinese college entrance examination (the Gaokao), and 41 percent enrolled in selective institutions (defined as the top fifty major research and top twenty liberal arts colleges). Chapter 3 shows that Chinese students consider the top fifty national research universities and top twenty liberal arts colleges as selective institutions based on the rankings of the *U.S. News and World Report*. This book utilizes this criterion in differentiating selective versus nonselective institutions.

Their parents' occupations were quite diverse; they ranged from business executives to professionals in education, health, and science fields. Figure 1.3 shows the occupations of the parents of the participants.

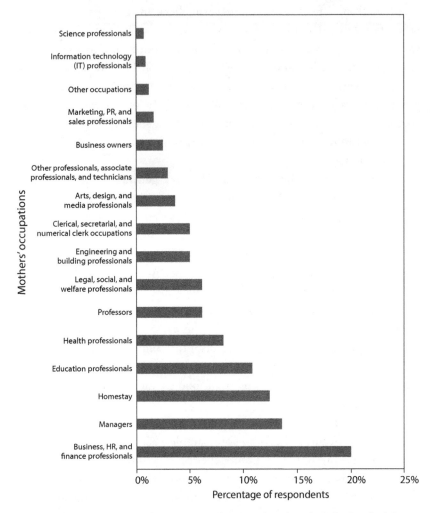

FIGURE 1.3A Occupations of survey respondents' mothers, based on the Standard Occupation Classification Codes in the United States

Note: "Other occupations" includes a wide range of blue-collar jobs, such as cashier, driver, factory worker, etc.

Source: Author's study

A PREVIEW OF THE BOOK

The chapters ahead explore and explain various aspects of experiences among this new wave of Chinese undergraduates in American higher education with both quantitative and qualitative data.

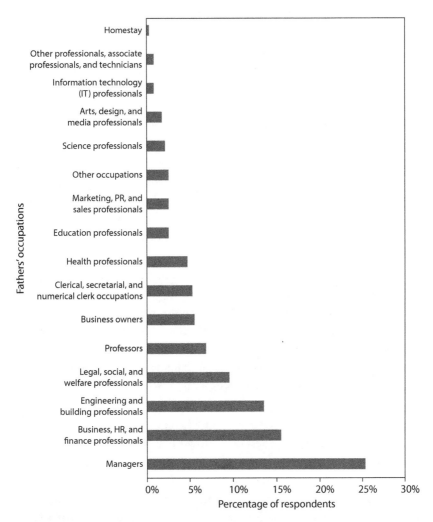

FIGURE 1.3B Occupations of survey respondents' fathers, based on the Standard Occupation Classification Codes in the United States
Note: "Other occupations" includes a wide range of blue-collar jobs, such as cashier, driver, factory worker, etc.
Source: Author's study

Chapter 2 examines the motivations for studying in the United States and the process of college choice. I argue that a culture of studying abroad has emerged in urban China over the past decade; so much so, that studying abroad has become the new education gospel. This new gospel stands as an alternative to the old gospel of the Gaokao, in that students and their parents believe that access to college—in this case, an overseas college—can promise a brighter future with more options and potentially a global platform. In the process of choosing a college, rankings guide the way, and counselors and agents facilitate it. Parental networks, if any, also affect the choices.

Chapter 3 identifies four main pathways Chinese students travel to arrive on American campuses: (1) through regular classes in Chinese public high schools, (2) through international classes in Chinese public high schools, (3) through Chinese private schools, and (4) through American high schools, usually in the private sector. In general, the cost of tuition stratifies these pathways. Navigating this unknown territory is challenging, which creates the demand for new professions and services—college counselors in Chinese schools (with international classes) and a billion-dollar industry of for-profit agencies making their living off of the anxieties of Chinese students.

Chapter 4 focuses on Chinese students' experiences and reflections about the education systems in China and the United States. This chapter presents their voices and experiences on the following topics: creativity, critical thinking, attitudes toward math, the transition between secondary and postsecondary schools in the United States and China, and their encounters with academic integrity.

Chapter 5 examines the question of social integration of Chinese students and focuses on both external exclusions from American networks and internal withdrawal into Chinese enclaves. This chapter discusses the rationales and benefits of voluntary segregation for this new wave of Chinese international students, who nonetheless desire to go beyond their own groups and make American friends. Chapter 5 also examines what makes a difference, at the individual and institutional levels, in improving social integration.

Chapter 6 situates the choice of a major within the social contexts of Chinese and American societies and examines the strong culture of STEM fields in China and the emerging interest in business and economics in an era when China has embraced a market economy. I argue that pragmatic collectivism can help us understand Chinese students' preference for lucrative and marketable college majors, in spite of their relative economic privilege. Pragmatic collectivism stands in contrast to the American creed of expressive individualism.[57] The contrasting cultures set some Chinese students on a journey of self-discovery.

Chapter 7 examines the question of why Chinese international students tend not to speak up in the classroom and the various factors that lead to behavioral variations among them. Drawing from W. E. B. DuBois's notion of double consciousness, I find that Chinese students often internally criticize their own English—a crippling barrier to free expression. They look at themselves through the eyes of an imagined speaker of "native English," which thwarts their efforts at communication. In addition to language, I argue that the traditional culture of valuing action over words, and the Chinese exam-based education system, which orients students to giving *only* the right answer, are key contexts to understanding Chinese students' classroom behaviors in American higher education.

Chapter 8 focuses on reflections of Chinese international students on the changes in their lives after studying abroad. The chapter discusses these changes along the following three dimensions: global citizenship, attitudes towards China and the United States, and personal transformation. Overall, the students become more active and engaged, and more reflective and reflexive than before, although sometimes these changes entail tensions and conflicts with their parents and families. However, this has not estranged them from China. Their interest in Chinese society and in being Chinese is renewed and refreshed from afar. Some scholars believe that American higher education is central to American soft power and helps to transmit American values,[58] but this chapter finds mixed evidence regarding such a claim.

Chapter 9 examines the future plans of this new wave of Chinese international students. Approximately 60 percent of them intend to return to China, and most intend to return within one to three years upon graduating; this finding casts doubt on the "study-to-migrate" notion, which is upheld mostly by data on graduate students, particularly doctoral students.[59] This finding reflects the allure of the new and ever-stronger China for its students overseas. For those who intend to stay in the United States, most prefer America over China out of concerns over the costs of development in China, such as corruption, pollution, over-work, and lack of family time.

Chapter 10 concludes the book. It summarizes the major findings, paying particular attention to how these students have brought their ambition and anxiety from China to bear upon their study in the United States, in such areas as applications, college experiences, and social relations. The concluding chapter also considers the theoretical significance and policy implications for American higher education institutions.

CHAPTER 2

A Love for Separation

STUDY ABROAD AS THE NEW EDUCATION
GOSPEL IN URBAN CHINA

In late 2016, the TV drama series, *A Love for Separation*, ignited widespread discussion within China and among the Chinese community in America. The drama centers on three families in Beijing, each pondering the pros and cons of sending a child to study abroad in the United States.

The children differ in socioeconomic status: Xiaoyu's father is a wealthy business man; Duoduo's father is an eye doctor and her mother is manager in a multinational corporation; Qingqing's background is more modest—her father is a taxi driver, her mother works at a community health center.

The students also have different academic backgrounds. The show's writers challenge a general pattern recognized by social scientists—the idea that higher socioeconomic status (SES) predicts higher academic achievement[1]—by inverting the relationship between SES and academic achievement. Qingqing has the lowest SES of the three families but the most outstanding academic record; she is a viable candidate even for the most elite universities in China. Duoduo is an average student and feels increasingly stressed by the highly competitive education system in China, and Xiaoyu hails from the most well-heeled family among the three but has the poorest academic record.

A Love for Separation frames a hot-button issue facing millions of Chinese families: students from diverse socioeconomic backgrounds with different academic abilities invariably consider going abroad as a viable option for pursuing their studies. The show won number one ratings for eleven consecutive days during summer 2016. In addition, 4.6 billion viewers streamed it online as of September 6, 2016. This highlights the strong impact of studying abroad on popular culture and on the lives of ordinary people in China.

In this book, I argue that in recent years a culture of studying abroad has emerged in urban China, so much so that it has become the *new education gospel*, challenging the old gospel of the Chinese college entrance examination (hereafter, the Gaokao). I use the term *education gospel* to refer to a system of belief, sometimes not entirely rational, that education is liberating and worth investing in and even sacrificing for, because it leads to a bright future, broadly conceived. As in any society, what a bright future means for a child depends on the student's SES and academic background, as can be seen in *A Love for Separation*. For upper- and middle-class children such as Duoduo and Xiaoyu, the purpose in education is to maintain their socioeconomic standing and privilege; for less privileged students such as Qingqing, it is to achieve upward social mobility.

The Chinese Gaokao once served these purposes almost exclusively until recently, when studying abroad has provided a welcome alternative. The Gaokao is relentless and cruel, and many parents do not want their children to go through the ordeal. In other words, what used to be the exclusive determining factor of college placement in China has now become optional, at least for some urban Chinese students. In this sense, for a large swath of urban Chinese students and their parents, studying abroad offers salvation, in several ways. This saves some from participating in the tortuous Gaokao, or if they have already participated, it can rescue them from their undesirable Gaokao scores and the lackluster college placement. Studying abroad liberates others from an oppressive test-oriented education system in China, which, ironically, many of their parents survived and thrived by obtaining professional jobs and middle-class status, yet these parents want to provide alternative education opportunities for their children—ones that afford a more well-rounded human development unbridled by test scores than what they themselves experienced.[2]

By the "culture of studying abroad," I mean the shared values and expectations of Chinese families and their children who place their faith in an overseas education as an admission ticket to a bright future.[3] This culture of studying abroad emerged initially in economically advanced megacities such as Beijing and Shanghai, then diffused into second- or even third-tier cities and towns, and it has now become a dominant mode of thinking for millions of families in urban China in planning their children's future. This chapter presents evidence of the strong desire of young Chinese to pursue their educations in the United States and explores the motivations and rationales prompting these students and their families to make such a decision. I will also explain how the students choose their American colleges and universities, guided by the institutional ranking and aided by parental networks.

Nevertheless, it's important to note that however influential this culture of studying abroad appears to be, it will never replace the Gaokao— even in urban areas, the number of Chinese students taking the Gaokao and attending domestic universities in China is still the majority. In 2017, 9.4 million Chinese students took the exam. This is often because, for many, the cost of studying abroad is still prohibitive. Although studying abroad is not the norm in a statistical sense, China's privileged class has made it nearly normative, in the sense that parents, especially from urban areas, feel urged to at least consider it despite its exceeding their economic capacity. This is the case for Qingqing in *A Love for Separation*—her mom has little means to support her overseas education but still wants it for her, just because she believes in it.

WHY STUDY IN THE UNITED STATES?

What does Qingqing's mom really believe about studying abroad, despite her inability to afford it? She believes that an American education can broaden her daughter's horizons, and she hopes for a more exciting and inspiring life for her daughter, one that differs from the life she has lived as an ordinary worker in China. In other words, studying in the United States represents broader life aspirations in addition to just educational aspirations.

Education scholars have described the college choice as a complex multi-stage process that progresses from aspirations to information gathering about different schools to the choice of one school over others.[4] This model effectively explains the process for domestic American students, but the process for international students adds an additional layer of complexity. The aspiration phase typically involves the key decision to study in the United States, but this entails a two-stage decision: the choice to study abroad instead of attending a domestic education and the selection of the United States as the destination country. The question is: Why choose to study in the United States?

China is often perceived to be lacking in educational opportunities, so when high demand cannot be met, students with the means flee to seek opportunities elsewhere. This perception is only partially valid, however. Chinese higher education has become much more accessible in recent decades due to a massive expansion that began around the turn of the twenty-first century. In 1999, the Plan to Revitalize Education in the Twenty-First Century, proposed by the Ministry of Education, launched the expansion of college enrollment in China. Under the auspices of the plan, annual college enrollment increased from one million in 1998 to 6.3 million in 2009. This expansion was unprecedented, both in and outside of China.[5]

In other words, the timing of the educational expansion precedes and overlaps the advent of the era when Chinese students began to study in the United States at an unprecedented level. Therefore, it is not the lack of access to college, per se, that drives Chinese students abroad. Rather, it is the advantages associated with an American education, such as access to good colleges and high-quality educational experiences, that appeal to Chinese students and their parents (see figure 2.1). In spite of an increasing number of higher education institutions and rising enrollments in China, only two

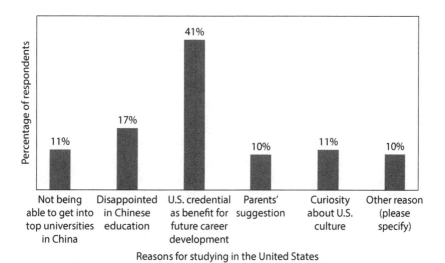

FIGURE 2.1 Distribution of the most important reasons for studying in the United States
Source: Author's study

institutions are ranked among the top 100 best universities in the world, while 41 out of these top 100 are located in the United States.[6] Admission into these two institutions—Peking University and Tsinghua University— is fiercely competitive: less than 0.1 percent of the test-takers in regions outside of Beijing are accepted each to Peking and Tsinghua Universities, although residents from Beijing have higher admissions rate—which is still less than 1 percent.[7] Moreover, after several years of massive expansion, the supply of new college graduates has outpaced demand, and Chinese college graduates now confront a shrinking domestic job market,[8] which also pushes students and their families, at least those who are financially able, to seek credentials abroad so that they can gain more advantages.

It is useful when studying population migration to understand the push-pull model,[9] and student migration is no exception. The push factors are those that push international students out of their home countries, and the pull factors those that attract students to a host country. In the case of Chinese international students, certain push and pull factors converge, such as the quality of education. Figure 2.1, which shows survey results on the reasons Chinese students give for studying in the United States, tells a convincing story of how quality of education serves as both a push and a pull factor. The foremost reason is that a "U.S. credential is beneficial for future career development" (a pull factor), and the second most important reason is "disappointed in Chinese education" (a push factor). The Gaokao represents the most gruesome and ruthless part of Chinese education.

Gaokao: A Push Factor

To understand Chinese education, it is imperative to understand the Gaokao—the Chinese college entrance examination. Unlike American college admissions, which consider test scores as one of many factors for selection decisions, Chinese Gaokao test scores alone can determine whether and where students go to college, and often, what they study (as college majors are linked to a hierarchy of scores, as detailed in chapter 6). A popular saying links the Gaokao with the meritocracy ideal: everyone is equal before test scores. Scholars have demonstrated that the Gaokao system is just "the meritocratic façade of higher education selection,"[10] in that there is much inequity in education resources and opportunities in precollege education leading up to the Gaokao.

To prepare for the Gaokao, high school students in China are tracked as either science or humanities/arts students in grade 10 or 11. The track choices are largely up to individual students and their families. These tracks affect different exams in the Gaokao and later college major choices.[11] The exam takes place only once a year, in June, and it includes Chinese, math, and English for both science- and humanities-track students. In addition to the above three common components, for science-track students there is a comprehensive exam in science subjects including physics, chemistry, and biology; for humanities-track students there is a comprehensive exam in the humanities that includes such subjects as history, political science, and human geography. Students can retake the Gaokao but they have to wait another year. This system has been in place for decades now, and the pilot for reform just started in a few selected regions recently to allow students to take the exam earlier in high school and multiple times if they want.[12]

It is easy to imagine the crucial importance of the Gaokao in Chinese students' lives and the pressure this creates. The high stakes mean that all precollege education has become preparation for the Gaokao, and Chinese students and their families bear an enormous emotional and psychological burden throughout this process. When students are able to opt out of the Gaokao and study overseas, they often leap at the opportunity. Figure 2.2 shows that the number of Gaokao test-takers declined steadily from 2008 to

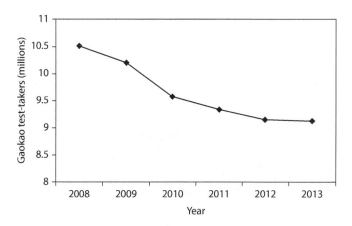

FIGURE 2.2 The number of Gaokao test-takers, 2008–2013
Source: Author compilation of data from the Chinese Ministry of Education, http://en .moe.gov.cn/Resources/Statistics/

2013, driven in part by the decline of the college-going population due to one-child policy, and in part by the number of students opting out of the Gaokao in favor of other alternatives.

Of our survey participants, a little more than 30 percent took the Gaokao before coming to study in the United States; most of them opted out. Some students explicitly mentioned that they wanted to study abroad to escape the exam. For example, Zhong, a psychology major at Vanderbilt University, said:

> I did not want to take the Gaokao in China, so I decided to study abroad. In high school, you have to be good at every subject to stand out on the Gaokao, to get into elite universities in China. But I was not good at physics, which is part of the science track. I liked the humanities track, but I was not good at political science—a required subject for the humanities track. So I opted out of the Gaokao to study in the U.S. There were eighty students in my high school cohort opting out of the Gaokao.

Zhong later added that there were about 400 students in his graduating class, about 20 percent of his cohort chose to avoid the Gaokao and study overseas, and most of them came to the United States. It is important to note that he is from a key high school in Guangzhou, one of the most economically advanced megacities in South China. Zhong's father encouraged him to study abroad as early as in high school, but he resisted because he was afraid of being homesick. So he waited until after his high school graduation in 2012. Dim prospects of going to a good college in China drove him overseas.

Students like Zhong are able to opt out of Gaokao, in part due to the booming international education sector in China—schools and industries supporting overseas studies for aspiring students and their parents, which chapter 3 elaborates. The international education sector in China helps spread the information about the superior educational resources in the United States. Figure 2.3 is a photo I took in 2013 during my fieldwork at a public school located in Jiangsu Province. This photo was presented at the graduating ceremony of this international division to showcase the advantages associated with studying abroad, as opposed to taking the Gaokao and going to a Chinese college. The figure lists three types of benefits associated with studying abroad: first, in regard to the opportunities to take tests, the Chinese Gaokao is offered once a year, while the SAT is offered multiple

	高考	留学
考试机会	一考定终身	托福雅思 40/48次 SAT 6次
考核维度	只看成绩	成绩＋课外活动 (交流、潜力、责任心、领导力等综合素质。有个性、有兴趣、有想法，能坚持)
名校录取	中国名校录取几率低	世界名校录取几率高

FIGURE 2.3 Graph highlighting the advantages of studying abroad in Chinese presented by the principal of an international division in Jiangsu Province, China
Source: Photo by author

times per year; second, in regard to evaluation, Chinese admissions are based exclusively on Gaokao test scores, while test scores are just one of the considerations for college admissions abroad; third, the admission rates of elite Chinese universities are much lower than those of selective universities abroad; so the conclusion is self-evident: studying abroad has overwhelming advantages over taking the Gaokao.

Disappointment with the Chinese Education System

Figure 2.1 also shows that the second most important reason for Chinese international students to study in the United States is that they are disappointed by the Chinese education system. During the interviews, this sentiment was palpable. American education gleams like a beacon of hope for them.

Yang, an undergraduate student at Penn State, came from Wenzhou, Zhejiang Province, a southeastern province boasting a successful economy and a strong entrepreneurial spirit. However, the education system there is stifling and gruesome. Yang described his pre-Gaokao schedule: "We had to study fifteen to sixteen hours per day, and I was really tired of that hellish life. So I wanted to have some changes." Ironically, as will be elaborated in chapter 4, Yang also attributed his academic success at Penn State to the strict study schedule and habits that he developed in China. He was one of the top-ranking seniors majoring in earth science at Penn State and is now a doctoral student in the earth science department at an elite private university on the East Coast. Chapter 4 provides elaborations and reflections of students like Yang about the strengths and weaknesses of Chinese and American education as they straddle them firsthand.

Sometimes, the ultracompetitive nature of the Gaokao pushes students who do not score as high as they wanted to study in the United States as an alternative. Jane, from Nanjing, did not score high enough to go to a top college in China, so she took a gap year at home and worked on applying to American colleges. Jane eventually enrolled at Ohio State University, majoring in business. She later said that she would still prefer to study in the United States even if she'd achieved her desired score on the Gaokao:

INTERVIEWER: So would you be willing to go to a top Chinese college if you were admitted?

JANE: I am not sure. I probably would still prefer coming here [to the United States].

INTERVIEWER: Why is that?

JANE: I've heard that even in good colleges in China, students do not have good experiences in learning. Professors are not invested in college students. Chinese students are also unmotivated to learn after getting through the ruthless Gaokao.

Jane's point that Chinese college faculty are not dedicated to education is further validated by students whose parents are college professors. Shantell, a history major at Georgia State, noted:

My mom is a college professor. She felt college education in China has many problems. Professors are not into educating students. Teaching is not taken seriously. Professors spend most of their time pursuing money and fame for themselves. They either teach/lecture outside for money, or focus on doing research and publishing papers. They do not pay attention to students' development.

Shantell's comments show that parents, who are college professors with insider knowledge of Chinese higher education, actually discourage their own children from attending college in China. The survey data shows that "professor" is listed as one of the top five occupations of fathers and as one of the top seven occupations of mothers. The nontrivial presence of college professors among the parents of these Chinese international students is quite revealing: the quality of higher education in China is worrisome to these insiders.

The notion that Chinese education is disappointing at the college level becomes all the more credible in light of reports by a few students who had first-hand experience in Chinese colleges and later transferred to American colleges. Samantha, a student currently enrolled in Indiana University at Bloomington, was an exchange student at the University of California-Riverside who came from a reputable university in Southern China. She described her experiences in both Chinese and American universities:

> I found myself much more motivated to learn in the U.S. than in China. My friends and I felt we had bleak futures [as college students in China]—no good jobs, no bright prospects—and studying hard made little difference. But here [in the United States], we are very motivated to learn.

Her feelings about the bleak future for college students in China are associated with the astronomical growth of college graduates in the country as a result of the expanding enrollment in Chinese universities. The dire employment situations facing Chinese college graduates who are often disappointed with their college education are one of the key unintended consequences of China's college expansion policy.[13]

Superior American Universities

In contrast to the disappointing Chinese education system, many students envision American universities are far superior. Hudson, from Changsha in Hunan Province, now an engineering student at the University of Washington at Seattle, is such an example:

> My top choices in China were Fudan University in Shanghai or Sun Yat-sen University in Guangzhou, but I knew it would be extremely

hard for me to be admitted by these top schools. My teacher told me that, based on my high school records, my safest bet was Hunan University in China. This was not ideal. So coming to the U.S. provided an alternative.

Hunan University in China is perhaps the best university in Hunan Province, but it remains a provincial university in China, roughly equivalent to a state university in the United States. Ultimately, the University of Washington at Seattle, although also a state university in the United States, proved more prestigious in his eyes than a provincial university in China.

Nevertheless, it is wrong to presume that students who study in the United States consist of those who cannot attend top universities in China. They are academically diverse. For example, Brian, a native from Guangzhou, prepared to study in the United States; he successfully landed offers from several schools in April 2011, and he accepted an offer from the University of Wisconsin at Madison. In June of the same year, he took the Gaokao, and scored high enough to get him into Zhejiang University—one of the top-tier universities in China. When I asked why he took the Gaokao with offers from American universities in hand, he said he wanted to take on the challenge of seeing how well he could do on the Gaokao—a test he considered to be the culmination of his twelve years of schooling in China. He is satisfied with the result—more for self-affirmation than for any tangible purpose. However, what made him forgo one of the best universities in China and opt to study at the University of Wisconsin at Madison? The simple answer is that he, along with countless other Chinese students, believes that American higher education is superior.

How did this belief come into being? There are both instrumental and idealistic reasons for this belief. The instrumental reasons pertain to the quality of American liberal arts education and the perceived higher value of American degrees.[14] The perception of higher value of American degrees is inexplicably tied with the ranking order that put forty-one American universities among the top 100 world best universities. On an idealistic level, what Chinese students and their families are seeking is cosmopolitan capital—a kind of global social and cultural capital[15]—a concept further explored in the next section. American education is considered a transmitter of such capital, an asset that will give them an advantage in their future careers.

Students often refer to liberal arts education in America as a symbol of the advantages associated with American universities. Some students explained that American colleges give students the option to remain undecided about their major for the first two years of college, affording them opportunities to explore their interests. Other students cited faculty excellence. Brian marveled at the fact that Nobel laureates teach undergraduates in America, claiming, "This is unimaginable in China." The Chinese mainland did not produce a single Nobel laureate winner until 2015, when a female researcher named Tu Youyou was awarded the prize in medicine. Brian was very excited to think about the possibility of getting first-hand access to Nobel Prize-winning teachers.

To further understand why Chinese students choose to study in the United States, two concepts can advance our understanding: one is the intergenerational transmission of inequality in China; the other is cosmopolitan capital. In a nutshell, Chinese parents often drive their children to study abroad with the aim of transmitting and solidifying their resources and status across generations. They also want their children to acquire cosmopolitan capital in the United States, which is perceived as the epicenter of globalization and a place where higher educational resources are concentrated.

The Intergenerational Transmission of Inequality in China

The defining feature of the current Chinese society ever since the launching of reform and opening up policies in 1978 is the increasing social inequality and the more salient role of family backgrounds on the status attainment. There is a robust body of literature on the stable and strong relationship between family backgrounds—mainly in terms of socioeconomic status—and educational attainment. Researchers have identified the influences on vertical educational outcomes,[16] such as level of education attained, and on horizontal educational outcomes,[17] such as high school course selection and elite college attendance. This persistent effect of family background on both the vertical and horizontal aspects of education has led sociologist Samuel Lucas to examine them jointly and propose the concept of effectively maintained inequality (EMI), which posits that high SES families "secure for themselves and their children some degree of advantages wherever advantages are commonly possible."[18] The advantages generally take two forms: quantitative differences (e.g., in the level of education) and qualitative differences (e.g., in the quality of education). Studying in the United States involves both qualitative differences in obtaining education credentials in the country that boasts the largest number of best colleges and universities in the world, and quantitative differences in accessing college, and even graduate school, down the road. The question then is, Who in China can access this vast reservoir of higher education institutions in the United States?

What has happened in China over the past few decades can be characterized as phenomenal economic growth coupled with widening social inequality.[19] Family resources are quickly concentrating in the upper-middle classes in urban areas, leaving the working classes and remote rural areas in the dust. The single-child policy spurs Chinese families to devote their resources to developing their children; anthropologist Vanessa Fong has vividly described the single child as "many parents' only hope."[20] The concentration of resources among the upper-middle classes in urban areas are transmitted through children's education—children from richer families have more education choices including studying abroad. The intergenerational transmission of inequality through education is magnified in China by longstanding traditions in Chinese culture that place a high value on education. Anthropologist Andrew Kipnis examines the deeply entrenched desire for education among Chinese citizens and argues that university education has such an "aura of prestige" and that the desire for this prestige "inhibits the application of strict economic reasoning" and instead serves as an object of desire in itself. [21]

As China has become integrated into the global market, Chinese citizens, especially those from urban areas with more resources and exposure to the West, have expanded their desire for education beyond their own country. Studying abroad, especially in the United States, has taken on a new "aura of prestige" and has become more accessible than before. In the past, only the elites—including the political, economic, and academic elites—who had the connections, money, or academic credentials could gratify this desire to study abroad. However, with today's rising middle class and its ever-increasing capacity to pay for tuition at American universities, many students from ordinary Chinese families have expanded the league of those who study abroad. This "aura of prestige" has given rise to a study abroad culture, with the United States as the most popular destination. Middle- and upper-class Chinese families create and reinforce this culture. On the one hand, their rising economic power has enabled the middle class to afford an expensive international education; on the other hand, most of them have achieved their economic success within a single generation over the past two or three decades, and they have anxiety and a strong urge to preserve their newfound wealth and status.[22] Their children's education remains one of their top priorities for maintaining and strengthening their family advantages.[23] Sometimes parents directly push their children to study in the United States. Ying, a native of Nanjing studying at Pacific Lutheran University, considered his mother's push a deciding factor in his studying abroad. She had studied abroad herself in Japan for medical school, and she has several close friends currently living in the United States. She said, "You must study in the U.S., by all means." Apparently, she saw American higher education as more appealing than Japanese higher education, where her mother's generation tended to study because of the geographic proximity of Japan to China. Japan is still one of the top destination countries for Chinese international students.

As figure 2.4 shows, among all the survey participants, more than 60 percent of their parents had played a somewhat important to very important role in their choice of a college in the United States. Many parents are, like Ying's mother, with a college education. The survey data

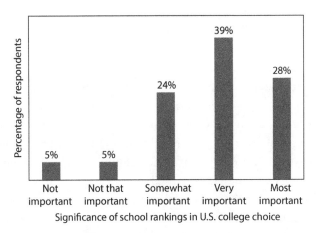

FIGURE 2.4 Significance of school rankings in survey respondents' choice of a college in the United States
Source: Author's study

from this study show that more than 80 percent of the respondents' parents had a college education, and more than 40 percent had an advanced graduate degree. Interviews with individual students often brought up a snippet of their parents' biographies, which sometimes involved a change of fate through education or, more specifically, through taking the Gaokao and getting into a Chinese college. For example, Sunny, an accounting major at Syracuse University, talked about her father, who starved during his childhood in the 1960s with his illiterate parents before becoming the first person in his village to go to college in Shanghai. He became an engineer and is now the head of an engineering firm in Shenzhen. It is ironic that people like Sunny's father, who changed his life primarily through the Gaokao, want a different kind of education for their children. Sunny explained:

> My dad has lived a hard life through relentless studying and working. He grew up without much to eat. But he persevered and finally went to college and changed his life. He has a successful career and can provide a good life for me. Now, he wants me to have a different life, more choices, more fun. In terms of education, he wants me to have a more education and life. He was not able to have that himself, but he is able to provide that for me.

Sunny's father apparently considers American education to be well-rounded, the sort of education that he, regrettably, did not have, and he paved the way for Sunny to have one. When asked what her father meant by "well-rounded education," Sunny was not exactly sure: "Something like not very test-oriented. You do not spend all your time working on exams, you can pursue other interests, I guess." The notion of a well-rounded education is related to the concept of the whole child, the development of children in all areas—academic, athletic, musical, artistic, and social.[24] This perception that American higher education is more amenable to well-rounded development than Chinese education reflects Chinese social imaginaries about American liberal education, driving the influx of Chinese international students to the United States.[25] Chinese parents such as Sunny's father, who achieved success through the test-oriented education, are among the most receptive towards American liberal educational ideals. They desire a well-rounded education for their children, and they believe an American education to be superior to a Chinese education in achieving that aim.

There is a misconception that the new wave of Chinese students comes entirely from wealthy families. Of those who are from upper-middle class families, none of their parents are idle scions of great wealth, lounging comfortably on family fortunes. Instead, students often describe their parents as coming from humble beginnings, sometimes growing up dirt poor as the descendants of peasants. Most of them changed their destiny through education, and specifically, by succeeding through the Gaokao and going to college. Now, as they become part of the rising middle class or upper-middle class in China, they want something better for their children, and studying abroad in America is what they desire—and can afford.

In contrast, some students come from lower-middle class or working-class families whose parents have to sell their apartments to afford an American education for their children. Jack from Shanghai, enrolled in Boston University, is an example—his parents are both factory workers. The only reason that he can afford to study in the United States is the rising property values in Shanghai. His mother was able to sell their apartment in downtown Shanghai for a good price. Now they live in a smaller apartment far from downtown. He majored in computer science, a highly popular major among Chinese students, and he hopes to land a job someday in Silicon Valley so that he can pay back his mother's investment.

Peter, another student from Shanghai, is also from a working-class family. His father is a driver for a company and his job often involves sending guests to and from the airport, but he has never taken a plane himself—he put most of his savings into Peter's education. Peter had never boarded a plane until he went to take the SAT in Hong Kong. He took the SAT two times, once in Hong Kong and another in Taiwan, as the test is not administered in mainland China. Every time his father drove Peter and his mother to airport and then continued with his work. Peter did not let his parents down and he successfully got offers from several top fifty American universities, and now studies at the University of California-San Diego. When asked why his parents want him to study in the United States in spite of his family's modest background, Peter said: "Chinese parents tend to sacrifice for their children and want the best for them. Here in Shanghai people consider studying in the U.S is the best. It is just natural to follow the trend."

Students often described how natural it was for them to be on the path to studying abroad. The very term *natural* speaks to the pervasive study abroad culture in urban China; studying abroad is no longer reserved for a few academic or economic elites.

Cosmopolitan Capital

Other than a quality education and American credentials, what these students and their parents are seeking could be termed *cosmopolitan capital*, which is rooted in cosmopolitanism. According to sociologist Don Weenink, "cosmopolitan capital is, first of all, a propensity to engage in globalizing social arenas. . . . Cosmopolitan capital comprises bodily and mental predispositions and competencies which help to engage confidently in such arenas."[26] American institutions of higher education embody such a globalized arena, with the largest international student body in the world and a full spectrum of prestigious academic programs,[27] ranging from science and engineering to fashion design and computer art. Sending students to America, the epicenter of globalization, is an effective strategy for acquiring cosmopolitan capital, which is a form of social and cultural capital. Weenink further theorizes: "It provides a competitive edge, a head start vis-à-vis competitors." Like any other capital, cosmopolitan capital can bring power and privilege. Studying in the United States can help Chinese students acquire and master a near-native level of English language use, meet and maintain a global network of classmates and friends, and access and consume intellectual and media content that reaches a global audience. These students, influenced by their parents, are keenly aware that they need to equip themselves with the language, knowledge, and cultural know-how to navigate the global world. Ultimately, they aspire to feel comfortable and confident in living as a world citizen, and they see studying in the United States as an effective way to realize this goal.

Related to the desire for cosmopolitan capital is a strong notion instilled early on in these students' minds that studying in the United States can broaden their horizons. This notion has been seeded and reinforced sometimes at a remarkably early age. Nicole, a native from Nanjing, was enrolled at Emory University as an environmental science and environmental health major. She visited the United States for the first time as a four-year-old, as she has an aunt living in Maryland. Her grandparents took her there for a summer vacation. Ever since then, she was infatuated with the idea of coming to the United States. During that trip, her family took her to many places, and the highlight was a visit to Harvard University, which made a long-lasting impression on her. "The lawn so beautiful with pigeons all around," Nicole reminisced fondly. Addressing my question of when she first wanted to study abroad, Nicole replied without hesitation: "I wanted to study abroad as early as I can remember."

Other students share Nicole's desire for a Western education from an early age. For example, Sabrina, a student from Guangzhou who was studying at the University of Wisconsin at Madison, recalled when her dream to study abroad began. She said:

> I have wanted to study abroad since kindergarten. Back then, everyone was watching TVB (a Hong Kong TV station), because around 1997, Hong Kong was officially returned to mainland China. As I was growing up, I watched many TV shows about the U.S. and the UK, and I was really impressed: "Wow, how good life is, modern and high-class. . . ." So at that time, I think, the dream of studying abroad was already sown.

Unlike Nicole and Sabrina, who had early aspirations to study in the United States, Jennifer, a student at UCLA, had no such idea until later in high school. She is from Zhuhai, only a one-hour boat ride from Hong Kong. She said she could have studied in Hong Kong, but she still wanted to study in the United States and experience the larger world. She said:

> I just wanted to go to see the outside world. I think perhaps I can still acquire knowledge very well in China, but I do not think that is the most important thing. I want to broaden my horizons. While I am young, I want to go out and see the larger world. This is priceless to me.

Jennifer was able to differentiate knowledge acquisition from horizon broadening, and it is the latter that she valued most and intended to achieve by studying in the United States. Interestingly, knowledge in Chinese (*zhishi*) consists of two characters: 知识. The first character means "knowledge," the second means "horizon." Jennifer is not alone in differentiating the two.

Brian also made an insightful differentiation between them; he specifically linked his education in China with knowledge:

> A horizon is different from knowledge. Knowledge is like a stock, a kind of preparation, but a horizon can give you a platform. Without a platform, knowledge can go nowhere. My schooling in China provides a lot of knowledge and I've learned a lot of material, but now I need the horizon to put the knowledge to good use. That is why I came here [to the United States].

Brian specifically names horizon broadening as his reason for studying abroad after forgoing his chance to go to Zhejiang University, one of the very best universities in China. Equally important, students' desires for an American education are entangled with strong yearnings for Western life, which, as Sabrina described it, is "modern, high class." As the superpower among the Western developed societies, the United States, and its society and culture, have been romanticized and imagined with help from American brand-name products, Hollywood films, and other American media platforms.[28] As a result, there is a consistent theme among these aspiring students of wanting to broaden their horizons, and in their minds studying in America will achieve this goal. Alfred, a Shanghai native studying at Boston University, echoed this feeling:

AFRED: From a very young age, I felt that going abroad is an honorable thing, a goal that I should pursue. I feel now this was like a superstition. I had a cousin, much older than me, who went abroad to study, first in Australia and then in the U.S. My family and extended family always pointed to this cousin as a good role model for me.

INTERVIEWER: What makes you think it is like superstition?

AFRED: I don't know. Just a feeling, perhaps, because you can never prove it, but we just believe in it.

Alfred's analogy of studying abroad to superstition brings to light an irrational belief in the value of studying abroad. The benefit of studying abroad lies not so much in terms of concrete skills and credentials as in the belief in its broader advantages—even if that belief is not entirely rational at times.

Once this belief is seeded, how do these students and their parents actualize it? Chapter 3 examines the various pathways from high schools to American colleges and universities. The remainder of this chapter zeroes in on the processes by which students select the American institutions at which they decide to enroll.

HOW DO CHINESE INTERNATIONAL STUDENTS CHOOSE THEIR SCHOOLS?

In short, school rankings largely direct students' choices: Chinese students will go to the highest-ranking school they possibly can. Rankings provided by the *U.S. News & World Report* are the bible in this process. In addition, family networks and knowledge about specific schools sometimes play a determining role in Chinese students' college choices.

Ranking, Ranking, Ranking . . .

Just as real estate has the mantra of "location, location, location," Chinese students have the mantra of "ranking, ranking, ranking." Sociologists Michael Sauder and Wendy Nelson Espeland argue that school ranking works to shape public opinion and receptivity, and thus recreates the social world.[29] Ranking has indeed recreated the American higher education landscape— the one of an absolute hierarchical order—in the eyes of Chinese students and their families. Our survey data provide evidence for ranking as the most important factor for college choice among Chinese international students. Figure 2.5 shows that close to 70 percent of the students thought that school ranking was either the most important or a very important factor in their choice of a college in the United States. Other secondary factors included parents' advice and the type of program.

This was corroborated by the in-depth interviews. Rankings guided students through their application process, from their initial selection of schools, to applications, to their final decision of enrollment. Stefanie, a native of Changzhou, a city in Jiangsu Province, hired an agent in Nanjing, the provincial capital. The agent helped her select ten schools to apply to,

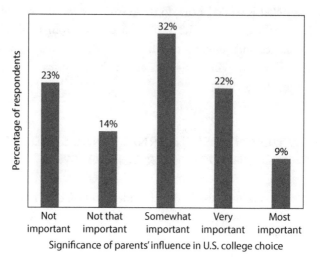

FIGURE 2.5 Significance of parents' influence on survey respondents' choice of a college in the United States
Source: Author's study

based purely on the best college rankings published by the *U.S. News & World Report*. According to her:

> The ten schools ranged from number ten to number forty in the rankings. The top fifty were my bottom line, and the top ten to twenty were my dream schools. I finally got offers from several schools in the top twenty to thirty, such as Berkeley, Rice, and Boston College. I decided to go to Notre Dame, which was ranked fifteen. This was the highest-ranking school that made me an offer, so I went there.

Stefanie had an excellent academic record, so for her, the top fifty schools were a safe bet; many other students expanded their pool to the top 100 schools. Schools outside this range are far less appealing to students, unless under circumstances of academic partnership between Chinese schools and American institutions.

Alexa was in the international division of the Guangzhou Foreign Language School, a prestigious public school in South China. The international division there has partnered with a third-party education company with programs that can send students directly to one of three colleges in the United States: Colorado State University, Georgia State University, and San Diego State University. None of the three schools ranks among the top 100 schools. However, students are spared the effort of taking the SAT, nor do they have to hire an external agency to go through the college application process, which most other students have to rely on. The only test they need to take is the TOEFL. Among the three schools, Colorado State ranks highest among the three, and it has become the most selective of students in this program. According to Alexa: "They [Colorado State] only gave two seats to us [her high school], based on GPA. I was not selected, so I came to Georgia State." Alexa further explained that she selected Georgia State because it has a high-ranking program in actuarial science, her choice of a college major. This indicates that sometimes the rankings of certain programs or fields are also relevant to helping students make their college choice, especially when the institutions they've been accepted to are not top-ranking.

This resonated with Wei's experience in her choice of a liberal arts college. Wei, a native of Hangzhou, studied at St. Olaf College. She applied to eight liberal arts colleges and two major universities. She prioritized liberal arts colleges because she knew that one of these would provide the small, intimate educational environment that she wanted. She too selected her schools primarily based on rankings. Her top choice was Mount Holyoke College, but she was wait-listed. So she went to St. Olaf College, which is well known for its math and music programs, subjects in which she was interested. After she came to St. Olaf, she realized that rankings are not as important as she used to think:

> I came to realize that rankings do not really reflect the educational quality of an institution. At least, Americans are not as much into rankings as we are. One of my close American friends originally enrolled at Barnard College and later transferred out, due to the larger classes at Barnard than anticipated, and my friend did not like this.

Among all the interviewees, there were four transfer cases who had in common the experience of transferring from a lower-ranked to a higher-ranked school. These transfers were: Jake, who went from Fisher College in Boston to Bentley in Boston; Diana, who transferred from the University of Washington at Seattle to Johns Hopkins; Joey, who transferred from the

University of Missouri at Columbia to Johns Hopkins; and Samantha from the University of California at Riverside, who moved to Indiana University at Bloomington. Their rationales for transferring were simple: they wanted to move to a higher-ranked school.

Diana, who enrolled at Johns Hopkins after transferring from the University of Washington at Seattle, told me that:

> Almost all my mom's friends' children are enrolled in elite schools in the U.S. So when I could only go to University of Washington at Seattle, we were a bit disappointed . . . so after two years, I transferred to Johns Hopkins.

The priority placed on school rankings is not unique to Chinese students' college choices in the United States. Research based on the UK also shows similar patterns. A recent study using nationally representative data confirms that university prestige often measured by school rankings is the most important driver of Chinese students' college choices in the UK, while cost of study and marketing strategy are not that important.[30]

How can we make sense of this? I propose two rationales. The first pertains to the Chinese cultural value of saving face and family honor.[31] For many Chinese students, where they go to college, and the brand name of their college, are closely tied with their family face and honor. In other words, going to college is not purely an individual student choice; far from it, it is a decision of a collective nature and consequence. Parents, in particular, play a decisive role in this process.

The second rationale pertains to the lack of knowledge of, and familiarity with, American colleges and universities. What makes a program or institution attractive is elusive to many Chinese applicants. Americans sometimes choose a college because they like its athletic programs or certain social clubs like Greek society. In other cases, they choose a college because their parents or grandparents were educated there.[32] These reasons are largely irrelevant to Chinese international students.

Many international students have little information about American colleges and universities beyond the rankings associated with these schools. Rankings, therefore, fill a void of knowledge about American higher education. In particular, rankings capture the hierarchical nature of the American college and university system as a whole, in an oversimplified way, but still satisfy the needs of Chinese applicants. The test-oriented Chinese education system has instilled the sense of attaching a score/number to measure quality and determine access, the culmination of which is that a hierarchy of Gaokao scores determines access to a hierarchy of Chinese colleges and universities.[33] As a result, the straightforward numbers of rankings lay bare the hierarchy of colleges and universities—an almost mirror image of the Gaokao scoring system.

Family Networks

In addition to rankings, family networks and information can help with the enrollment decision. Coco attends Emory because her mother, a college professor in medicine, was once a visiting professor there when Coco was in seventh grade. Coco visited her for a month one summer, and it left a lasting impression. When she was applying to colleges, Emory was her first choice, and she was admitted on an early decision (ED). Figure 2.5 shows that parents play an important role in affecting Chinese students' choice of a college in the United States. More than 60 percent of the respondents reported that their parents played a somewhat important role in their college choice decision. Sometimes the importance of rankings is conveyed through parents or parental networks.

Parents are sometimes embedded in strong social networks that consist of other parents who have children studying abroad or who plan to send their children abroad.[34] These networks create a race-to-the-top mindset among China's new middle and upper classes. To them, education is the best investment in maintaining and elevating their economic and social status. This is even more evident in the case of students whose parents are successful entrepreneurs. These students study in the United States with a clear intention to acquire the advanced business and cultural know-how that will enable them to grow and expand their family business upon completing their studies. Jake, a student from Bentley, corroborated this:

> My parents want me to study here, as the U.S. has the most advanced business and financial market. They hope that I can acquire skills to help our family business succeed.

Bentley has a highly ranked business program, higher than its overall institutional ranking, which attracted Jake.

Occasionally, Chinese students will forgo more highly ranked schools in favor of lower-ranked ones. Some parents have been to the United States before, either on business trips or during their own educational training, and they have information beyond the rankings to guide their children. Brian was accepted by Rice, which has a higher ranking than the University of Wisconsin at Madison, but he chose the latter because his mother, a business woman in the field of international trade, had formed very unpleasant impressions of Texas, the state where Rice is located, during a business trip there. His mom dissuaded him from going to Rice.

In addition, some of the study participants have extended family members living in the United States, who were often themselves international students of an earlier generation. As will be explored in chapter 9, the stay rate for Chinese international students in the 1990s and early 2000s was among the highest among all the sending countries, and many of these students attracted their nieces and nephews, who had grown up in China, to study in the United States. Angela from Shanghai has an uncle who graduated from Georgia State University in Atlanta in 1999. He had a great educational experience at Georgia State and ensuing professional success, so he settled his family in Atlanta. When Angela was applying to American colleges, she wanted to study only at Georgia State, close to her uncle's family. With the help of her uncle, she got in seamlessly and was happy with her choice, in spite of the fact that the institution is not in the top 100 colleges.

The central role of family information and networks about American institutions further proves the point that had Chinese families had access and information about specific American institutions, their enrollment decisions would not have been necessarily driven by rankings. This points to the importance of institutional outreach and information sharing if we'd like to reduce the overwhelming impact of rankings.

SUMMARY

This chapter focuses on understanding why Chinese students are motivated to study in the United States and on how they choose their institutions. More educational opportunities, higher quality programs and schools in the

United States, and a chance to avoid the Gaokao in China—all rational considerations—stand out as reasons for studying in the United States. However, encapsulating all these rational considerations are notions and beliefs that studying in the United States is a promising, and even honorable, thing to do. These beliefs are sustained and reinforced by strong social networks of family, peers, and friends who have either studied in the United States or are well on the path to doing so. Hence, it is a path "just natural to follow," as Peter described it. It is not an exaggeration to say that, in China, studying in the United States has grown into an education gospel that people believe in, and given the necessary resources, act upon.

This new education gospel satisfies the ambitions of rising middle- and upper-class Chinese parents; that is, to elevate their children's future in this global world. They aim to maintain their social position and grow their competitive advantage. This ambition, largely emblematic of the Chinese middle and upper class, also affects some working class. Notwithstanding a few exceptions, parents play a decisive role in this process, from the decision to study in the United States to the choice of a specific institution. For the most part, published rankings serve as the key signposts to American colleges, and in some cases, networks of family members and relatives help students decide where to go. In the end, the reliance on rankings coalesces with the cultural value of saving face, in that students and their families are in a race to get into high-ranking schools to bring honor to themselves and their families, and parents often serve as the enablers of this process.

In a nutshell, there are both instrumental and idealistic dimensions to the belief that studying abroad can help advance the future of Chinese international students. Instrumental considerations mainly relate to the perceptions that American college credentials are a gold standard for career development and that English proficiency is an admission ticket to full participation in the global world. Idealistic considerations relate to the perception that an American education provides more freedom and autonomy for students and to parents' desires to provide opportunities for their children to develop fully and realize their human potential. In the case of some parents with idealistic concerns, their children may already excel in the Chinese education system and qualify for admission into elite colleges in China; yet they still want their children to study abroad, because they feel American colleges are of higher quality than even good colleges in China. If acquiring American credentials represents the concrete goal of studying in the United

States, the more abstract or idealistic goal is to broaden one's horizons by acquiring cosmopolitan capital in order to display confidence and comfort in this era of globalization. Altogether, they help to create and maintain the education gospel of today's urban China: studying in the United States is going to advance your child's future, in terms of both academic and personal development.

CHAPTER 3

"From Hello to Harvard"

THE PATHWAYS TO AMERICAN HIGHER EDUCATION

D uring the summer of 2013, as I walked through a gated residential community of high-rise apartments in downtown Guangzhou, I noticed a banner with the slogan "English First" hanging outside the main entrance of one apartment building. Throngs of grade-school kids, ranging from kindergarten to elementary school, trooped in and out of the building, accompanied by parents or grandparents who lived in the neighborhood or close by. These kids came to study English and to practice their spoken English with teachers who are often native speakers from English-speaking countries. Nothing was more revealing than the numerous and colorful flags reading "From Hello to Harvard" hanging from the ceilings.

English First (EF) is a multinational education service company with diverse portfolios, among which preparing students to study in English-speaking countries is one of its core missions. Their motto is "learn English as well as your native language," and they focus on teaching it through listening and speaking—not by teaching grammar, as regular schools do. EF has opened branches in almost every major city in China; its offices are scattered throughout, in business districts, residential neighborhoods, and shopping malls. The curriculum of EF has encouraged and enticed many Chinese students to enroll in supplementary classes in English. Some students enroll in supplementary English classes as early as kindergarten.

The path of Chinese students to the United States often begins with English language tutoring. This is because the college application process often requires two exams: the TOEFL and the SAT. The former is purely an English language test, the latter a scholastic test, also in English, required by college admissions at a large majority of American colleges.[1] Consequently, English language education has become an integral part of the industry of the international education sector in China, which has grown to meet the education desires of millions of families.

Two parallel streams of new development in the Chinese international education sector have emerged in recent years: One stream is the burgeoning of international education in both the public and private sectors within China. Starting in the early 2000s, key Chinese public schools, often ones with strong academic reputations, opened international divisions, where Chinese students study for an international curriculum—American Advanced Placement (AP) or British A-level courses, or to study under the International Bachelaureate (IB).[2] The second stream is a trend among Chinese families to send their children directly to secondary schools in the United States. As many Chinese students come to the United States alone, a large majority of them enroll in private boarding schools or stay with the American host families.[3] After high school graduation, both streams converge on the common destination of American colleges and universities.

This chapter takes a close look at Chinese international students' pathways to undergraduate study in the United States. My research has identified four main routes:

(1) From regular classes in Chinese public schools to American colleges
(2) From international classes in Chinese public schools to American colleges
(3) From Chinese private schools to American colleges
(4) From high schools in America, usually private, to American colleges

Close to 80 percent of the survey respondents in this book traveled via the first and second pathways to American colleges, with some students enrolling first in Chinese colleges and later transferring to an American institution (like Samantha). The second pathway, through international classes, often involves tuition equivalent to that of private schools in China. The annual tuition for these international classes in public high schools where I conducted fieldwork ranged from $8,500 to $14,000 (60,000 to 100,000 Chinese yuan), but this was less expensive than the American private boarding school route, which entails both tuition and living costs (like Joy). Eighteen percent of the survey respondents attended an American high school before enrolling in an American college. However, while there has been phenomenal growth in the number of students coming to American high schools,[4] students who travel the fourth pathway are still in the minority, as the costs of attending an American high school, in addition to four years of undergraduate education in the United States, are often prohibitive—not to mention parents' concern over sending their teenage children to a foreign land. Consequently, the four pathways are stratified based on the economic resources of the students' families, with the first pathway entailing the least cost and the fourth pathway the most.

Aside from economic resources, students on these pathways also differ in terms of their academic planning. Students on the first pathway are part of the regular Chinese public school system, which is primarily geared towards the Gaokao, while students on the other pathways are more likely to opt out of the Gaokao, as they have already decided to attend college overseas. They might also have different support on their college applications. Students on the second pathway, or those in the international divisions, often have access to counselors who can assist with applying to college abroad. For students on the first pathway, such support mechanisms are not available, so they have to resort to outside agencies for help. These agencies are entirely private, for-profit entities that provide a range of services, from helping to choose a college to test-prep (for the SAT, TOEFL, etc.) to paperwork (helping with personal statements and letters of recommendation, filling out application forms, etc.).[5] I conducted in-depth interviews with students, including their experiences with agencies and their rationales on whether to use one or not.

This chapter shows how overseas study at the postsecondary level has redirected and reorganized educational strategies for Chinese students and their parents at the secondary school level, including school choices, school curricula, and the use of educational consulting agencies. My fieldwork and survey analysis further demonstrate how economic resources and parental education influence the educational trajectories of these international students and their college placement, which points to the process of social reproduction, even among this relatively privileged population.

I conducted fieldwork in nine high schools in China: eight are international divisions of public high schools and one is a private high school. Specifically, the fieldwork in public schools included four schools in Beijing—the first city offering the international curriculum—one school in Shanghai, one school each in Wuxi and Nantong (two medium-sized cities in China's Jiangsu Province), and one school in Guangzhou in South China. Chinese private schools are on the rise, but some serve only foreign citizens. Since this book only concerns Chinese citizens, I conducted the fieldwork in a private school in Chengdu, which accepted primarily Chinese citizens. The fieldwork consisted of classroom observations and interviews with students who were preparing to study in the United States, their foreign teachers, their counselors, and school administrators.

INTERNATIONAL DIVISIONS IN CHINESE PUBLIC HIGH SCHOOLS

Beginning in the early 2000s, a handful of public schools in major Chinese cities began to incorporate international education into their curriculums, separating students either into regular classes or into so-called international classes. The regular classes are for students who are preparing for the Gaokao, while the international classes—which charge substantially higher tuition—are almost exclusively for students preparing to study abroad. With the rising popularity to study abroad as undergraduates, schools with these classes have mushroomed in recent years.[6] In megacities such as Beijing and Shanghai particularly, the quantity of these schools has increased exponentially within a few years,[7] and now these programs are spreading to many other schools in smaller cities and less-developed regions. While there are no official statistics on this as of yet, these schools number in the hundreds, and expansion is ongoing. An international division often teaches an American advanced placement (AP) curriculum, a British A-level curriculum, and/or an international baccalaureate (IB) curriculum.

My fieldwork in these public high schools addressed the following questions: (1) What are the students' academic and social backgrounds in these kinds of international classes? Do economic elites trump academic elites here? (2) To what extent has the test orientation been weakened, as these students do not have to take the Gaokao?

Economic Elites and/or Academic Elites?

International education is often associated with elites.[8] Due to the much higher tuition charged in the international divisions, the cost itself can exclude many students without means. Does that mean students can just buy their way into the international programs? In the eight public schools where I conducted fieldwork, the findings are mixed. International divisions admitted students based on their *Zhongkao* test scores, the test middle school students take before being admitted to high school. It is usually specific to each region, and the key high schools in each region use the test scores as the basis for admission. Among all eight schools in my fieldwork, five had admission scores for their international division that were lower than those for their regular division, on average twenty to forty points lower (about less than 5 percent of the total score). Three such schools, two in Beijing and one in Wuxi, have higher admission scores in their international divisions than their regular divisions. These students can be considered both academic and economic elites. In other words, international divisions at these three schools are extremely selective, on both economic and academic grounds. The extent of selectivity hinges upon the size of the pool, which increases in a region where educational and economic resources are concentrated. For example, Beijing has a large pool of students who can afford the international division and at the same time also have strong academic records.

In addition to considering Zhongkao test scores, international divisions usually require an interview with candidates—in English, to ensure their oral English proficiency. The interviews range from ten minutes to half an hour. In one prestigious public high school in Beijing, the international division requires Zhongkao test scores that are higher than the regular division of that school, and they also entail two sets of interviews, student interviews and parent interviews. The student interviews are in English, the parent interviews in Chinese. The purpose of the two sets of interviews is to ensure that students from the right kind of families are selected. The international division head of this school, Mr. Zhang, explained to me during the interview:

> We want to make sure that parents are on the same page with us in terms of educational philosophy and their approach towards their children. We want them to understand that their children studying in

the international division are going to be educated in elite institutions in the U.S., where equality and individual freedom are core values. We want to select parents whose values are consistent with ours. We do not want parents who are authoritarian and controlling. This will not help their children succeed in the U.S. That is why we want to interview the parents.

Equality and individual freedom are frequently touted as core American values. In other words, the international division gatekeepers aim to select those parents who have practiced the American way of educating children— associated with "equality and individual freedom." This is distinct from traditional Chinese parenting, where there is a clear hierarchy between parents and children and where parents are in a position of authority and control.[9]

However, the extent to which such a public school as the one described above, with a strong national reputation in China, intentionally avoids the traditional Chinese parenting style is nothing short of ironic. Interviews with parents can be regarded as tests for Western notions of cultural capital.[10] Here, I draw from sociologist Annette Lareau's definition of cultural capital to include the skills and knowledge needed to navigate the education system, particularly the skills and beliefs associated with the Western cultural values embedded in education and parenting. Shrouded under notions of freedom and equality, these values are almost opposed to traditional Chinese education and parenting, yet this prestigious public high school in China adopts them in admitting students and their families into its highly competitive international division, to cultivate future elites. This selection mechanism effectively excludes students who have good academic records and the capacity to pay for the tuition but lack the requisite cultural capital. Therefore, in order for students to be admitted, they have to harness all the appropriate resources: economic, academic, and cultural.

For those schools that accept lower admissions scores in the international division than the regular division, they have developed a reputation for enrolling the children of economic elites who are not so strong academically. Some students whose parents are financially able to send them to an international division ultimately choose to stay in the regular division, especially when the regular division has a track record of sending students abroad as well. Coco, from the Nanjing Foreign Language School's regular division, is now a student at Emory. She chose not to enroll in the international division of her school because she was able to get into a regular division that was more competitive and prestigious, even though her parents could afford the international division.

Has the Testing Culture Been Alleviated?

Chinese students and their parents bemoan the Gaokao and the test-oriented education system, and those students who are enrolled in the international divisions usually forgo the Gaokao because they are preparing to apply to colleges in the United States. Our survey data reveal that 68 percent of our respondents had never taken the Gaokao. The question then becomes: In the absence of the Gaokao, is the testing culture in the international division alleviated? The answer is yes and no. Yes, the insane pressures of the Gaokao are dissipated, and so are its associated test prep activities, but really the Gaokao is simply replaced by the pressures of new tests—the TOEFL, SAT, and AP—and more testing, because many students take them multiple times to achieve the best scores possible. Although these new tests seem not to inspire as much nail-biting and are not as hell-ish as the Gaokao, years of testing anxiety still wire these students to work their hearts out.

Students from Nantong reported that they had a more-or-less standard timeline for testing to study abroad. At the end of senior one (comparable to tenth grade in the United States), students take the TOEFL tests. So for the whole senior-one academic year, they take TOEFL prep courses in addition to their regular academic classes. Why do they take the TOEFL at the end of senior one? Because many of them want to take it repeatedly to get a higher score. At the end of senior two (eleventh grade in the United States), in June, they take the SAT, and some also take SAT subtests. During this time, they also travel to Shanghai to take AP tests. The testing season falls in the midst of the regular semester, so many students often skip their regular classes. This deeply frustrates their teachers, their foreign teachers in particular.

When I visited the high school in Nantong, it was the end of May. The Chinese academic semester was still in session, and would not end until a month later, but most of the eleventh grade students had left to take SAT-prep courses. Bill, an English writing teacher, said that he had no students showing up in his class. He was visibly upset, "Nobody likes this—sitting around and doing nothing." He was referring to the fact that he would have no students in his class the following day, although the course was not over. "I very much want to teach the students how to write, but the students seem not to be interested."

Another foreign teacher, Thomas, who was teaching human geography for a senior three AP class (twelfth grade in the United States), also expressed frustration with low attendance. Both teachers found the senior-one students, those who had just started in the international division, to be the most engaging group, as they had not yet embarked on their testing journey. He lamented, "Students here are only interested in tests. I am worried about it. Because testing skills are very different from the skills needed to succeed in college."

Are students really interested in tests, as their foreign teachers assume? Students gave out their rationales: they feel they are plagued by an ever-rising bar for admissions and that their scores have to be exceedingly higher than in previous years, which means they have to work especially hard to get higher scores. This is because, as the overall number of applicants from China grows significantly, the admission rates of the select schools do not increase proportionately, so the process is increasingly selective and competitive, and the anxiety levels of Chinese students and their parents grow along with it.

One female student, Heng, who had already taken the TOEFL twice by senior two, described her dilemma:

> American universities are becoming more and more selective now. Their score requirements are higher and higher. Previously, a TOEFL score of 95 was fine, but now we all agree that it has to be over 100. Previously 100 was considered excellent, but now it is required. Only scores like 110 are excellent.

In 2017, when I did fieldwork in Beijing, a senior-two student said that she had already taken the TOEFL twice, and her score was 105. She planned to take it a third time, as "now everybody says we need to exceed 110." Moreover, those who take the TOEFL and SAT multiple times do not just aim to study in the United States; they have their eye on the top schools in the United States.

Is the threshold for top college admissions in the United States getting higher for these Chinese students? This is a common message perceived by various stakeholders, including counselors and teachers at top public schools in China, students, and their parents. They are fully aware that increasing numbers of Chinese students are applying to selective American colleges, which nonetheless do not proportionately increase their enrollment of Chinese students. According to Ms. Wang, working as a counselor in the International Division at the Beijing National Day School, which is one of the best public schools in Beijing:

> We started the international division around 2009, and we knew little then. But our average student could go to a top-fifty school in the U.S. We didn't know much, and the students' materials were not as polished as they are now. Now we have had more experience, and the students' application materials are of much higher quality, but it's much more difficult to get into the top schools now.

This rise in admissions standards not only reflects the expanded applicant pool in China but also results in part from the students' exclusive preferences for, and choices of, top-ranked schools in the United States. Only recently have college counselors tried to dissuade students and their parents from their laser focus on rankings. The effect is transient at best. According to Ms. Wang:

> Yes, we always try to educate parents that the ranking of the school is not that important. We try to communicate that message during our meetings with parents. We should focus on specific programs that their children are interested in. These parents seem to be willing to listen and change their perspectives. But once the meetings are over and the parents go back to the outside society and resume their routine, they tend to forget about this, and again are influenced by the broad societal emphasis on rankings.

In light of this, the Chinese obsession with top-ranked schools, coupled with the increasing selectivity of such schools in the face of an ever-expanding applicant pool, has sustained the testing culture in China,[11] even in the absence of the Gaokao.

THE DEEP STORIES OF AGENCIES

A majority of students who complete high school in China do not have access to college counselors, as Chinese college admissions are entirely exam-based. For those with in-house counselors, students sometimes still hire an external agent for extra support. Students usually face an initial, primary decision: whether they will use an agency to help with their college applications or instead do it themselves. Because the American college admission process is entirely different from the Chinese counterpart, most students feel the need to use an agency in China. There are more than 4,000 agencies in China, and their numbers are still growing as demand continues to increase. The for-profit agencies fill the void, and it has turned into a billion-dollar business.[12]

For Chinese Students, "Using [an] Agency Just Makes Sense"

Stefanie found her agent to be very helpful. She was one of a handful of Chinese students who got a sizable merit-based scholarship. She applied to more than ten schools that were ranked between ten and forty in *U.S. News and World Report*. She was admitted to Notre Dame, the highest-ranked school among all her offers, and she was also admitted to its honors college with a $25,000 scholarship. She owes her success in part to the help of her agent.

> As someone from our [Chinese] education system, I felt it was really hard to figure out how to craft a personal statement. So the agent was really helpful. We met for one day, with my parents there, brainstorming my experiences and extracurricular activities, and we collectively decided what to highlight in this essay. Then I drafted it, and the agent helped me revise. It was really helpful. The agent also knew all the logistics stuff well, such as the application deadline, the application materials required by different schools. They specialize in this. With their help, I could concentrate on preparing for tests and so forth.

Coco, a premed student at Emory, initially tried to get admitted into a top private high school in the United States before going to college, and she tried doing it herself, but failed. She attributed this failure to not using an agency. Ultimately, she remained in her Chinese high school, but she had learned her lesson, and she used an agent for her college application. She described her experience in glowing terms:

> They [the agents] provided excellent service. My agent provided comments and annotations for what I should revise, and I had to do the work. I felt I made a lot of progress during this process. I really feel that there is nothing wrong with Chinese students' using an agency. I think using an agency just makes sense, as the education systems are so different.

Sometimes, agents have connections with specific institutions, which create institutional pathways. Nicole, a graduate from Nanjing Foreign Language High School, used an agent who used to work as an advisor for her school. This agent, with a PhD in psychology from Emory, was well versed in writing and American culture. He opened an independent college counseling business in China and has developed a good reputation for sending students to elite American universities. Nicole explained:

> All the students [from her school in China] going to Harvard and Yale were advised by him, so he is very famous. Emory, in particular, has become the backyard of our school. They really like our students. In my cohort at Emory, there are more than ten from my school [in China].

This agent is in high demand, but he is very selective. According to Nicole:

> He charges 125 thousand yuan (about $18,000) per student, but he accepts only twenty students per year. Every student and his or her parents have to go through interviews with him. He only wants the academically strongest students, so that he can send them to the top schools in America. I am perhaps among the academically weakest he has counseled. He likes my personality, and he thinks that would be helpful for my case, so he accepted me.

This agent typically accepted students when they were in the tenth or eleventh grade, and he would assign a peer mentor from the twelfth grade to each new student. These mentors were chosen from his former students, a number of whom had already gotten an offer of acceptance, and they would provide peer support to students who had just signed up for the service. This agent served mainly as an advisor to students on how to revise their essays. He did not provide help with test-taking, so Nicole took SAT test prep classes elsewhere, incurring additional costs.

June, a native from Shandong Province in North China, enrolled later at Colby College. In 2011, she was among the first cohort of her high school's international AP class. Despite the fact that her high school offered in-house counseling, she felt that the counselors were inexperienced, so she hired an external agent who was a graduate of Stanford and had companies in Beijing and Shanghai. She explained how she came to hire this agent:

> I think looking for an agent is like looking for a mentor. I interviewed several agencies in my hometown, but I was not convinced they would be really helpful. Some of them, their English is no better than mine. This guy [from Stanford], at least his English was excellent, and I felt his knowledge and sense of American universities were compelling. I took a two-hour class with him first before I hired him as my agent. I found him convincing, so I hired him.

This agent helped June only with her essays. She was on her own when it came to choosing a college and preparing for tests. As a result, she paid less than 40,000 yuan (about $5,800) for the agent fee. Later, at Colby, she found that many of her Chinese friends had paid more than 100,000 yuan (about $14,500) for their agent, but they often had lower scores than hers. So she felt "it makes sense that they have to compensate for their lower scores with more money for their agent fees."

Student Dissatisfaction with Agent Services

As is the case with any kind of business, customers can be dissatisfied with the service. Writing a personal statement is critical, and it is often the most unnerving part of the college application process for Chinese students. Many turn to agents for help, some of whom ask standard questions and have a standard template to help students piece together their statements. When she was a college sophomore, Yan transferred from her hometown college in Dalian, a city in North China, to Syracuse University.

> They gave me a list of questions: my name, my experiences, what I had done before . . . they seemed to have a template for the personal statement, and they squeezed my information into it. This would not yield a good statement. Later, I met some graduate students here; they had written their statements on their own and asked for help only to polish their language. I think that is better. Had I known more, I would not have asked them to handle this for me.

Other than standardizing the whole process of writing essays, her agent also failed to do a good job helping her transfer her credits. According to her:

> They had many students to handle and they did not want to bother to communicate with my school in China about transferring course credits. For example, I only transferred three-credit courses, but many courses in China have 2.5 credits, which are really comparable to three-credit courses in the U.S. My agent neglected to communicate this to my school. Many of my courses are wasted. They ruined my application process.

She went on to describe how she did not even have access to the final version of her personal statement: "I did not even read my final personal statement, because the agent claimed that it was a business secret."

The discovery that their agents would not give them the final version of their personal statement kept resurfacing in various students' interviews. Jane at Ohio State University explained: "Perhaps they do not want you to access the final version, afraid that you'll send it to other agencies . . . some sort of intellectual property, I guess." Although Jane was not able to see the final version, she felt that the agency had not done a good job. She complained that she could have been admitted to a better school than her current one. Instead, her preferred schools, which were mostly small liberal arts colleges such as Mount Holyoke and Richmond, all rejected her application.

JANE: This school was last on my list of the eight schools I wanted to get into. It is a large public school where the classes are big and the Chinese students are many, and I had heard many negative stories about it.

INTERVIEWER: Why do you want to avoid Chinese-heavy schools?

JANE: I am studying in America. Why do I want to be surrounded by Chinese?

Jane's desire to avoid schools with a high concentration of Chinese seems to be in conflict with the tendency of Chinese students to hang out with only each other, a topic chapter 5 focuses on. It is possible that they desire to venture out of their Chinese group, but they are not sure how to do it. So Jane tried to avoid schools with a high Chinese enrollment in the first place.

Sometimes it is not just that their personal statements are inaccessible to these students, but that the entire agency-aided application-to-admissions process is marked by opaqueness. The lack of communication and transparency in this process deeply bothered these students. Hudson gave a vivid account of how cryptic the process had been for him:

I drafted my personal statement and sent it to my agent. The agent refused to let me see the final version. They actually did not tell me anything except for the final results: which schools admitted me and which schools rejected me . . . and they never would show their work or their communications with the schools. I asked to see the email exchanges, but my request was turned down. I started to become suspicious. I privately told my mom—who knows how many schools the agent had really applied to for me? I asked them to apply to ten schools for me. They might only have applied to four schools and said the other six all rejected me. . . . They did not even give me my admission letters and came up with various kinds of excuses, saying the letters were lost, or because I could not commit, the schools had not sent an official letter. They just told me which schools had accepted me, and I decided to go to the University of Washington at Seattle. I had to keep pushing, and I finally was able to see the admissions letter from the University of Washington, but that is the only letter I was shown, even though they told me I had also been accepted by Purdue, Ohio State, and Penn State.

The lack of transparency in the application process directly leads to an ero-sion of trust, and Chinese students become suspicious that their agents have not done the job that they promised to do. It is possible that the Chinese students and their parents were exploited and taken advantage of by for-profit agencies due to their lack of knowledge about the college application process in the United States.

Do It Yourself (DIY)

The students who chose to apply to colleges themselves, without the help of an agent, usually had access to someone they trusted—friends or family members to whom they could turn for help. For example, Angela, a student at Georgia State University, has an aunt that has been living in suburban Atlanta for the past two decades. Her uncle got a degree from Georgia State University and raved about his alma mater. They offered to help Angela to apply to Georgia State, which was the only school to which she applied. Her aunt helped her to polish her essays, and she was admitted. In her case, the thorny issue of college choices, which leads many other students to seek help from agencies, wasn't an issue at all.

Lei, an education major now at the University of Portland, is another example of the DIY path. A native of Nanchang, Jiangxi Province, she knew an English teacher, Ms. Zhao, who persuaded her not to use an agency. Ms. Zhao had studied at the University of Southern California and returned to settle permanently in Nanchang. According to Lei:

> Ms. Zhao helped me a lot during the application process. I asked for recommendation letters from high school teachers. They were in Chinese. Then I had to get them translated into English. Ms. Zhao helped me with the translations. I worked very hard on my personal essays. I also got help from my good friend, who was then studying in Singapore. She helped me with my English writing. This process was so new to me that I took painstaking efforts to complete it.

Personal statements and recommendation letters are genres of writing that are new to Chinese applicants. In the absence of trusted family and friends, a majority of Chinese students felt a strong urge to find an agency to help them with their college applications. The perceived necessity of using an agency is deeply rooted in the lack of familiarity with the holistic admissions system of American higher education, to which I turn next.

Holistic Admissions Push Students to Agents

Chinese students that feel the need to rely on study-abroad agencies to handle their applications are concerned that, however competent they themselves might be, the professional agency will give them a better chance of being admitted to the school that they want. However, application materials processed and embellished through agencies are often called into question by American universities. Chinese students are entrapped by their belief that an agency can help them and that their own efforts cannot generate a desirable outcome.

Using third-party help to craft essays is not unique to Chinese students; American students use this tactic to boost their applications as well.[13] I argue that what Chinese students encounter is confounded by the profound differences between the Chinese and U.S. education systems, which exacerbate the need and near necessity for them to seek external help. Chinese colleges and universities rely almost exclusively on test scores from college entrance examinations. Numerous research studies have shown that this college admissions policy shapes Chinese precollege education to be largely, if not exclusively, test-oriented.[14]

American college admissions, on the other hand, adopt holistic admissions principles and consider standardized test scores to be only one factor in the whole package of students' application files.[15] Holistic admissions, however, have created a cultural bind for Chinese students. These youths are fully aware that test scores are not the single factor that determines whether they get into a good American university, as it would do in China; individual biography is important, as are community activities. Nonetheless, the Chinese education system has not yet woven extracurricular activities and community engagement into their formal schooling. In other words, Chinese students are not trained to be the kinds of applicants the American higher education system expects, and in order to be competitive in the applicant pool, they have to learn quickly how to equip themselves with interesting experiences and present themselves in a way that meets the expectations of American institutions. This entails a drastic change of behavior and a deep learning curve in a short period of time; Chinese students need help and guidance in one way or another, and for-profit agencies satisfy this need.

AMERICAN HIGH SCHOOLS

Some parents decide to send their children abroad during high school, believing that this will help them make a more seamless transition to an American college given the disconnect between the two education systems. This choice is a hard one for many parents, entailing additional costs of both a financial and psychological nature. Financially, few parents can accompany their children to the United States, which means that Chinese students often attend a private boarding school or stay with a host family. These students often plan to stay on and attend college in the United States, and years of private school tuition plus four-year college tuition impose a hefty financial burden on parents. In addition, psychologically, many Chinese parents are worried that their teenage children could face insurmountable cultural and social challenges alone in a foreign land, thousands of miles away from family.

Notwithstanding the above concerns, the number of students coming to American high schools as a pathway to the American higher education is on the rise.[16] Many parents hope their children can adapt to the American education system better by arriving earlier and developing their English. Our survey data show that 18 percent of the respondents started their American education here as high school students. The survey analysis examines what differentiates those who started their American education in high school from those who started in college. Figure 3.1 shows that those who started in high school were more likely to have parents who did not have a college education. In other words, they were more likely to be first-generation college students. Figure 3.2 shows that those who attended American high schools were more likely to think their English was good or excellent than those who had not attended high school in the United States. However, attending an American high school may not necessarily lead to advantages in enrolling in a selective higher education institution. Figure 3.3 shows that the percentages of students in selective institutions were almost identical between those who attended American high schools and those who did not.

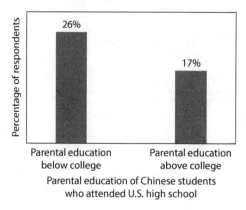

FIGURE 3.1 Distribution of parental education among survey respondents who started their American education in high school
Source: Author's study

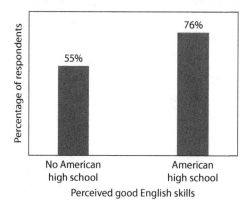

FIGURE 3.2 Relationship between attending American high schools and perceived good English skills among survey respondents
Source: Author's study

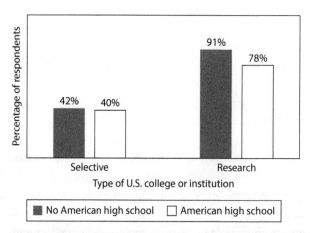

FIGURE 3.3 American high school attendance and college enrollment in selective and research institutions among survey respondents
Source: Author's study

So what really influences enrollment in different institutions among Chinese international students? This question is vital because, as shown in both chapter 2 and this chapter, Chinese students and their parents maintain a laser focus on rankings and admission to selective institutions, and that has driven them to engage in relentless testing and enormous investment in the college application process. (Selective institutions include the top fifty major research universities and top twenty small liberal arts colleges in the eyes of Chinese students.) I ran separate analyses for the outcomes of enrollment in a major research university versus a small liberal arts college. Table 3.1 presents the results. There is virtually no gender disparity in enrollment in selective institutions, but Chinese males are much more likely than females to enroll in a major research institution rather than a liberal arts college. Parents having had a college education is positively associated with admission to a selective institution but negatively associated with enrollment in a major research institution. In other words, students whose parents went

TABLE 3.1

Multivariate Analysis on Enrollment Into Institutions of Different Types (Odds Ratios)

	SELECTIVE INSTITUTIONS		RESEARCH INSTITUTIONS	
	I	II	I	II
Male	1.096	1.071	3.105***	2.978***
	(0.208)	(0.207)	(1.014)	(0.994)
Parents with college education	1.726**	1.376	0.564	0.373*
	(0.467)	(0.394)	(0.258)	(0.192)
Good English		1.893***		1.221
		(0.390)		(0.397)
American high schools		0.851		0.310***
		(0.22)		(0.11)

*** p<0.01

** p<0.05

* p<0.1

Note: Standard errors are in parentheses. "Good English" refers to students' self-perception that their level of English is either good or excellent, as opposed to poor and fair. "Selective institution" includes both research institutions and liberal arts colleges. The sample size does not allow for the intersectional analysis of the two dimensional institutional differences (for example, selective research institutions vs. selective liberal arts colleges).

to college are more likely to enroll in a liberal arts college than their first-generation college counterparts.

Attending an American high school does not yield any benefit in selective college enrollment, which defies the expectation of many parents who shoulder both financial and emotional costs to send their children as young as fifteen or sixteen years old abroad. Strengthening the college application and providing a better transition to American colleges are largely the rationale for the pronounced increase in Chinese international students' attending American secondary schools, as stated in the report on "Global Mobile Youth" released by the Institute of International Education.[17] Allen and his parents exemplified this rationale when Allen came to a private high school in Maryland as a tenth grader. He was initially reluctant to go, but his mom was persistent. He explained:

> My mom was disappointed with Chinese education and she wanted me to go as young as possible, so that I could adjust to the American education system and get into a good college. That is the ultimate goal. My mom believes that a private school in the U.S. leads to a good college in the U.S.

In spite of his reluctance, he went to a private school close to Baltimore. A growing number of Chinese parents are, like Allen's mom, coming to believe in the positive role of American high schools for selective institutional enrollment. However, our data show that while attending an American high school can boost English proficiency, when English proficiency and other factors were controlled (table 3.1), students who attended American high schools were no more likely to enroll in selective institutions.

As for the divide between research institutions and small liberal arts colleges, students who come to the United States as high school students are more likely to enroll in a liberal arts college than those who complete high school in China. This is perhaps because students who have been in the American education system for a longer period have a better understanding and acceptance of liberal arts colleges. Back in China, many small American liberal arts colleges lack name recognition, aside from a handful of elite ones. Many parents and their children would easily recognize the names of such major universities as New York University, the University of Southern California, Purdue, and Boston University, but would hardly know Williams, Pomona, or Carleton.

PRIVATE SCHOOLS IN CHINA AS A ROUTE
TO THE UNITED STATES

Since the Chinese government first adopted the private education law in 2003 to systematically develop the private education sector, Chinese private education has been growing steadily.[18] According to statistics published by the Chinese Ministry of Education, as of 2015, 7 percent of all primary school students and less than 6 percent of all high school students attended private school.[19] Barbara Schulte from Lund University has identified five types of private schools in China, differing in their levels of fees and student body clientele.[20] One of the five types—high-fee private schools offering international education—often sends their students abroad for an overseas college education. Schulte has not further differentiated this type; however, my fieldwork identified two subcategories of these high-fee private schools that prepare students for a college education abroad. Simply put, one category admits only foreign-passport holders, such as children from expatriate families; the other category serves Chinese citizens. I have done research in both types of schools, but in what follows, I will focus on the latter category—schools that serve Chinese citizens—given the scope of this book.

Pioneer, a private school located in Chengdu, China's southwestern region, had fifteen full-time teachers and forty-seven students, ranging from twelve to twenty years of age, as of spring 2017. Starting from fall 2017, it added an elementary division, open to students aged six to twelve. The expansion from middle school and high school to elementary school was due to the demands of many parents who find this kind of alternative schooling attractive. The founder and principal of this school, Mr. Shen, preaches and practices an educational philosophy quite contrary to that of the mainstream Chinese education system: he discourages testing and promotes individual students' free exploration of learning. Mr. Shen explains how he came to found this school:

> I used to be a college teacher before I pursued my graduate education in the U.S. majoring in education in the early 1990s. After graduation, I went back to China and first started to work in the government, but I always wanted to do something to change Chinese education. Then a friend approached me and asked me to tutor his son, who was not doing well in a regular Chinese school. I tried a different way to

teach this boy, by encouraging him to explore his interests, rather than studying for tests. This boy was learning well and has been on the right track since then. Other colleagues and friends referred more kids to me, so for a while, I had a few kids studying in my home. That is how this all got started.

Mr. Shen quickly found that his home was not large enough to accommodate his quickly developing clientele. Then, a former student, who had become a successful real estate developer, offered him a place—a former real estate sales center. Mr. Shen converted the space into his new school, which contains its own classroom space, lounge, library, and so forth. The annual tuition is 70,000 yuan (about $10,000). As most of Mr. Shen's students come from out of town, they have to pay room and board as well, and they live in apartments rented by the school.

Perhaps due to his own graduate education in the United States, Mr. Shen's education philosophy deviates from the central goal of mainstream Chinese education. He focuses on interest-based learning and rejects testing. There is no testing at this school. Students are evaluated on attendance, participation, teamwork, project work, and presentations. Some courses require a defense as the culmination of learning. The school does not reject applicants. Students go there either proactively, seeking out this educational opportunity, or passively, having been unable to survive the regular education system in China. The former category of students could survive, even thrive, in the regular system, but they opt out because they yearn for free, exploratory learning. The latter category of students has had trouble with the regular test-oriented education system. The school has something of a reputation as a home for students who struggle with the regular system.

Because this school operates outside of the regular education system, it does not have to abide by the curriculum regulations set by the local education bureau. Students customize their curriculum based entirely on their interests. During the time of my observations, many students shared a common interest in video gaming, which is often considered in ordinary Chinese families and schools as a disruption to learning. However, the school offers two courses based on video games. Their motto is: Play videogames with earnestness and professionalism. No casual gaming is encouraged.

Mr. Shen regularly visits American liberal arts colleges and works on building relationships with them so that he can recommend his students to those schools. He also invites the leaders of these colleges to visit Pioneer during recruitment season, so there has been a tremendous amount of trust built between Pioneer and a number of liberal arts colleges. Mr. Shen explained that Pioneer is a small school, and he thinks his students would adjust better at small liberal arts colleges in the United States rather than major universities. So far, Pioneer has established relationships with sixteen small liberal arts colleges in the United States, none of which are among the top twenty liberal arts colleges—the criterion of selective schools in the eyes of Chinese international students. Through the relationship building, Mr. Shen negotiated admissions requirements and privileges for his students. For example, he negotiated merit-based scholarships for his students and the waiving of the SAT exam; his students on average receive scholarships amounting to $20,000 annual support. His students need to take TOEFL, but they seldom go to cram lessons for testing services, as Mr. Shen discourages that.

Mr. Shen teaches one course on college success. He is also the sole college admissions counselor for all the graduating seniors (no more than ten per cohort). When he showed me around, he introduced me to every student we came across, and he would talk about each student's special talents and interests. For instance, he introduced me to a female student and told me that she had just completed an ethnographic project in a school that provided special education and had written a report and published it on their school website. He introduced me to a male student who was very interested in birds and geology. He got to know the students over several years and wrote very detailed and personalized letters of recommendation for each of them.

Jim is an example of a student who struggled in regular schools and then moved to Pioneer. He was not doing well in the traditional Chinese public schools, despite the fact that he was enrolled in one of the three best high schools in Chengdu at the time. His mother had invested much in his early education, which helped to give him a leg up in elementary school. However, that lead quickly faded in middle school, and by high school he was struggling and resistant to learning. His parents were able to provide various kinds of resources, including outside tutors. One tutor earned the trust of his family and turned out to be transformative in Jim's life. This tutor went on to work as a full-time teacher at Pioneer, and he convinced Jim's parents that transferring to this private school might be a good option for him. So Jim did.

He joined the first group of ten students. Now, Jim is an undergraduate philosophy major at St. John's University in Minnesota. Unlike other Chinese students, who spent the majority of their time preparing for tests, he took only the TOEFL, with a score of eighty. St. John's University was the only college he applied to, because he was confident he would be admitted with a recommendation from Mr. Shen, who arranged for one of St. John's college administrators to visit Pioneer and meet Jim before he applied.

Jim said his experience at Pioneer changed his life trajectory. His love for his alma mater is palpable: he plans to come back to this school as a fulltime teacher after he gets his degree in the United States. Pioneer has been a rising star in the alternative school sector in China. Over the summer of 2017, it hosted a Chinese education innovation conference. Jim served as a volunteer, helping with the conference organizing and hosting.

SUMMARY

This chapter focuses on the four main pathways Chinese international students take to get into American higher education institutions: (1) through regular classes in Chinese public high schools, (2) through international classes in Chinese public high schools, (3) through private schools in China, and (4) through high schools in America, often in the private sector. These different pathways entail different resources, educational experiences, and options. On a general term, the first pathway is the least expensive, and the last is the most expensive, in terms of tuition costs and living expenses. Academic requirements and the value of students' grades vary depending on the selectivity of the individual schools, but students in the first pathway do not necessarily opt out of the Gaokao, as students in the other pathways do. So, to some extent, students in the first pathway are the most academically burdened, as they have to prepare for the Gaokao and for study abroad for an extended period of time before they ultimately decide which option they will follow.

However, regardless of the heterogeneous resources and experiences associated with the different pathways Chinese students travel, they share some commonalities. They are all very ambitious about their future, and this ambition directly translates into aspirations to attend a high-ranking college in the United States. In their minds, studying in the United States is not sufficient; studying in a top-fifty or, even better, a top-thirty school is the goal. However, they were very anxious and frustrated in their efforts to decipher the value codes of American college admissions. The elaborate story-telling of personal statements and elusive admissions standards were alien to the Chinese students and their parents, who yearned for concrete measures to guide them. Frustrated and insecure, they often resorted to the only concrete standard—SAT scores and GPA—for reassurance, and they engaged in a relentless race to boost their test scores. They also feel that they have to depend on for-profit agencies. Due to the heterogeneity in terms of qualities of agency services, Chinese students and their parents are vulnerable to agencies' exploitation and mistreatment.

In addition, this ambition to get into a good college in the United States has sometimes driven Chinese parents to send their children to study abroad as early as high school—in the belief that American high schools are a better bet for selective college admissions. However, our survey data do not support this assumption. If anything differs in terms of college placement, the data show that those who attend an American high school are more likely to attend a small liberal arts college than those who completed high school in China, who are more likely to attend a major research university. What matters for college placement is parental education and students' English proficiency. In particular, first-generation college students are less likely to enroll in the selective institutions. This indicates a pattern of social reproduction among this relatively privileged population.

CHAPTER 4

Navigating and Comparing Chinese and American Education Systems

The stellar academic performance of Chinese students grabbed America's attention in 2009 when students from Shanghai, the city with the largest population in China, participated in the Program for International Student Assessment (PISA) and ranked first. PISA is a worldwide evaluation of fifteen-year-old students' performance on mathematics, science, and reading. Soon after, in 2011, Marc Tucker of the National Center of Education and the Economy in Washington, DC published a monograph, *Surpassing Shanghai*,[1] in an explicit effort to target Chinese schools as the primary competitors of U.S. schools. Tucker's text also expressed concerns over the American education system and, in turn, the future of American leadership in the world.

However, droves of Chinese parents are eager to send their children to American schools. They may be unaware of the first-place ranking of Chinese students in the PISA and, even if they are aware, they are concerned about Chinese education being too test-oriented. Instead, they want their children to have a quality education that transcends test scores. The question is: What do we make of this fascinating paradox, that Chinese and Americans are looking to each other in search of better education? Often, a lack of sufficient understanding tends to bias our judgment. I argue that Chinese international students are better positioned to compare the two systems and potentially help address this paradox, as they have had first-hand experience with both education systems.

Given that Chinese international undergraduates have received their primary and secondary education in China and their college education in the United States (those who start their American education in high school experience the secondary school systems in both societies), they have a unique understanding of the two systems. What do Chinese students think of the Chinese and American education systems as they experience them? Through both surveys and in-depth interviews, this book identified five key aspects of Chinese and American education into which Chinese students provide important insights. These are: (1) creativity and critical thinking, (2) ability-versus effort-based learning mindsets, (3) attitudes toward math, (4) the contrasting disconnects between the precollege and college experiences, and (5) academic integrity. Through their eyes, the strengths and weaknesses of each system emerge, which shed new light on some hot-button issues, such as which attributes of education are amenable to innovation and why the Chinese system is able to produce innovation despite its tendency to repress creativity.

CREATIVITY AND CRITICAL THINKING

In the West, academics and the public alike often perceive East Asian education systems to prioritize standardization and conformity at the expense of creativity and critical thinking.[2] The priority on standards and conformity may be rooted in the collectivist orientation of East Asian societies.[3] The distinction between individualism and collectivism is salient in American and Chinese education systems, as well as broad societies. Geert Hofstede and Gert Jan Hofstede, in their groundbreaking book *Cultures and Organizations: Software of the Mind*, identified the cultural dimensions that underlie Chinese and Western societies;[4] in particular, the divide between individualism and collectivism. This distinction manifests itself in the beliefs and practices of the education systems. While the American system is based on the belief that each student is an individual with unique abilities and interests, the Chinese education system subscribes to the belief that students should be taught at a given grade level as a given age group.[5] That is why tracking occurs much earlier and more often in the United States than in China, where generally, students are not separated until later (approximately around eleventh grade) into science versus humanities tracks to prepare for the college entrance examination.[6]

Chinese education shares some key features of East Asian education in its value of a standardized curriculum, high-stakes testing, and so on. Academic and public discourse both promulgate images of rote learning, memorization, and drill practices associated with East Asian education.[7] The problem with such discourse is that creativity varies across cultures and societies, and scholars use quite different conceptualizations of creativity.[8] Without a consistent definition and measure of creativity, reliable empirical evidence is extremely hard to come by.

In 2014, Hyunjoon Park, a sociologist of education at the University of Pennsylvania, published a book titled *Reevaluating Education in Japan and Korea: Demystifying Stereotypes.*[9] In chapter 4 of his book, Park turns to psychology: "Psychologists have long believed that their study of problem solving would provide insight into creative thinking . . . [C]reative thinking is a form of problem solving."[10] Park used PISA data to compare students from Japan, South Korea, and the United States on their performances in problem solving. He found that Japanese and Korean students outperformed American students in both high- and low-performing student groups (the ninetieth and tenth percentiles) and that they had higher averages. Park does not claim that problem solving is the only component of creativity, but he argues that it is an essential element. By showing that the United States lags behind East Asian countries in problem-solving skills, Park questions the notion that American education is superior in cultivating creativity. He concludes:

> The biggest problem I have with the current literature on creativity is its dichotomous thinking that simply assumes that homogeneous and standardized curricula in Japan and Korea necessarily hurt students' creativity, while the United States' individualized and non-standardized curricula necessarily enhance students' creativity. This all-or-nothing thinking only reinforces the stereotype that higher academic achievement among Japanese and Korean students is at the expense of independent thinking and creativity and mainly the outcome of memorization and rote learning under the "same"

curriculum for everyone. The stereotype diverts the imminent concern about the poor basic academic skills of U.S. students by disproportionately highlighting the supposed strength of U.S. education in creativity.[11]

This all-or-nothing thinking about creativity, criticized by Park, could be due to a lack of empirical research on the subject. Park's research on conceptualizing and measuring creativity in terms of problem solving, while helpful, is still limited. Creativity may encompass traits and skills well beyond problem solving that are hard to measure quantitatively. In-depth interviews with Chinese students illuminate their insights on creativity and critical thinking and the extent to which Chinese and American education help to cultivate this trait.

Creativity

CONNECTING CREATIVITY WITH MULTIPLE PERSPECTIVES

Chinese students consider creativity in terms of multiple ways of thinking, and they believe American education is conducive to cultivating it. Kathy was a public health major at Eastern Tennessee State University. In 2011, she came as an exchange student from Guangzhou to join the eleventh grade at a magnet high school in Tennessee. When asked what impressed her most about American education, she mentioned "creativity." Here is how she understood creativity in the United States and how she perceived the problem with Chinese education:

> I think here in the U.S. education does not expect you to give one right answer. It encourages you to think about multiple perspectives, and come up with your own ideas. Chinese education wired me to search for one single answer. I could not get used to American education with open-ended questions. American education wants you to have ideas, but I have few ideas, as in China, teachers give you an idea, and you learn to copy that idea. So when I applied to American colleges, the application form asked why I want to go to this school,

what kind of person I was, what kind of contribution I could make to this school? I felt very dumb before these questions—I didn't know myself, and I didn't know why I wanted to study at this school.

Kathy spent two years in American high school before enrolling in Eastern Tennessee State University. She struggled with the aforementioned problems during the greater part of her high school; namely, discomfort with open-ended questions, lack of self-knowledge, and a paucity of ideas. However, she worked hard and made significant improvements; in college, she came to feel more confident in courses such as history and social science, where multiple perspectives are intensively dissected and discussed.

This connection between creativity and multiple perspectives rather than one way of thinking emerged consistently in my interviews with students. Sabrina is a physics major at the University of Wisconsin (UW) Madison with a second major in art history; below, she described how she was attracted to art history:

> I found that every time I look at an art work, I have new understandings. We often used to pursue the single perfect answer, but [art history] can allow multiple interpretations, as long as they make sense. I find this is also a feature of American education, which is open to different answers, not necessarily one answer, as long as you can provide support.

In China, Sabrina wanted to study physics. She didn't anticipate studying art history, but she found that she enjoyed learning about the subject so much in the United States that she added it as a second major. Chinese students sometimes choose to double major, as this reflects their interest in making full use of the American liberal arts education system. This topic will be further explored in chapter 6, which focuses on the process of choosing a college major.

CREATIVITY REQUIREMENT CONTINGENT ON DIFFERENT FIELDS

The students in my study often referred to art as a creative form of expression. Some of them tried to follow in Sabrina's footsteps and develop their artistic creativity through coursework by choosing a second major in art. Others lamented that their capabilities in the creative arts had atrophied before coming to the United States. Peng was among the first cohort in his international classes in Wuxi, and he was able to transfer over 20 AP credits to the United States, claiming a triple major in mathematics, finance, and information management at Syracuse University. However, he said he regretted his loss of artistic creativity:

> I was very impressed by my American classmates' ability to design and create artwork, and I wished that I could be that creative, too, but I just cannot. When I was a small kid, I also enjoyed drawing and doing artwork. But later academic studies totally stunted my development in that area.

Education scholar Yong Zhao's argues that creativity is hard to cultivate, but it can be killed.[12] But the question is: Was Peng's creativity killed in all domains? While Peng felt the loss of his creativity in an artistic sense, he did not feel the same way about math and science. Indeed, he is very happy with his logical and analytical skills. He sailed through his entire math and technical curriculum in college and graduated with flying colors. After a brief stint working as a financial analyst in New York City for a year, he returned to China in 2016 to start his own fund. He has joined China's new generation of financial entrepreneurs. He credited his academic success and early career take-off to the Chinese education system: "Without a solid foundation in math, I would not have been able to work in this field and start my own company. This is what my Chinese education has paved the way for, my current creative pursuits in finance."

Many students shared a similar sentiment: On the one hand, they lashed out against their prior education in China as stifling their creativity, describing Chinese education as dead and dull. On the other hand, they felt grateful for their solid foundation in technical subjects, which paved the way for technological innovation. As paradoxical as it seems, this parallels another trend, that China now has become the world leader in various cutting-edge industries, such as artificial intelligence, electric cars, and nanotechnology.[13] These successes in innovation hinge upon a solid supply of technology talent with strong training in math and science. Through their experiences of learning in both education systems, Chinese international students affirm that the solid foundation in math and science is indeed the strength of the Chinese system. Their complicated views of their Chinese schooling also shed light on why the Chinese system can cultivate creativity despite the potential to suppress it.

Domains do differ in utilizing creativity. Some fields can let people freely engage in their creativity without much drill or hard-core practice, while other fields require prior training so that people can utilize their creativity. Sociologists of science define the hard-soft dimension of different fields of study based on paradigm development and the degree of mathmatization.[14] Whether a discipline has a dominant paradigm or allows multiple and competing paradigms reflects the degree of consensus about problems and knowledge in the field.[15] *Hard fields* are characterized by a dominant paradigm and a sequential knowledge structure, as opposed to *soft fields*, which have no rigid sequence. Hard fields include subjects such as math, the natural sciences, and engineering; soft fields include the humanities, the arts, and some social science fields. It is worth noting that there is no clear-cut boundary between them, but is more of a spectrum of hard and soft fields. Due to the sequential knowledge structure of hard fields, such as math and science, students need to accumulate certain knowledge and skills before they can effectively utilize their creativity. A good example is the fast-growing computer science field, as math training is absolutely essential for software creation. Thomas L. Friedman quoted Bill Gates's words in his book *The World is Flat*: "I have never met the guy who doesn't know how to multiply who created software."[16] Many American students, low-income minorities in particular, have lost the opportunity to enter high-tech fields, sometimes because they are woefully unprepared in math during their pre-college years.[17] This theme is further explored in the section below on attitudes towards math.

Critical Thinking

Chinese students in this book consider critical thinking as the defining feature of American higher education, and the interviews yield their understanding about critical thinking in three major aspects: (1) from dualistic thinking to multiplistic thinking, (2) truth seeking and challenging authority, and (3) emphasizing process over outcome.

FROM DUALISTIC THINKING TO MULTIPLISTIC THINKING

Chinese students often mention critical thinking when discussing creativity, especially as it relates to approaching a problem from multiple angles. They also talk about critical thinking in the context of challenging authority and focusing on process over result. From this perspective, creativity is an end, and critical thinking provides the means to achieve that end.

Stefanie, a finance student at Notre Dame with a second major in applied math, mentioned critical thinking during the first few seconds of our interview. When asked why she wanted to study in the United States, she said that for her, developing critical thinking skills was the main allure of American education.

INTERVIEWER: How do you understand critical thinking?

STEFANIE: Let me think. . . . I feel it means every position and opinion is not strictly right or wrong. They are culturally dependent. We can all have our unique perspectives, based on our cultural backgrounds and personal experiences.

INTERVIEWER: How does American education cultivate critical thinking?

STEFANIE: I think independent course selection is really important. For example, I am now interested in psychology, so I can explore my interest in courses in psychology. This is really helpful, because it allows you to explore your interest beyond your major field of study. Also, I do not know whether Notre Dame is particularly so, but in philosophy and theology courses, they are all seminar discussion style. No exams, all discussion and essay writing. Professors are very interested in our own thoughts and pay much attention to our essays, and cultivate our individual perspectives.

In Stefanie's eyes, critical thinking is the defining feature and crown jewel of American higher education; she refers to the ability to go beyond dichotomous right-or-wrong thinking and develop a unique perspective. In contrast, Chinese students learn to find the answer in their test-oriented education. Often, the answer is definite, which is hardly compatible with the open-mindedness that accepts multiple answers and interpretations. William Perry's theory of cognitive development and critical thinking proposes a number of stages that describe college students' intellectual development

(1970, 1981).[18] Simply put, there are three stages through which most college students progress. The first stage is dualism, when students view the world in dichotomous categories (right/wrong, good/bad) and believe there is a single correct answer. The second stage is multiplicity, when students recognize that there are multiple perspectives to problems, but they cannot evaluate every perspective. The third stage is relativism, when students can identify knowledge as relative to particular frames of reference and can engage in informed comparison, analysis, and evaluation. Chinese students such as Stefanie are transitioning from being dualistic learners to being multiplistic and relativistic learners.

TRUTH-SEEKING AND CHALLENGING AUTHORITY

According to education scholar Jin Li, "Critical thinking is first and foremost about truth-seeking."[19] In order to seek truth, a necessary component in the learning process is to cast doubt on existing knowledge and to ask questions. Therefore, a much-valued attribute in the American learning process is challenging authority. American professors encourage and expect students to raise pointed questions in the classroom. Small-group seminar classes are designed to provide intimate environments for the faculty-student exchange of questions and ideas. Other key elements of critical thinking are open-mindedness to different views and questioning one's own potential bias. Students are also expected to embrace questions and challenges to their own thinking.

These elements of critical thinking—challenging authority (the teacher's) and challenging one's own biases—pose difficulties for students who are steeped in the Chinese education system, which is heavily influenced by Confucianism, particularly its emphasis on hierarchy and obedience.[20]

This helps account for how Sabrina was shaken when she asked her professor a question at University of Wisconsin at Madison:

He said: "I do not know." I was totally shocked for the first few seconds. How could you be a professor and say, "I do not know"? After a dozen seconds, I started to feel awed by this. He is really a deep person to do that. He did not want to guide me in the wrong direction. Had this happened in China, my teacher would say, "Oh, do not worry, you do not need to know this, as this is not going to be tested."

Brian, another UW Madison student studying industrial engineering and psychology, understood critical thinking as evidence-based truth-seeking. He said:

> In China, we used to equate believing in someone with believing in their ideas. I do not agree with this. In the U.S., you do not have to follow this. If you want me to believe in your ideas, you need to provide evidence, and I then will see the logical connection between the evidence and your argument. I like this way of making judgments.

This stance inevitably involves challenging authorities, who are supposed to be the keepers of truth, including teachers. Brian went on to describe his perception of teachers and his relationships with teachers in China:

> I agree with you, not because you are my teacher, but because what you've said is convincing to me. I liked to debate with teachers in China, which often got pushback. Now, in the U.S., I feel freer to do so without getting much pushback.

Chinese students in America are confronted with a different type of authority figure, one who makes them reflect and develop new understandings about knowledge and authority. In turn, they develop their own critical thinking skills.

EMPHASIZING PROCESS OVER OUTCOME

Many Chinese students like to compare their American teachers to their previous Chinese teachers, and some students have provided vivid examples of how American teachers approach teaching in ways that are remarkably different from those of their Chinese counterparts. Jack, a biochemistry major at Boston University, mentioned the following point, echoed by many participants: Chinese education teaches you knowledge, and American education teaches you how to find the knowledge on your own. He gave an example in his math class in the United States:

> My math teacher taught trigonometric functions, and the teacher started the lecture just a bit, then let us work in teams and make

presentations about this. The teacher asked us to use Google, wikis, and other math software to teach the class. The process is not easy, and sometimes uncomfortable, as we need to figure out many problems and collaborate as a team to complete the task, but going through that process is very good. We know the material pretty deeply, how to divvy up the work, and how to collectively work on a project. We finally make our little PowerPoint presentation, which we are quite proud of. In China, the attention is on the result, and teachers care about whether the result is wrong or right; in the U.S., the focus is on the process.

Jack's insight about process versus results, emphasized by the American and Chinese education systems, respectively, helps explain another student's choice to retake many gateway courses in America that he had already taken in China. Unlike most Chinese students, who are eager to transfer credits to their American universities to save time and money, Brian enrolled in several intro-level classes in math and science at UW Madison that he had taken already in his high school in Guangzhou. He did not think it a waste of time to relearn the material in America, because he found that the ways his American professors taught the same materials zeroed in more on the essence of a problem. He gave the example of a math function:

In China, the teacher asked us to write down $f(x) = y$, without explaining why. We also did not ask, assuming it is what it is. My American teacher went into detail explaining what a function is. According to him, "f is like a magic box, x entering a magic box, like a procedure, turns into y." I was very impressed. Asking questions in the process is very important, because then we can really understand why.

This focus on *why* is exactly what critical thinking entails, and the Chinese education system does not orient students to questioning.[21] A majority of the interview participants lamented the lack of critical thinking in Chinese education. The expectation of dualistic right or wrong answers effectively shuts down alternative options and thinking, which could be venues for creativity.

Nevertheless, despite their criticisms of their prior education in China, these students are appreciative of other aspects of their Chinese education;

notably, the effort-based learning approach helped them develop tenacity and endurance, which they found to be very beneficial to their studies in America.

ABILITY VS. EFFORT AND FIXED
VS. GROWTH MINDSETS

One of the most influential cross-national studies of American and East Asian education is the book *Learning Gap: Why Our Schools Are Failing and What We Can Learn from Japanese and Chinese Education*, by Harold W. Stevenson and James W. Stiger.[22] The authors conclude that Chinese people, including parents and teachers, believe in effort over innate ability, in driving the process and outcome of learning, while American educators and parents believe in innate ability over effort in academics.

Similarly, social psychologist Carol Dweck and her colleagues have identified two types of mindsets for understanding intelligence: a fixed mindset and a growth mindset.[23] A *fixed mindset* is the belief that one's abilities are largely innate and that the room to improve them is limited. A *growth mindset* is the belief that one can grow and improve one's performance through effort, perseverance, and mentoring. Recently, Angela Duckworth's book *Grit: The Power of Passion and Perseverance* hit a nerve and made *grit* a buzzword in the education world and beyond. *Grit*, as defined by Duckworth, refers to perseverance combined with passion, driven by interest and purpose. Duckworth has collaborated with Dweck, and what they found is that grit and a growth mindset always go together: people with a growth mindset tend to have higher grit scores.[24]

Jennifer Lee and Min Zhou[25] have drawn from Dweck's theories to explain how Chinese and Vietnamese immigrant children had a growth mindset instilled in them at home by their immigrant parents, who believed that their children's performance could be improved through increased effort. They argued that this contributed to their children's academic performance in school. So, where did these Chinese and Vietnamese immigrant parents obtain their growth mindsets? Lee and Zhou argue that they were influenced by the educational norms and structures of their home countries in Asia.

Similarly, Chinese international students deeply believe in the pivotal role of effort in driving learning outcomes. The survey and interview findings in the following section corroborate their belief in hard work and intense effort.

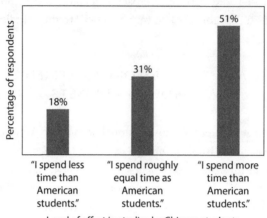

FIGURE 4.1 Percentage of Chinese students reporting their level of effort in their studies compared to American student peers
Source: Author's study

Survey Findings on Effort

Over half of the interview participants reported that they put more time into studying than their American peers, while less than 18 percent reported that they put in less time (figure 4.1). This investment in studying paid off in their GPAs. Over half of the students had a GPA over 3.5, and about 87 percent had a GPA over 3.0 (see figure 4.2).

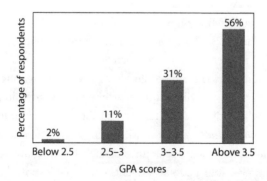

FIGURE 4.2 Distribution of GPA scores of Chinese international students
Source: Author's study

Differences exist among Chinese students on this measure. Figure 4.3a shows that female students were more likely than males to report that they put more effort into studying than American students. Fifty-four percent of Chinese female students reported that they spend more time studying than their American peers as compared to 48 percent of Chinese male students. On the other hand, 24 percent of Chinese male students reported that they spend less time studying than their American peers, compared to 12 percent of Chinese female students. This is consistent with the worldwide pattern that girls tend to put more hours into academic work than boys.[26] Another differentiator is college major. Figure 4.3b shows that STEM majors and business majors were more likely than humanities and social sciences majors to report that they put more effort into studying than Americans.

Table 4.1 presents the multivariate analysis for Chinese students' effort, examining which factors influence the outcome of spending more time in studying than American peers while holding other factors constant. Model I includes background variables. Gender turns out to be insignificant when taking into account parental education, length of stay, and whether or not the students take the Gaokao before they study in the United States. Notably, the length of stay in the United States was negatively associated with effort; namely, the longer Chinese students had stayed in the United States, the less likely they were to report putting more effort into studying than their American peers. Specifically, one additional year of time in the United States can reduce the odds of putting in more effort than American peers by 14 percent. Interestingly, taking the Gaokao will increase the odds of a student putting in more effort by 53 percent. This indicates that the Chinese Gaokao, with its relentless nature, cultivates endurance and strong study habits in students, further evidenced by their interview responses in the next section.

Model II adds academic background variables, including GPA, perceived English proficiency, and college major. GPA is positively associated with effort. Social sciences/humanities majors are less likely than STEM fields to put in more effort than American peers.

Model III adds institutional-level factors. Chinese students from selective institutions are more likely to put more time into studying than their American peers, compared to their peers from nonselective institutions. In the final model, length of stay remains negatively associated with effort. The robust negative association between length of stay in the United States and effort-making across different models provides evidence to support classic

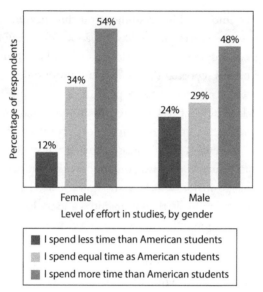

FIGURE 4.3A Chinese international students' survey responses of their level of effort in their studies compared to American student peers, by gender
Source: Author's study

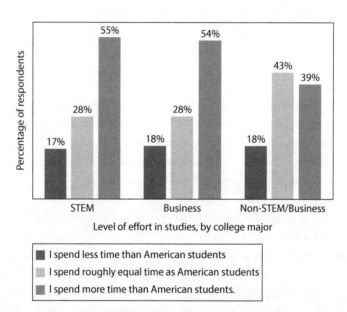

FIGURE 4.3B Chinese international students' survey responses of their level of effort in their studies compared to American student peers, by college major
Source: Author's study

TABLE 4.1

Multivariate Analysis of Chinese International Students' Effort in Academic Studies (Odds Ratios)

	MODEL I	MODEL II	MODEL III
Male	0.813	0.876	0.872
	(0.147)	(0.172)	(0.183)
Parents with college education	0.969	1.035	1.003
	(0.233)	(0.269)	(0.278)
Length of stay	0.858**	0.871*	0.850**
	(0.058)	(0.063)	(0.064)
Taking Gaokao	1.531**	1.37	1.366
	(0.127)	(0.149)	(0.161)
Business majors		1.138	1.134
		(0.264)	(0.279)
Social sciences/humanities		0.676*	0.668
		(0.159)	(0.165)
Good English		0.841	0.880
		(0.174)	(0.193)
GPA		1.599***	1.678***
		(0.217)	(0.247)
Selective institutions			0.604**
			(0.127)
Research institutions			0.813
			(0.256)

*** p<0.01

** p<0.05

* p<0.1

Note: Standard errors are in parentheses. "Effort" is defined as those Chinese students who put more time into studying than their American peers. "Good English" refers to the perception that the student's level of English is either good or excellent, as opposed to poor and fair.

assimilation theory: the longer migrants stay in the host society, the more they resemble the members of that society.[27] In other words, those who come to the United States at a younger age (e.g., those who come to attend high school) are far less likely to work hard than their Chinese peers who start as college students.

In-Depth Interview Findings on the Meaning of Effort

CHINESE EDUCATION TRAINS FOR TENACITY AND ENDURANCE

Jenny is a junior majoring in both Global Studies and French Studies at Colby College in Maine. During our interview, she recounted an experience in her French class at Colby with her American classmates:

> In my French class, my American classmates tend to associate learning with talent. They would say, "Oh, I am not good at this." But I would say, "Hey, you have not worked hard. The effort you have shown in learning French is not even half of mine in learning English. How could you know that you cannot do it?" I think that is not a right attitude—not being able to accept setbacks.

Jenny expressed gratitude toward her Chinese schooling, which helped cultivate her "right" attitude towards learning—that is, "being able to accept setbacks." Coco, a premed student at Emory, is fully aware of the challenges in gaining entry into an American medical school, which is her goal. However, some state universities' medical schools do not even admit international students. Still, she wanted to aim for the few coveted seats available for Chinese students like her. Her GPA was 3.9. She said that she "worked dead hard," and that the journey ahead is promising; she became a teaching assistant for her biology class last semester after only one year in college.

Yang graduated from a high school in Wenzhou, Zhejiang Province, before matriculating at Penn State. While in China, he taught himself AP courses, took exams in Hong Kong, and successfully transferred 30 credits to Penn State— roughly equivalent to the entire first year of course credits. As a result, it took him only three years to graduate from Penn State, and he graduated among the top four in his program. He was awarded a fellowship to study earth science at Johns Hopkins. Nevertheless, in spite of his academic accomplishments at Penn State, he still thinks his study hours in the United States do not compare to his prior academic regimen in China. He described his gruesome study schedule in China:

> Usually I got up around 5:30 A.M. in the morning and went to bed around midnight. I studied about fifteen hours per day, except for some

brief periods for meals. Not just me, everybody around me studied like that. So you do not have time to think, and you have no choice.

Yang maintained pretty much the same schedule in the United States, except there were not as many study hours. He filled in his time with sports and exercise. He also took a part-time job as a sandwich maker at one of the on-campus restaurants at Penn State, and he volunteered to tutor math in the local city school district. He said his work ethic had been "instilled in China." He did this kind of work not just to make money but also to gain some experience, just like his American peers.

Not all of the Chinese students interviewed for this book were academically strong. Some carried an effort-based learning orientation to the United States despite the fact that they were repeatedly ridiculed and put down by their teachers and peers in China due to their weak academic abilities. Phyllis, at North Carolina State University, did not have good grades in China, where she said she had often let down her teachers and parents. She deemed her opportunity to study at a U.S. college a second chance and wanted to prove herself. Interestingly, although education scholars point to Americans' belief in talent over effort as a driver of learning outcomes, the American education system seems to be structured to offer multiple opportunities and second chances to reward people for extra effort, unlike the Chinese system. Phyllis made the following observation:

> In China, if you fail in one test, you are doomed. But here in the U.S., there are usually several tests for one course, and professors give extra credit, chances for revision. . . . Just more opportunities to improve yourself. I like this system better. I was not a good student in China, and that is it. I cannot change it. But I feel that I can be a good student in America, because I am willing to work hard and improve myself, and the system here rewards it. I really work hard. I am so mad that my friends in China sometimes think I am just having fun in the U.S.

Phyllis identifies a very paradoxical attitude towards effort in Chinese and U.S. education: the Chinese believe effort drives learning, while Americans believe that talent drives learning. However, the Chinese education system does not give people as many second-chance opportunities as the American education system. Perhaps it is exactly because of these limited opportunities and the fact that there are no second chances in China that Chinese students work especially hard—for fear of missing their one shot.

GOING BEYOND AN EASY A FOR FURTHER FEEDBACK

A highly competitive education system such as China's can also orient its learners to strive hard even after they leave the system. These learners often hold themselves to a high standard and are not easily satisfied with their performance. Kathy, a public health major at Eastern Tennessee State University, came to the United States as an exchange student at a local high school in Tennessee, then stayed on as a college student. She knew American teachers tend to encourage and give positive feedback, and she made great efforts to solicit critique. Whenever she got an A, she would approach her teacher and ask why, to make sure her work deserved an A.

INTERVIEWER: Why are you so motivated to do this?

KATHY: I do not want to be contented with A, and I want to keep making progress. My English teacher always gave me detailed feedback. I always read it very carefully. Sometimes on midterm exams teachers would only give you grades, but no comments. So I would approach them and ask for comments. I learned a lot from that.

INTERVIEWER: Were you like this in China as well?

KATHY: Not at all. All the tests and homework were challenging. I always made mistakes. That consumed my energy. Also, Chinese teachers were strict, and I was always afraid of them. Here, teachers are nice and approachable. I feel encouraged to talk with them.

Kathy felt challenged by the academic intensity and daunting teacher authority in Chinese education, yet she carried her attitude of seeking academic excellence to the United States. Even in situations where she was not being challenged academically, she took the initiative and sought input from the approachable American teachers to better herself. This belief in effort has particularly salient effects on her performance in math courses, which entail substantial practice. Chinese students report that they have very different attitudes towards math than Americans.

MATH ATTITUDES

Americans Legitimize a Dislike of Math

In 2012, a professor of political science wrote an op-ed piece in the *New York Times* titled "Is Algebra Necessary?" arguing that algebra has cost American students too much psychological pain, so it is not worth the effort.

> A typical American school day finds some six million high school students and two million college freshmen struggling with algebra. In both high school and college, all too many students are expected to fail. Why do we subject American students to this ordeal? I've found myself moving toward the strong view that we shouldn't.

His assertion that studying math has a negative impact on a student's psychology is not necessarily unfounded. Notably, Tom Loveless, an education expert at the Brookings Institution, found that there is a negative correlation between students' confidence in their math abilities and their math scores, based on data from the Trends in International Mathematics and Science Study (TIMSS)—the study that provides comparisons of math and science achievement for fourth and eighth graders from the United States and other countries.[28] His findings indicate that countries with higher math scores on average tend to have students who are less confident in math. This seeming paradox is easily reconciled: math is a killer of confidence—one of the most prized attributes of American educators and parents. As a result, inadvertently, American culture legitimizes a dislike of math. As math is so foundational in STEM fields, the general sentiment of disliking math can help us understand why so few American students earn degrees in STEM fields (see figure 4.4), in spite of the appealing job markets that STEM graduates enjoy. The American government has long felt the need to encourage more domestic students to pursue science and engineering majors. In his 2010 State of the Union address, President Barack Obama stated, "We should make the winners of science fairs as proud as the winners of the Super Bowl." However, American leaders cannot solve this problem until they change the culture of math and science learning in the United States. In their book *Is American Science in Decline?* sociologists Yu Xie and Alexandra Killewald report on the paradoxical attitude towards math and

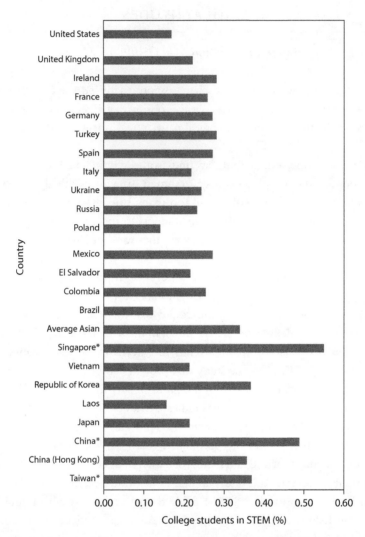

FIGURE 4.4 Proportion of college graduates in STEM majors by country, 2005
Source: UNESCO and NSF (data for those countries with * is from NSF)

science held by the American public. That is, although the American public holds math and science in high regard, they do not think these fields are for most people but for only a few who are intrinsically good at math.[29]

Amy Chua, the author of the best-selling memoir *Battle Hymn of the Tiger Mother* (2011), claims that American parents put too much of a premium on their children's self-esteem, and in so doing, they underestimate their children's strength to overcome setbacks and withstand pressures. Learning can be fun and rewarding, but it can also be temporarily frustrating. Some subjects, such as math and science, require arduous work at first, and enjoyment may ensue after a certain level of mastery. This is consistent with Chinese international students' earlier observations about creativity in math and science fields requiring some foundational training. American students, growing up and being socialized in an environment in which they are showered with praise and encouragement, may be vulnerable to feeling discouraged at learning math, where mistakes are mistakes, and no sugarcoating can be made.

Chinese Valorizes Math

An old Chinese saying goes: "Mastering math, physics, and chemistry, you are fearless wherever you go." So competence in math is valorized in China; and more important, is expected of common people, not just a few gifted minds. This positive attitude towards math has enabled Chinese students to stick to math learning despite not feeling like they are initially good at it. This attitude can reduce the odds of students quitting too soon, thereby closing off opportunities in the future. This math attitude apparently benefits many students who are not especially gifted in math but who, through practice, can become confident enough to enter math-intensive fields. Jennifer is a great example of this.

Jennifer was majoring in mathematics and economics with a minor in accounting at UCLA. She came to America during her last year of high school. In her Chinese high school, she had been on the humanities track, as she was not strong in math by local standards. At UCLA, however, she switched tracks from humanities to math-intensive fields. She did this quite strategically, as she knew she could get a job more easily in a math-intensive field in the United States than in a humanities-related field. (Chapter 9 offers more detail about Jennifer's rationale for staying in the United States after graduation.) Fully aware that her math was not up to the requirements of an innovative research position, she envisioned that perhaps she could apply math in some corporate setting, and her later trajectory largely confirmed her plan. She graduated from UCLA with a bachelor's degree in applied mathematics and economics, and she now works as a data analyst in the San Francisco Bay area.

Jennifer's story illustrates how, in spite of her awareness of her lack of talent in math, she was not intimidated and made the effort to be employable in a position that required math skills. She was able to differentiate between those who are really talented in math and able to make creative contributions to the field and those who are able to learn and apply mathematical knowledge and skills. She knew that she belonged to the latter category and took advantage of an opportunity in the U.S. labor market where math-intensive skills are in great demand.

The push to learn math and science in China, however, has mixed results. Embedded in a social context that considers performance in math and science the main measure of intelligence and a surefire path to success, those who cannot excel are vulnerable to enormous insecurity and subject to peer ridicule, teacher contempt, and parental disappointment. Interviews with students reflect these experiences mired in pain, humiliation, and resentment.

Han was enrolled in the international division of his public high school in China before he came to Syracuse University as a freshman. He was criticized by his math teacher and his classmates before he enrolled in the international division, as he was bad at math and good at English. He vividly described how his math teacher, an older Chinese lady, ridiculed him for spending all of his energy studying English and neglecting math. His status among his peers dropped and his self-esteem suffered. However, he recovered his lost self-esteem in the international division, as English was prioritized. He has a great relationship with his current teacher, and all of his classmates admire his English.

Phyllis recounted a similar story. She painfully recalled how her math teacher was strict and mean to her. He would look down upon students who did not do well in school. Once Phyllis even worked very hard and then scored high on a test, but this teacher still publicly humiliated her, saying in front of the entire class, "Do you know? Even Phyllis got a good score this time." Phyllis felt totally humiliated. She recalled, with a sense of vindication: "Now, when I visit my hometown during summer and see that teacher, he is still there, stuck in the same old place and the same old job, but I am already moving on, and I am in America."

Although the perception that math kills confidence sometimes rings true for some in China, the hardship in learning is not without its value. One consistent message that Chinese students conveyed in the in-depth interviews is that they felt that their prior education in China laid a solid

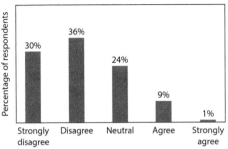

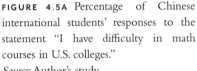

Responses to "I have difficulty in math courses in U.S. colleges."

FIGURE 4.5A Percentage of Chinese international students' responses to the statement "I have difficulty in math courses in U.S. colleges."
Source: Author's study

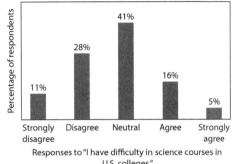

Responses to "I have difficulty in science courses in U.S. colleges."

FIGURE 4.5B Percentage of Chinese international students' responses to the statement "I have difficulty in science courses in U.S. colleges."
Source: Author's study

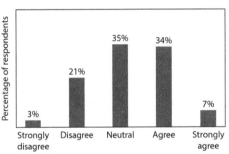

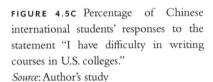

Responses to "I have difficulty in writing courses in U.S. colleges."

FIGURE 4.5C Percentage of Chinese international students' responses to the statement "I have difficulty in writing courses in U.S. colleges."
Source: Author's study

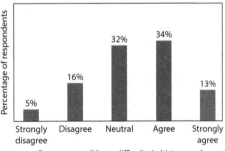

Responses to "I have difficulty in history and liberal arts courses in U.S. colleges."

FIGURE 4.5D Percentage of Chinese international students' responses to the statement "I feel difficulty in history and other liberal arts courses in U.S. colleges"
Source: Author's study

foundation for them in math and science. Figure 4.5 presents their perceptions of the difficulty of coursework in different subjects in the United States. Less than 10 percent of Chinese students agreed or strongly agreed that math courses in U.S. colleges were difficult for them. A bit over 20 percent of them agreed or strongly agreed that science courses in U.S. colleges were difficult for them. On the other hand, over 40 percent of them agreed or strongly agreed that writing courses were difficult, and close to 50 percent agreed or strongly agreed that history and other liberal arts courses were difficult for them. Their advantages in math and science are quite evident, which is all the more noteworthy, given that a considerable number of them major in STEM, economics, and finance fields—math-intensive fields. This speaks powerfully to their prior preparation in these fields in China.

TWO OPPOSITE DISCONNECTS: FROM HIGH SCHOOL TO COLLEGE

Chinese international students, straddling the education systems in China and the United States, have also identified two distinct but rather opposite disconnects in transitioning from high school to college in the two countries. Simply put, American universities require much more effort than secondary schools (barring a small number of exceptionally competitive high schools), while Chinese universities demand less from their students than secondary schools. Ping, a female journalism major at Syracuse University, gave a vivid account of this:

> I really envy my friends studying in Chinese universities now. They live such a relaxed and carefree life. They do not have homework or papers to write. College is like heaven for them after their hard work in high school. I have never thought American colleges are this hard. I am really unfortunate, because I went to Chinese high schools, which were like hell, and now an American university. I have to study hard every day here.

Ping considers herself "unfortunate" in part because the challenges in American colleges exceed her expectations. So I asked her, what were her expectations, and how were they formulated?

INTERVIEWER: So what did you expect American colleges to be like?
PING: I thought it would be easy and fun.
INTERVIEWER: Who told you this?
PING: I don't know. Everybody said so. . . . I certainly imagined this before I came here.

The "easy and fun" social imaginaries about American education give rise to an expectation gap about college academics. However, such imaginaries may not be unfounded. In the National Survey of College Freshmen,[30] less than 40 percent of first-year students reported they did homework in high school more than six hours per week. Homework came after socializing with friends, exercise or sports, and working for pay. This is evident in the Chinese international students who come here as high school students. The finding that the younger Chinese international students arrive in the United States, the less time they spend on studies, underscores the fact that American high schools in general are not very academically demanding. National statistics show that, as a result, American students are underprepared for college. The National Center for Education statistics show that 60 percent of students in two-year colleges enroll in at least one remedial, noncredit course to prepare them for college. At four-year colleges, 20 percent of first-year students are in remedial courses.[31]

On the other hand, Chinese students are overwhelmingly hardworking before college, largely because they are preparing for the Gaokao. Once they enter college, the academic pressures are no comparison to those at the precollege levels, as college admissions almost guarantee graduation.[32] The low requirements for college graduation in China have their roots in the era of elite higher education, when college admissions were extremely competitive and only a few academic elites could access higher education.[33] As China has transitioned from elite to mass higher education over the past decade, graduation requirements have remained low, perhaps due to institutional inertia. This has created unique problems for China in both the quality of its higher education and in the transition from college to the workplace.[34]

Alisa, a public health major at Bryn Mawr, echoed this idea:

> In the U.S., students could still be very relaxed and fooling around in high school. But once in college, professors have high expectations, and students have a lot of work to do. In my college, the library is open twenty-four hours, and you can see students studying all the time. This is different in China. Colleges are relaxed and you cannot learn much, as opposed to the rigorous high school life there.

Are Chinese students such as Alisa, who experienced rigorous high schools, prepared for demanding American colleges? The answer is yes and no. Chinese students generally feel they are well prepared in terms of testing but not necessarily for other means of evaluation. Dan, a self-described mediocre student in Chinese schools, described her experience studying at the University of Saint Louis:

> I was studying very hard in China but still was an average student. After I came here, I realized that I am a better test-taker than my American friends. I guess it is because I just took so many tests in China, and I could even guess at test questions. My American class-mates do not have such an ability [*laughing*]. I almost have an instinct to know what is going to be tested, so I am able to take better notes in class. My American classmates always borrow notes from me.

This test-taking ability was further confirmed by Jessica, from Smith College, who summarized where Chinese students' strengths and weaknesses lie:

> Chinese students generally have high test scores and GPAs. Anything with a clear structure, Chinese students are good at. Chinese students are not so good at open-ended learning. We are accustomed to sit-ting in the classroom and taking tests, and boom, we get our grades. American colleges tend to have various means of grading and differ-ent deadlines for projects. We are not quite used to that.

What Jessica describes as "different deadlines" and "various means of grad-ing" has often led to issues with time management and procrastination. Some very good Chinese students find themselves bothered by a new aca-demic ailment—procrastination. They are annoyed, shocked, and angry with themselves but not sure where this problem comes from. Cheng, an inter-national relations major at Boston University, struggled with this. She was academically strong in China and aced all her courses with the same strate-gies she used when cramming for exams. Apparently, these strategies did not work for her at Boston University, where her courses required multiple projects due at various times. She found herself struggling to stay on top of each task, and her old habit of cramming for exams backfired. She later realized that she was suffering from procrastination.

In part, this academic disease has structural roots in the differences between Chinese and American education and particularly in grading practices. In Chinese schools, grades are almost entirely, if not exclusively, based on test scores. This is true for the entire precollege system. Even when it comes to college education, one final course exam or paper largely determines the final grade. Under such a system, students are primarily evaluated at a single point in time. Although students still work hard during the entire semester, they do not need to worry about various deadlines and the associated time management skills. In American schools, grades are based on a diverse set of assignments and projects spaced out over a given semester. In addition to a final paper or exam, every assignment and project contributes to the final grade. Sometimes a project might span several weeks, if not months. Early stages of planning, researching, drafting, and fine-tuning are often required to conduct and execute the task. Any serious delay in one of the components can compromise the quality of the work—and even worse, threaten its completion. These are the injurious impacts of procrastination on academic studies. Psychologically, the damage is even more profound. Students are often fraught with guilt, anxiety, and even self-hatred, all of which can be debilitating.

ACADEMIC INTEGRITY

Academic integrity is an area in which Chinese international students encounter challenges as they navigate the American education system after transitioning from the Chinese system. There have been some grave violations, followed by high-profile media coverage about them, which have contributed to negative profiling and stereotypes.[35] This has led to much anxiety on the part of Chinese students in America about their performance and self-image. Chris, a first-year student majoring in nursing at Georgia State, experienced constant questioning and ridicule from her American peers when she got high grades in her classes.

> I had done very well in my class, and I got 3.9 GPA last year. But my American friends kept asking how come I could have high test scores, and they couldn't believe that I could have achieved them through my own work. "You've got to be cheating," they said. I always laughed this away, saying, "I didn't cheat at all." They're just jealous of my good grades. In fact, my American friends asked me many times whether I cheated. I just denied it and told them, "Just work hard and you'll have good grades, too."

Confronting such skepticism and ridicule, Chris chose to laugh it off. However, other students can be more sensitive. Bethany, a finance major at the University of Illinois, expressed discomfort with the university administrators' tone and attitude when they talked about academic integrity issues. She recalled one instance during the orientation for international students:

> Someone from the school orientation committee explicitly stated, "No matter what you are used to in your own country, the U.S. does not tolerate cheating or plagiarism." I am not at all comfortable with this; this sounds as if we are all cheaters already! My friends and I attending the orientation all felt the same way.

Participants like Bethany and Chris clearly felt the negative impact of academic integrity violations by certain individuals or groups of Chinese students on international students at large. They felt uncomfortable but helpless in the face of the cheating scandals caused by fellow Chinese students. What really accounts for the nontrivial cases of academic integrity violations by these Chinese international students? Other than the intentional violations that are sometimes backed by the for-profit industry, I suggest that we need to look more deeply into what may confound Chinese students' understanding of academic integrity.[36]

Academic integrity is a formal expression that carries grave consequences. Many Chinese students equate it with "no cheating." But what does it really mean? It seems fairly straightforward in the matter of formal testing. Most Chinese students, who often progress in their academic careers through formal testing, readily understand what "no cheating" means. However, once they study overseas, they find that exams are far from the whole evaluative system. Essays, papers, and projects are often mainstays of evaluation. Often, term papers require external research and citation. Many American students have had instruction on this in high school: write in your own words, and if you need to use others' words, you need to quote them. Such clear-cut rules are obvious to most American high school graduates. However, many Chinese students are not familiar with these practices, which did not become part of their education until college.[37] Therefore, what is often assumed by American professors to be something basic and fundamental requires arduous effort from Chinese students trying to familiarize themselves with it.

In addition, Chinese students' understanding of academic integrity is often confounded by the language barriers encountered by international students in general. Sometimes clear guidelines are written on the syllabus, and/or conveyed verbally by professors in class, but these might not register in the minds of new foreign students. Peng, a triple major in math, information technology, and finance at Syracuse University who graduated with honors after four years of study, had a close encounter with a cheating violation. He once took a special calculator—one he used with permission during his SAT exams—to a math exam in college, because the message on the syllabus that this special calculator was forbidden in this class did not register in his mind. He assumed that a calculator acceptable during SAT exams must be fine for other exams. He was seized on the spot by his professor, who accused him of cheating. Before the professor filed the formal case against him, however, another professor in his department came to his rescue. In a previous course, Peng had stood out as an exceptional student with strong talent and a conscientious attitude, and his professor served as a liaison between the accusing professor and Peng. Through rounds of communication, they ultimately decided this was an isolated event arising purely out of a communication failure, and thus saved him from a potentially disastrous situation. Eventually, the professor dropped the charge.

Some universities are aware that differences exist in the understanding and practices of academic integrity across cultures and societies, and to address this, they have incorporated workshops into orientation programs for new international students, providing a clear definition of, and clear expectations for, academic integrity. This is potentially helpful; however, it has to be handled with care and cultural sensitivity, as it can be interpreted by new foreign students as condescending and distrustful.

SUMMARY

As they straddle both the Chinese and American education systems, Chinese international students are in a good position to address the paradox of China and the United States often looking to each other for better education. In short, they see that American education and Chinese education each have unique advantages and issues. The students provide important insights on creativity, critical thinking, and math attitudes, and on the transition between secondary and postsecondary schools in the United States and China. They consider American education to be better than Chinese education for cultivating creativity and critical thinking. The two are closely related, and Chinese students often refer to them interchangeably. On closer examination, however, creativity is an end, and critical thinking is the means to achieve that end. There was a consensus among the students that their previous Chinese education stifled their creativity, while American education fostered it by encouraging multiple interpretations when approaching a question. Because their previous Chinese schooling emphasized one correct answer to a question, these students were challenged in humanities and social science courses, where open-ended questions are the norm.

On the other hand, Chinese students gave much credit to their previous education in China for helping to cultivate their perseverance and persistence and for making them into assiduous students in general. This effort-based learning attitude had a positive impact on their overall academic performance and in particular helped them to excel in math and science. This is particularly relevant to creativity in STEM fields, which require a solid foundation in math and science. This helps account for the paradoxical notion that Chinese education is able to cultivate innovation while having the potential to suppress creativity. The positive attitude towards math and effort-based learning models is amenable to building a strong foundation in STEM learning, which paves the way for technology innovation.

In light of the opposing disconnects between precollege and college education in China and the United States, Chinese students are uniquely positioned to harvest benefits from both the rigorous elementary and secondary education in China and the demanding postsecondary education in the United States. They are challenged and inspired by the stark contrasts between the Chinese and American education systems. Benefiting from their solid foundation in learning cultivated in Chinese education, and recognizing their challenges in the area of critical thinking, they are motivated to combine the best of the two worlds.

However, the students in this study were dismayed by the academic integrity violations committed by their fellow Chinese students and felt negative profiling and stereotypes leveled against them by their American peers. The voices and experiences of Chinese international students, often neglected by the mainstream American media reporting these violations, highlight that the issues surrounding academic integrity are confounded by the social and cultural differences underlying the two distinct education systems.

CHAPTER 5

Protective Segregation

CHINESE STUDENTS HANGING OUT AMONG THEMSELVES

I can understand why Chinese students like to hang out among themselves. It is hard to find common topics without sharing common interests. Actually, American students are also in their own groups: Whites with whites, blacks with blacks . . . this is human nature. . . . I do not think this is something to be critical about.

—Kathy, a public health major at East Tennessee State University

K athy arrived to the United States as a tenth-grade exchange student from Guangzhou to Tennessee in 2009. She was the sole Chinese student in her entire high school, so she had no conational peers to start with. She cried a lot but ultimately was able to make American friends. In our interview, she compared herself to Chinese peers who started American education in colleges that had established communities of Chinese students:

Perhaps I do not have the peer pressure they have—they've got to hang out with their Chinese friends. I do not have this pressure, as I was here alone, and I was forced to venture out to make friends.

So she did. However, she fully recognizes the social challenges facing her Chinese peers. Kathy is right that the tendency to socialize with people like oneself, identified as *homophily* by social scientists,[1] is human nature.

It's understandable; more importantly, it's useful. Homophily can provide the social cushion necessary for newcomers to survive and thrive in a new environment. It can offer a soothing familiarity for those who may feel disoriented and confused.

As valuable as a homophilic network can be, two major issues of concern emerge. One is internal: Chinese students' lack of satisfaction with their social lives. Studies have shown that one of the most common complaints of international students is their lack of friendships with host nationals, and international students from East Asia (from China, Japan, and South Korea) are more likely than students from other countries to have no American friends.[2]

Once they get over the initial stage of learning new routines and familiarizing themselves with their new environment, international students feel motivated to reach beyond their own conational network. After all, they are voluntary migrants[3] who, for the most part, aspire to broaden their horizons by forming new social ties and building meaningful relationships. Chapter 2 provides evidence that the Chinese international students in the study wanted to broaden their horizons as one of the key purposes of their study-abroad journey. Friendships with locals would be a meaningful and effective way to achieve that purpose.[4] Therefore, when that social aspiration is not fulfilled, the students are disappointed. The second issue of concern is external: American institutional leaders insist that the presence of international students will enrich domestic students' learning and campus experiences by bringing a much-needed variety of perspective.[5] However, in the absence of social integration, the mere presence of international students does not yield the desired benefits for either domestic or international students.[6]

Previous research has painted a less-than-optimistic portrait of Chinese international students' social integration. For example, Chinese international students in general had a higher level of acculturative stress than European international students and found it harder to integrate into their American institutions.[7] Faculty members and American college peers saw Chinese students as being uninterested in socializing with Americans.[8] To explain this, studies have often focused on issues of English proficiency, communication competence, and cultural differences. These issues are indeed critical to understanding the barriers to integration facing international students from any foreign country. However, we might go deeper and ask: What makes international students from China unique, particularly the new crop of undergraduates from a rapidly changing China? For those who stick to their own circles, what are the reasons behind their seemingly voluntary self-segregation? Some Chinese students have successfully integrated with diverse communities on campus. What has enabled these students to break out of their conational network?

This chapter addresses the above questions. The explanatory framework focuses on two processes: one is the process of exclusion—explaining how Chinese students are excluded from American networks due to neoracism—discrimination based on language, culture, and/or country of origin—I will further discuss this concept later in the chapter; the other is the process of the voluntary withdrawal of Chinese students into their own group. I propose the loss of an imagined America on the part of Chinese students is helpful to understanding their withdrawal. My interviews point to two major sources of such a loss: one is that these students are disappointed with the economic development of America, especially of rural and small town America, a perspective that is unique to this generation of Chinese students who have grown up with the prosperity in urban China. The other is the individualistic American culture, which pushes away group-minded Chinese students. American colleges and universities vary in offering buffers against the individualistic culture, and for most Chinese students, they need more support from their institutions. When external networks are not readily accessible, their natural coping mechanism is to resort to their own group.

The two processes are interrelated and complementary. For different students, one process might be more dominant than the other, and sometimes they are at work simultaneously. The important factors identified by the traditional literature[9] on international students, such as adjustment issues, communication competence, and the role of English proficiency, are encapsulated in these processes of exclusion and voluntary withdrawal.

LANGUAGE AND CULTURAL DIFFERENCES

It is not surprising that participants in this study almost universally invoked language barriers as a key impediment to forming friendships with Americans. The survey data highlight the critical importance of English proficiency to Chinese students' social integration, as shown in figure 5.1. One of the survey questions asked respondents to evaluate their own English

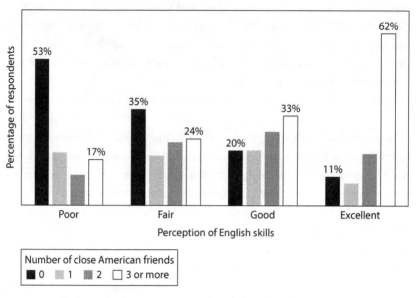

FIGURE 5.1 Relationship between perceived English skills and number of close American friends
Source: Author's study

proficiency, as their self-assessment of language has bearings on their confidence in communicating and interacting with Americans. The scale ranges from poor or fair to good or excellent.

In general, there is a positive relationship between English proficiency and the number of close American friends. The contrast in friendship patterns between students who perceive that their English is excellent and those who perceive that their English is poor is striking. Among those who felt that their English was excellent, 62 percent had three or more close American friends, and about 10.7 percent had no close American friends. Among those who felt that their English was poor, more than half had no close American friends, and only 16.7 percent had three or more close American friends.

The in-depth interviews revealed that language barriers are often related to the nuances of language as it is used in popular culture, such as the language of jokes. As Sara at Syracuse University noted:

Once the conversation started, the American friend would mention some names and facts, and I would quickly lose track of it. Especially those jokes—I do not know why they are laughing. It is just awkward to be present when others laugh and you do not know why. I think if one understands American jokes, it would just be natural to form close friends with Americans.

Sara considers jokes to pull people closer, but she cannot understand American jokes, so she has to fall back into her old circle of Chinese friends and speak their native language.

Other than language, a staple of American college campuses—party culture—also seems to get in the way of intercultural friendships. Sociologists Elizabeth Armstrong and Laura Harrington have presented rich evidence in their book *Paying for the Party* of the exclusivity of the party for upper-middle-class students, and many of their lower-income peers, all of whom were American domestic students, felt marginalized and excluded.[10] Chinese international students, though not disadvantaged in economic terms, are marginalized social-culturally.[11] Almost all of the Chinese international students in this book felt at best ambivalent towards, and at worst, scared, by the party culture on campus. Some claimed that American party culture was definitely a barrier to their positive social experiences on campus. The majority described their shock when they witnessed, often for the first time, the American college party scene. Many were aware that they ought to attend college parties to be fully socialized on campus, so they tried. When they did, however, they witnessed things they typically shunned as bad behaviors based on their prior socialization in China. According to Sabrina, from the University of Wisconsin at Madison:

> I went to parties a few times and did not like them at all. I saw people taking drugs. Others were drinking. Those things were unappealing to me, and I did not want to take up those behaviors. I know a few Chinese friends hanging out with Americans who have started taking drugs, too. So for us, we want to stay away from these, so we stop going to parties.

Sabrina tried to avoid drug use at the party, and associated activities at party scenes with bad behaviors. Other students found drinking, and sometimes drinking games, distasteful. Kaisy, from Lehigh University, was quite puzzled about the drinking games American students play: "They are silly games, not fun at all. My American friends at the party like to play many drinking games

around beer. When I saw them play with beer and then drink them afterwards, I feel it is not even sanitary." Both Sabrina and Kaisy stopped going
to parties, knowing this might cost them opportunities for social integration.

Other students mentioned overt sexual scenes disconcerting and even fright-
ening, especially to the female students. According to Jennifer from UCLA:

> I only went to a party once. I was really scared. Those grinding, and
> dirty dance. I do not want to go into details, but I ended up with most
> of my Chinese friends, and we do the typical Chinese girls' things to
> relax and socialize: shopping, eating in restaurants, etc.

These party behaviors go directly against the normative expectations of
Chinese femininity. Chinese males are uncomfortable with the party scene,
too. It goes fundamentally against the school culture these students were
socialized to in China—one of discipline and restraint.[12] Justin, from UCLA,
shared descriptions of parties and pubs with his family back in China. "My
grandma was really concerned and urged me not to go," he said with a grin,
explaining that although he was far away from his parents and other family
members, he was very close to his family, apparently including extended
family members, and he cared about their opinions.

Previous studies also found that Chinese international students feel a
lack of belonging at American college parties.[13] They are not alone—as
mentioned above, some American students, especially low-income students,
feel this way as well. Armstrong and Harrington propose the rationale of
protective segregation in *Paying for the Party*, referring to social spaces where
students can avoid the dominant party culture and seek comfort and support
from one another. Although Chinese international students are different
from American domestic marginalized groups, they are also marginalized
due to their race and foreign status, and feel removed from the party culture.
The concept of neoracism is helpful in accounting for the lack of belonging
on the part of Chinese students in American higher education.

NEORACISM AND PROTECTIVE SEGREGATION

Jenny Lee and Charles Rice proposed the concept of neoracism in the context of international students for the first time in an article titled "Welcome
to America: International Students' Experiences with Discrimination."[14]

Neoracism refers to discriminatory behaviors or attitudes based on language and cultural barriers and sometimes on country of origin. Often, negative stereotypes based on country of origin lead to neoracism, yet only a few studies have specifically examined the stereotyping of Chinese international students.[15] In one such study, Ruble and Zhang identified five stereotypes that Americans hold in regard to Chinese international students: They are (1) smart and hardworking; (2) kind, friendly, nice, and polite; (3) bad at speaking English, friends only with other Chinese, not well assimilated, and socially awkward; (4) quiet, shy, solitary, not very social; and (5) oblivious, loud, intrusive of personal space, conceited, annoying, strange, and unwilling to adapt.[16] The first four stereotypes resonate with previous research on stereotypes about Asians and Asian Americans, both positive and negative, and the fifth stereotype is exceedingly hostile and disconcerting.[17]

Phyllis, from North Carolina State University, described such an experience of encountering neoracism:

> Every time our groups of Chinese students in our language class walked together on the street, American students drove by in the car and they were always very rude, screaming and yelling at us. I later realized that they were having fun; they were probably drunk. I do not think they liked us, and actually my Chinese friends also did not like them. We often laughed at Americans when we took elevators with them. We spoke Chinese and laughed together. I know that now American students are afraid to take elevators with us, and they avoid being in the same elevator with a group of Chinese students.

Interestingly, Phyllis felt that her American peers were loud, mirroring the findings that Americans felt the same about Chinese students. However, Phyllis took it as Americans' hostility towards Chinese students, and Chinese students returned the sentiment with similar tactics of resistance and exclusion. This just deepened the divide. Phyllis had only Chinese friends during her entire first year in the United States, and she felt that that it was not right.

> I need to make more American friends. I am studying in America, after all. I should have been more open. But how? I do not know. I feel stuck. I probably will only have Chinese friends next year as well, because we've already decided to take courses together.

Phyllis's story illustrates a very complex ambivalence and a deep sense of helplessness among Chinese students in handling friendships in the United States. While she experienced exclusion from Americans and engaged in mutual exclusion and resistance with her Chinese friends against Americans, she yearned to make American friends and found the divide between them troubling and insurmountable. In this process of exclusion from and her desire for American networks, she resorted to her Chinese peers for comfort and community—an act of protective segregation—albeit with reluctance and regret.

Phyllis had no close American friends, but her perception of American peers' resistance towards Chinese students resonates with those who do have close American friends. Zhong, from Vanderbilt University, mentioned that his close American friend finds Chinese students hanging out together speaking Chinese in public spaces very uncomfortable and offensive. Zhong said, "A good friend of mine, who is white, once confessed to me that he felt a group of Chinese students speaking Chinese in the public space on American college campuses made him feel that Chinese people have colonized American universities." He added by saying that, as shaken as he was by this comment, he was appreciative of the candor his American friend showed him. Zhong added: "After all, had we been not real friends, how would I ever have known this?"

Chinese students sometimes also find Americans' comments outdated and biased. Guo, an information science major at Syracuse, described such a situation:

> Once I was approached by a friendly, middle-aged American woman on campus, asking me whether the Chinese government still kills Christians. I mean, come on, my grandma is a Christian. I find these kinds of questions laughable. How come they know so little about China? I am not happy, but I kind of get used to it. Many Americans label China as "Communist China." They do not know the real China.

Contemporary Chinese people, including most of the Chinese students in the United States, feel their lived realities could not be further from the political labels Americans often apply to China. Guo further explained: "If Americans go to China, they will find a different China from what they observe through the Western media." This sentiment resonated with the feelings of other Chinese students. The improved quality of life in China has eclipsed the perceptions of some Americans who are still steeped in memories of an impoverished China. Sunny, who worked at the campus football stadium at Syracuse University, described an encounter she had when she was serving drinks: "One American student asked me whether I was eating potatoes every day in China. I was like, what? Are you kidding me? Perhaps my grandma's generation did, not mine." Sunny almost felt insulted by this question, which reflected American ignorance about the social changes happening in China. These students, proud and sometimes spoiled, have grown up in a prosperous China and feel alienated and loss of their social status in America. This is consistent with sociologist Henry Hail's finding that "some Chinese students complained that host country students want to talk with them about China but exhibit misinformed, prejudiced and offensive views of Chinese current events."[18] Hail further shows that misinformed and prejudiced comments Americans make about China alienate the Chinese students, leading to a growing identification with their home country and giving rise to what he terms "patriotism abroad"— a theme further explored in chapter 8 where Chinese students reflect on their journey in the United States.[19]

THE LOSS OF AN IMAGINED AMERICA

Since China's market reforms, the Chinese people have increasingly been exposed to Western markets, media, and culture. As the superpower among Western developed societies, American society and culture have been romanticized and coveted, with help from Western name-brand products, Hollywood films, and other media platforms. Vanessa Fong draws on Benedict Anderson's concept of "imagined community"[20] in her book *Paradise Redefined*, arguing that Chinese youth and their families imagine the Western developed world as a paradise. In particular, Chinese students are motivated to study abroad in Western institutions of higher education, primarily driven by their desire to be part of this "imagined developed world community composed of mobile, wealthy, well-educated and well-connected people worldwide."[21]

This longing for an "imagined developed world community," coupled with the desire for Western higher education—American colleges still remain the envy of the world—has brought millions of Chinese international students to American college campuses. However, they change from having American fever to American disillusionment after their arrival in the United States.[22]

The Loss of America—"I Never Imagined It Would Be So Middle-of-Nowhere"

What fuels this disillusionment, among other factors, is the lack of city life when many students find themselves in small-town America. Given that about 95 percent of the survey participants hail from urban China, which teems with high-rises and urban amenities such as cafés and shopping malls, these students described their American university locales as "villages" or "the country." For example, Wen, a native from Beijing studying at Beloit College in Wisconsin, said:

> Before I came, I thought the U.S. was all like New York City, full of glittering high rises and rich city culture. I could never have imagined American society so rural and boring. I imagined this would be a remote place, but I never imagined it would be so middle-of-nowhere. It is even hard to find a taxi here.

While these thoughts may seem innocuous and matter-of-fact, they are telling of a dissatisfaction with American life. China has a pronounced rural-urban disparity and a profound culture of urban superiority.[23] In these students' eyes, the countryside signifies backwardness, and it is nothing like their imagined modern America. This sentiment was vividly articulated by Joey, a computer science major at Johns Hopkins University in Baltimore. He transferred from the University of Missouri at Columbia when he was a sophomore. He described how he felt before and after he came to his first institution:

> Before, I watched a lot of Hollywood films and listened to American hip-hop. I adored the singers and Americans featured in the film. Their lifestyle is something I admired in China. I thought the U.S. must be a very cool and dynamic place. But then I arrived in Columbia in Missouri, a very boring town; little is going on. This was so unexpected for me.

The disconnect between the American media images Joey was exposed to in China and the small-town America he found himself in hit him hard. Joey felt the urge to leave and transfer to Johns Hopkins—a higher-ranking school, located in Baltimore, a bigger city than Columbia, Missouri. When asked about whether his life in Baltimore was better, Joey gave a reluctant "yes."

This generation of Chinese students has grown up not only watching Hollywood films and listening to hip-hop but also witnessing the modernization and urbanization of China. This has helped formulate a mindset that equates modern city life with the good life. When they are confronted with real American life, which is not as modern as they imagined, their disappointment is palpable.

Even students studying in major cities in the United States tend to compare them with the major Chinese cities they are from. The comparisons fill them with disappointment in the host country and pride in their hometowns. For example, Hudson, a student from Changsha in Hunan Province, studying at the University of Washington at Seattle, said, "I find Seattle is even less modern than Changsha, my hometown. But Changsha is not the most developed area in China, and it is no rival to Beijing or Shanghai."

Individualism as a Barrier—"I Never Imagined How They Want to Be Alone"

Not only do these Chinese students feel disappointed with America's developmental level, they are also taken aback by the highly individualistic orientation many Americans exhibit. Compared to their previous school environments, where they often walked in groups and did things together, these students were shocked to find that American students tend to do things on their own. They were equally baffled by the social distance their American counterparts liked to maintain. Han, from Syracuse University, described his impression:

> I never imagined how they want to be alone. Why [do] Americans choose to sit on the school bus alone, far away from other passengers, instead of sitting next to each other, as we do in China?

In spite of this, Han still made great efforts to make American friends, as he was very conscious about broadening his horizons, and he thought making American friends would help him achieve that. He chose to force himself to stay away from his Chinese community and spoke only English, to such an extent that many of his friends thought he was born in the United States. Then, after a year, he felt tired. His English had become impeccable, and he had made a few American friends, but he was not enjoying himself. According to him, "Friendship with Americans feels different. They do not want to be close, and they are very individualistic. This is nothing like what I expected from a true friendship."

The American tendency toward individualism makes Chinese students who are accustomed to a communal and collectivist lifestyle confused and uncomfortable. The literature on intercultural friendship notes that cultural similarities between the host culture and the home culture ease initial encounters and make intercultural friendships more likely.[24] Chinese culture, or East Asian culture taken broadly, is highly distinct from American culture in such basic aspects as collectivism vs. individualism. The United States is considered the world's most individualistic culture.[25]

In *Habits of the Heart*, individualism is identified as "the first language in which Americans tend to think about their lives":

> American individualism, then, demands personal effort and stimulates great energy to achieve, yet it provides little encouragement for nurturance, taking a sink-or-swim approach to moral development as well as to economic success.[26]

Chinese international students have strongly felt the effects of this "sink-or-swim approach" taken by American higher education institutions. In other words, very little support or "encouragement for nurturance" in regard to social relations and integration is available to them. What is missing here is an institutionalized, structured platform where Chinese students can make friends with local Americans. It is not only because they are new arrivals and need community and comfort but also because their culture shapes them to be group-oriented.

In their landmark book *Cultures and Organizations: Software of the Mind*, Geert Hofstede and Gert Jan Hofstede have vividly and convincingly shown that Chinese society is more collectively oriented than American society.[27]

The market economy kicked off social transformations in current Chinese society, where there seem to be more choices and mobility than ever before. This leads some scholars to argue that China has become increasingly individualistic.[28] I published an article in 2015 explaining that education seems to lag behind in this process of transformation and the system has remained steadfastly collectivist, from curriculum to college admissions to daily rituals.[29] That means Chinese international students come to the United States with their habits of the heart primarily socialized in their prior family and school contexts in China; they expect to organize their activities in groups and to seek comfort in groups.

To be sure, international students are not randomly selected from the Chinese population. Like any migrants, they consist of those who tend to be motivated to venture beyond their group, as they have already crossed national borders to study abroad. However, the motivation to interact with an out-group does not necessarily materialize on its own. As communication scholar Elisabeth Gareis has argued, "the set of social skills (e.g., small talk) that is necessary for establishing friendship in the United States may not be part of international students' repertoire and cannot be internalized without regular exposure."[30] In other words, institutions need to provide support for Chinese students to acquire those social skills to make American friends. In the absence of such institutional support, Chinese students' proclivity towards a group-oriented lifestyle, confronted with the highly individualistic American society, can cement a strong identification with their Chinese peer group network and produce seemingly voluntary segregation.

The next section discusses some individual and institutional practices that can make a difference and facilitate Chinese students' social integration in American higher education.

WHAT MAKES A DIFFERENCE?

June, from Colby College, said: "I find it much easier to make friends with other international students, and Colby has them from all over the world. My friendship circles consist mostly of international students, not necessarily from China. It is very hard to penetrate into domestic students' networks." This sentiment was echoed by Zhong, from Vanderbilt. Zhong's friends are mostly international students, too; his best friends are from the

Philippines. Given the barriers to making friends with domestic Americans, I used survey analysis to closely examine broad patterns of friendship formation with domestic Americans, who are defined as "people born and raised in the United States."

Broad Patterns

In addition to a perceived lack of proficiency in English, as shown in figure 5.1, other factors may also make a difference. Figure 5.2 shows that parental education matters and, as a result, first-generation college students are at a clear disadvantage. Close to 23 percent of Chinese students with college-educated parents had no close American friends, while more than 40 percent of their first-generation peers had none. Figure 5.3 shows that the arrival time in the United States may play a role as well. More than 27 percent of those who started their American education as college students had no close American friends, whereas those who started as high school students did somewhat better, at 20 percent and more. In addition, those who came here as high school students were much more likely to have three or more close American friends.

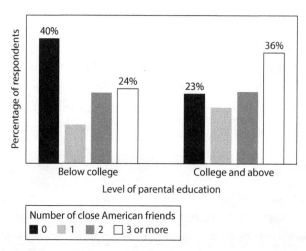

FIGURE 5.2 Relationship between parental education of survey respondents and number of close American friends
Source: Author's study

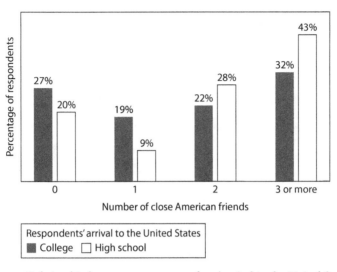

FIGURE 5.3 Relationship between survey respondents' arrival in the United States and number of close American friends
Source: Author's study

Another factor, participation in campus organizations, is positively associated with American friendship. Figure 5.4 shows that 18 percent of those who participate in campus organizations had no close American friends, compared to 38 percent of those who do not participate in campus organizations. Membership in campus organizations is a key part of social capital for American college students, and it undoubtedly boosts friendship formation with domestic Americans.[31] Figure 5.5 shows that those who chose their current college based on their interest in a particular program were more likely to have close American friends than their peers: 20 percent of those coming with interest in a particular program had no close American friends, compared to 30 percent of their peers coming without program interest. This indicates that interest-driven college choice is conducive to positive social outcomes during college. Interestingly, according to the survey data, institutional-level differences, including the selectivity level and whether a college is a liberal arts college versus a research-intensive institution, are not associated with friendship formation among the Chinese international students in this study, so we did not include them in the analysis. However, interview data reveal more nuances in terms of the relevance of institutional context.

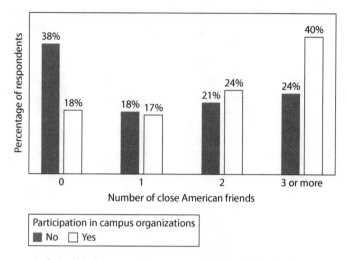

FIGURE 5.4 Relationship between survey respondents' participation in campus organizations and number of close American friends
Source: Author's study

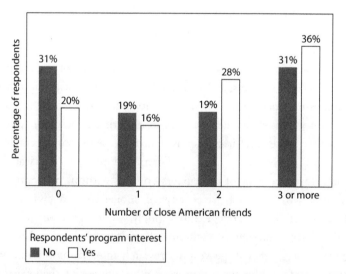

FIGURE 5.5 Relationship between survey respondents' program interest and number of close American friends
Source: Author's study

Table 5.1 presents the results of the multivariate analysis conducted to determine the independent effect of each of the above factors on the likelihood of having a close American friend. Gender and arrival time in the United States at the high school or college level seem not to matter after all other factors are considered. Chinese students with college-educated parents were still 2.5 times as likely as their first-generation counterparts to have a close American friend, taking into account all of the other variables (model III is the full model). This again highlights the powerful role

TABLE 5.1

Multivariate Analysis of the Likelihood of Having a Close American Friend (Odds Ratios)

	MODEL I	MODEL II	MODEL III
Male	1.124	1.414	1.345
	(0.237)	(0.324)	(0.329)
Parents with college education	2.279***	2.045***	2.505***
	(0.569)	(0.562)	(0.742)
Good English		2.074***	1.830**
		(0.490)	(0.458)
American high school		1.200	1.478
		(0.374)	(0.510)
Interest in program		1.814***	1.763**
		(0.418)	(0.427)
Campus organization		2.636***	2.876***
		(0.612)	(0.700)
Selective institutions			0.842
			(0.206)
Research institutions			0.991
			(0.386)

*** $p < 0.01$

** $p < 0.05$

* $p < 0.1$

Note: Standard errors are in parentheses. "Good English" refers to the perception that the student's level of English is either good or excellent, as opposed to poor and fair. "Interest in program" refers to being interested in a program as a reason for college choice.

of parental education and the disadvantages associated with first-generation college status in regard to social integration.

Those who thought they had good or excellent English were 83 percent more likely than those who thought their English was poor or fair to make a close American friend. Those who were interested in an academic program as the important reason for college choice were about 76 percent more likely to make a close friend than those who made their college choice *not* based on program interest. As chapter 2 shows, rankings remain the primary guide to most Chinese students' college choices; in contrast, these results highlight the role of intrinsic interest in programs in promoting positive social outcomes. Finally, those participating in a campus organization were close to 1.9 times more likely to form close American friendships than their Chinese peers who never participated in a campus organization. This is important in that, compared to parental education, good English, and program interest, participation in a campus organization is perhaps the factor most accessible and subject to institutional intervention. In other words, this finding underscores a specific mechanism that institutional support can work on; that is, helping Chinese international students participate in campus organizations can promote friendship formation with domestic students. After all, participation in campus organizations is in and of itself an important aspect of social integration on American colleges for all students.

These broad patterns provide an overview of what make a difference. The interviews further contextualize these factors and uncover in-depth information that can help with promoting the social integration of Chinese international students.

Prior Preparation in China

Yue took a gap year between high school and college. During her gap year, her parents hired an American tutor to help improve her English. Yue's tutor helped to open up a whole circle of friends and a foreign teachers' network for her while she was still in China. As she put it, "I experienced little culture shock when I started my studies here. I know how to initiate a conversation, how to get it going, and how to interact with Americans generally. . . . I have had a great time here in the U.S."

When I asked her about American jokes and the party scene, she readily replied:

I do not understand all of them [the jokes], and that is okay—as I am sure that not all Americans understand all those jokes, either. I move on to the stuff that I do understand and am interested in. In terms of partying, yes, I party too. Only sometimes, though. When I am not comfortable, I leave and move on to other activities. Some of my American friends do not like to party either.

It was her comfort and confidence with things she did not know more than her English abilities or social skills that made her different from most other Chinese students in the study. Where did that confidence come from? She owed it largely to her preparation for studying abroad. More specifically, she owed it to the private tutors who had equipped her with the cultural toolkit to effectively navigate the unknown territory. Undoubtedly, she was privileged to have parents who had both the vision and the resources to hire private tutors to help her prepare for overseas study. Both of her parents were college-educated, and her father had travelled widely in the world and recognized the vital importance of the ability to connect with people from different cultural backgrounds. As Yue recalled, "My dad always talked me into making new friends and broadening horizons. That kind of stuff . . . and it works." The concept of gap year is totally new in China, and her father told her about it and arranged for her to have a year of preparation for studying abroad. This was more to ensure her comfort and confidence in navigating the overseas culture and society than to boost her academic skills. However, this kind of knowledge and awareness is often beyond However, this kind of knowledge and awareness is often beyond reach of first-generation college students.

American High Schools

A minority of the study participants went to high school in the United States prior to enrolling in an American university. The survey data show that about 18 percent of them started their education at a high school in America first, and among those who did so, 20 percent had no close

American friends compared to 27 percent of those who started their educations in the United States in college. Attending an American high school, albeit a statistically small advantage, actually serves as prior preparation, as illustrated by Yue's case, reducing culture shock and smoothing the cultural transition to American colleges. Nevertheless, my in-depth interviews revealed a more complex and subtle picture of the trials and triumphs Chinese students experienced in American high schools.

KATHY'S AND ALAN'S STORIES

Kathy came initially as an eleventh-grade exchange student to a public magnet high school in Tennessee. Now she is a sophomore majoring in public health at Eastern Tennessee State University. Her early days in the United States were tough. She cried a lot. Her English was poor. Her understanding of American culture and society was limited. But two years of high school in the United States really helped her in her college studies. She got to know American pop culture and American movies and music, and she became active in her school's social activities. In college, Kathy worked as a residential assistant, so she got to know a lot of other residents. She cofounded the university's international student association and served as its president. She learned quite a bit from her high school experiences and recognized the significance of teamwork and student activities. She tried to collaborate with American domestic student organizations so that more students could get involved.

American high schools are not always happy places for international students. Alan, who was enrolled at the University of California at San Diego (UCSD), started his education in the United States as a ninth-grader in a high school in Maryland. He was the only Chinese student in the entire school, and he felt very lonely and upset. His only comfort and social support came from his host family, where a sibling of his age had become his close friend. However, this could not alleviate the struggles he went through in school. He was so unhappy that he transferred to another private school, in Connecticut, on the recommendation of a Chinese friend who was going there. It was a boarding school where a quarter of the student body were international students, the majority of whom were Chinese. Hanging out with so many Chinese students, Alan felt comfortable. However, by the end of his junior year, he started to feel uneasy and insecure—he felt that he should not have spent most of his social time with his Chinese peers in America, but he had felt strong peer pressure from his Chinese friends to stay within the group. He wanted to be open-minded, yet his Chinese friends made him feel awkward and odd when he was the only one hanging out with Americans. He attributed his willingness to reach out beyond his own group to his one-year stint at his previous school in Maryland, where he had been exposed to many Americans and stayed with a host family. Had he come directly to Connecticut from China, he would definitely have stayed within his Chinese network. At UCSD, he had not made a single Chinese friend; instead, his friend network shifted to the Asian American community.

> I found it most comfortable socializing with these Asian Americans, including Chinese, Japanese, Korean, and Taiwanese. UC schools have a lot of Asian Americans. I found them easier to make friends with than whites. A lot of them were immigrant children with Asian parents, so they were influenced by their parents in terms of Asian culture.

Ironically, Alan now feels closer to Asian American students than to Chinese internationals freshly arrived from China. He recounted how he once went to a welcoming party put on by the Chinese student association as part of orientation activities. During his first year in the United States, he had learned how to proactively greet others, so that's what he did. However, he got little response, and he felt the students were cold. He also felt that they shared few interests. He realized that the four years he had spent in American high schools had changed him, and he drifted away from the Chinese international student group.

Living Arrangements

American roommates sometimes provide a gateway for Chinese students to go beyond their own conational network. It worked well in Peng's case. Peng, a triple major in math, finance, and information management at Syracuse University, was among the group with close American friends, and he reported great satisfaction with his social life. Among his friends' circle, half were Chinese and half were Americans, some of whom he was very close to. One of them was his first-year roommate, who helped him with his writing, and who invited him to his home in Boston for the first Thanksgiving holiday. He said that he received more help with writing from his American friends than from the writing center at his school.

At the same university, Kai, a philosophy major, has had no opportunity to have American roommates, because he started off as a student in the English Language Institute (ELI), which is for students whose TOEFL score was below 90 points. During his time at ELI, he had a Chinese roommate, and then, a year later, when he graduated from ELI and became a freshman at Syracuse, he was not obligated to live in a campus dorm because he was considered a transfer student. He chose to live off-campus, mainly to save money:

> The off-campus apartments are a lot cheaper than on-campus dorms. But I feel that my Chinese friends living on campus with American roommates have better English and are also more likely to make American friends. I do not have good English vocabulary for daily life stuff. For example, if you ask me what is the English for that box on the table, I do not know. Had I had American roommates, I could have improved on that front.

Kai has no American friends, and he said he would welcome any opportunity to make American friends, but those are hard to come by. In his current dorm, neighbors rarely speak to each other, and they all seem to be very busy. Kai desires to have American friends, thinking he could have had one by rooming with Americans, but he was limited by financial constraints so that he could not live on campus.

Kai's financial constraints of living arrangement seem to prevent him from having American roommates and better social integration. The desire for American roommates is broadly shared among Chinese international students, but the effect is not always as expected. Jennifer, from at UCLA, said she let the system randomly select her roommate because she reasoned that by random assignment, her chances of getting an American roommate would be good. She was matched with a white girl who usually spent Thursday and Friday nights partying in fraternity houses. Her roommate once invited her to go to a party, and she went, but she did not enjoy it. She ended up socializing with most of her Chinese friends who went shopping and dined together. In her junior year, she moved out of the dorms to live with her Chinese friends. Jennifer spent last semester in Europe as part of her study abroad experience. However, she still hung out with her Chinese friends, because they signed up together for the program. In other words, her initial attempt to reach out of her old network by changing to a new environment did not materialize; instead, her old network followed her.

Institutional Differences

American institutions differ in their practices to support and integrate Chinese students. In 2015, the University of Illinois at Urbana Champaign, for the first time ever, had two Chinese students offer online Mandarin language broadcasts of its home football games. This was intended to attract more Chinese international students who otherwise would largely be absent from those games, as they typically do not understand the rules. Before that, the university's football coaches had offered "Football 101" camps to students and discount tickets to games, which are widely considered to be the social glue of students from diverse backgrounds.[32] Illinois's initiative was quickly adopted by Indiana University, the University of Washington, and Temple University, among others. They all recruited Chinese international students as sportscasters who could cover their football and basketball games in Mandarin.[33] The school officials reported that these efforts are succeeding in pulling some Chinese students out of their often closed-off social networks.[34]

The above institutions are all major research universities that host thousands of Chinese students. What about small liberal arts colleges? The survey analysis found no significant differences in friendship formation between major research institutions and small liberal arts colleges (see table 5.1). The interviews revealed that some liberal arts colleges have made conscious efforts to support and integrate international students. Alisa is such a beneficiary. She is a junior at Bryn Mawr, a women's college near Philadelphia. She is passionate about volunteer work. Her volunteer experiences started in China, but they became serious in the United States, because her college provided her with an institutional environment to participate in service activities. Through volunteer work, she has made many close American friends from diverse backgrounds. As they share a common interest in their work, their interactions and communication are spontaneous and smooth.

Alisa has not perceived a lack of social integration in her school. She attributes this to the fact that her college is a women's college with students from many different places; she hears English spoken there with all kinds of accents. She feels that when a place is diverse, people tend to be more open-minded and less judgmental. She talked at length about how her college provides support for international students. She works in the international student office, where there are four full-time employees and several student employees. Together, they serve each and every international student, offering a multitude of services that range from I-20 form consultation, airport pickups, and providing information on student employment to guiding students to mental and emotional support. Alisa's institution has provided her with opportunities to engage in volunteer work and international student work, activities she finds relevant and interesting, and through which she has also found close American friends.

Some students may wonder how they can access these opportunities for relationship building. As Sara at Syracuse University put it:

My only good American buddy is the boyfriend of my classmate. This guy took me to various kinds of American cultural events, such as standup comedy, movie shows, etc., from which I learnt a lot. This guy is very friendly to me because he has been to China before and is interested in Chinese culture as well. But the question is: This is a pure accident that I know this guy. How can I meet more people like him, so that I can have more friends like him?

Sara raises a very good question that resonates with many Chinese international students. Social interactions may be random and happenstance by nature; however, Chinese international students cannot expect random interactions to help them break out of their tight conational peer networks and broaden their social circles. Instead, they need institutional platforms to provide mechanisms that give them structural access to domestic students who can help them navigate the new environment and furnish them with rewarding social experiences. Previous research has also highlighted the lack of institutional support for international students.[35] The challenge is how to get domestic students interested and engaged. Some institutions have set up programs that partner international students with American students who are interested in Chinese culture. These programs are institutionalized, so that international students do not have to depend on their own individual efforts or pure luck to find American friends.

SUMMARY

A recurring theme of a heightened awareness of Chinese students emerges about their rather isolated social network. Contrary to widespread perceptions that Chinese international students want to remain within their own groups, this study found in them a strong and sometimes explicit yearning to reach out. However, this yearning is frustrated by the gulf between an imagined America and the real America, and it is thwarted by cultural and institutional barriers.

The expectation gap between an imagined America and the real America constitutes a mental context for Chinese students' social experiences in the United States. They expect America to be more prosperous than "the middle of nowhere." They expect Americans to be more welcoming and less individualistic. They also encounter concrete challenges. This study found that the challenges range from perceived English language difficulties to discomfort with the dominant culture of drinking and partying among American college students to a sheer lack of access to Americans who are interested in and hold unbiased views about China. Under these circumstances, sticking to their own group can at least help Chinese students find security and comfort when out-group friendships are hard to access without help. This situation highlights the shortage of outreach and support from American institutions of higher education.

Institutions can play a significant role in connecting students from different backgrounds. I have found that participation in campus organizations gives a strong boost to friendship formation with Americans. This is an area where institutional support and intervention can be effective. Intentional efforts can be directed at supporting Chinese international students' participation in campus organizations, given that participation in organizations is in and of itself a key aspect of social integration on college campuses. Contrary to media accounts that portray this new crop of international students from China as a uniformly privileged group, the survey data for this project highlight the heterogeneity among these students. In particular, Chinese students who are first-generation college students are at a distinct disadvantage. They are more likely to have poor English and less likely to have close American friends. Institutions need to be aware of this and provide targeted support to these first-generation college students.

As for the few Chinese students who are able to break out of their own circles, their stories suggest possible institutional changes that can be made to enhance the social experiences of the other Chinese students who yearn to make American friends but do not know how. The finding on the importance of prior preparation in bridging the cultural gap between the imagined America and the real one has clear implications for institutional change. For example, some institutions have developed summer bridge programs for international students, which consist of four- to six-week programs that involve writing, cultural instruction, and extracurricular activities meant to prepare students for the start of their academic studies in the fall. These programs could be of more benefit if they are longer in duration and provide sustainable support.

CHAPTER 6

College Major Choices, Rationales, and Dilemmas

William Deresiewicz, the author of *Excellent Sheep: The Miseducation of the American Elite* (2015), levels scathing criticisms at American elitist higher education, one of which targets the ever-increasing trend of college students at elite institutions to choose practical vocational fields over humanities and other liberal arts fields.

His critique is consistent with a recent analysis from Humanities Indicators (figure 6.1), which shows that in 2015 the number of bachelor's degrees conferred in the humanities was down 5 percent from the year before and down nearly 10 percent from 2012. Overall, about 12 percent of bachelor's degrees were conferred on majors in the humanities. However, while there is a clear sign of dwindling interest in the humanities, American college students' choices of majors do not always lean towards practical fields. While business degrees remain the largest category (18 percent) among bachelor's degrees conferred, the share shrank by 13 percent from 2006 to 2015. Engineering degrees have increased only slightly over the past decade, claiming 8.3 percent of all the bachelor's degrees conferred in 2015.[1]

Social class matters in students' college major choices. Previous research has found that, when academic ability and racial background are controlled, students from lower-socioeconomic status (SES) families are more likely to choose practical fields such as science, engineering, and business.[2]

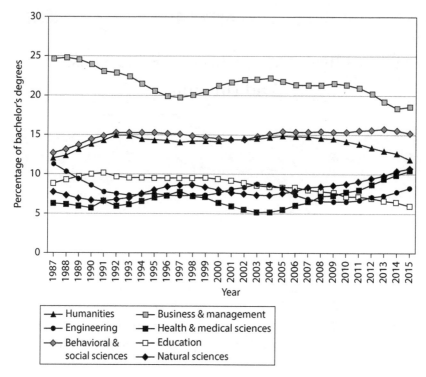

FIGURE 6.1 All bachelor's degrees awarded in selected academic fields, 1987–2015
Source: Humanities Indicators 2017, https://www.humanitiesindicators.org/content
/indicatordoc.aspx?i=34#fig197

The rationale is that the students from wealthy families are not as motivated by practical concerns such as jobs and money as their less well-off
counterparts.

Given their ability to afford American undergraduate tuition, Chinese
students disproportionately come from well-off families. Do their family
resources lead them to lean towards nonpractical fields? Does their family
privilege lead them to gravitate towards nontechnical fields such as humanities and social sciences? The short answers to the above questions are both
"no." Chinese international students, on average, overwhelmingly incline
towards practical and technical fields, such as STEM fields and business.
Despite their privileged backgrounds, they are even less likely than their
peers in China to choose humanities. Why is there such a paradox of

economically privileged students leaving liberal arts education for practical and lucrative fields? This chapter will focus on understanding the reasons for this paradox and examine the factors that produce in-group variations among Chinese international students.

Before proceeding, it is essential to understand the social contexts in China and the United States that affect the choice of a college major. Because most Chinese international students come to the United States no earlier than high school, they spend more time in Chinese schools than in American schools, and they are under the constant influence of their parents, family, and friends in China, even after they come to the United States. The important factors that influence their choice of a college major, which range from academic preparation to values and expectations concerning what they want to get from their college education,[3] are all embedded in the social contexts of China and the United States.

THE SOCIAL CONTEXTS FOR COLLEGE MAJOR CHOICES IN CHINA AND THE UNITED STATES

In China, college majors are demarcated by the hierarchy of test scores from the Gaokao.[4] Unlike American colleges, where students do not have to commit to a major right away and they are free to change majors throughout their college careers, Chinese students are admitted into college with a major, and admissions decisions are linked to test scores on the Gaokao. Usually, popular majors require higher test scores, and less-popular majors have a lower score threshold. Given that there is a clear, built-in hierarchy of college majors, it is very hard to change majors in China. Figure 6.2 shows the college major distribution in China among bachelor's degree recipients in 2015. The data are from the Chinese Ministry of Education. The disciplinary set-up is not entirely the same as in the United States. For example, medicine is an undergraduate major in China but a graduate field of study in the United States. Law in China is an undergraduate major, and often, traditional social science fields such as sociology are included under the category of law in the Chinese undergraduate certification process. Therefore, there is no separate social science category in the 2015 Chinese data.

Natural science and engineering in China are similar to majors in the United States, and together they constitute the so-called STEM fields.

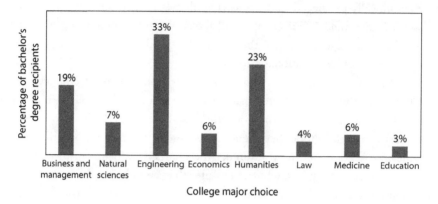

FIGURE 6.2 Percentages of college majors among bachelor's degree recipients in China, 2015

Source: Data from the Chinese Ministry of Education, http://www.moe.edu.cn/s78/A03 /moe_560/jytjsj_2016/

In this area, a comparison between the Chinese and American statistics is striking. A comparison of figure 6.2 with figure 6.1 shows that more than 30 percent of Chinese bachelor's degrees were conferred in engineering alone, and combined with natural science fields, the STEM fields garnered over 40 percent of all bachelor's degree holders in China. On the other hand, in the same year, only 8.3 percent of bachelor's degrees were conferred in engineering fields in the United States, which was even a slight increase over prior years. The combined STEM fields took up approximately 20 percent of all bachelor's degree holders, about half of the share in China.

If the percentage of college majors is an indication of a discipline's popularity in a society, we can conclude that engineering and STEM in general are much more popular in China than in the United States. The question is: Why are engineering and STEM in general so popular in China but not in the United States? Demand should not be a major issue in the United States, as the shortage of domestic talent has prompted American employers to fill the need by importing STEM professionals from all over the world.[5] Nevertheless, the shortage of American domestic students studying STEM has stimulated the creation of many policy programs to draw them into the STEM pipeline.[6] However, while STEM fields are valued and prioritized in national policy in the United States,[7] popular culture often portrays scientists and engineers as unpopular nerds and geeks.[8] Only students that are not very influenced by such a culture or have exposure to alternative cultural frameworks have the potential to succeed in STEM. Children of immigrants could be such students. For example, a *New York Times* article, titled "Math Skills Suffer in the U.S.," states that the United States has failed to develop the math skills of both boys and girls, and it especially notes that "girls who do succeed in the field are almost all immigrants or the daughters of immigrants from countries where mathematics is more highly valued."[9] That conclusion is based on a study of top-scoring participants in the International Mathematics Olympiad. My collaborative work with Dr. Amy Lutz, using the national representative dataset, also shows that the children of immigrants, by and large, are more likely to choose a STEM field as their college major and graduate with a STEM bachelor's degree than their third-generation coethnic and white peers.[10]

On the other hand, there is strong cultural value and social approval in studying in STEM fields in contemporary Chinese society. To be sure, nation building and modernization efforts since the Communist Party founded the People's Republic of China in 1949 have become the driving force for the priority accorded to STEM fields. China modeled itself after the Soviet Union in prioritizing STEM fields with an eye toward industrialization.[11] In 1970, the share of engineering degrees reached a peak of almost 60 percent.[12] Therefore, the 33 percent of engineering degrees in 2015 actually marks a decline compared to its ultradominant status before the reform era. Still quite dominant and popular, math and science subjects are vaunted knowledge in China. This has been deeply imprinted on the national ethos, and almost every schoolchild in China knows the saying: "Mastering math, physics, and chemistry, one is fearless in the world." There is no mention of engineering, because engineering is a college subject, and mastering math, physics, and chemistry lays the foundation for the study of engineering in college. Unlike Western politicians, who are often trained as lawyers with humanities and social science undergraduate degrees, recent Chinese political leaders have disproportionately specialized in science and engineering, with the latest exception of President Xi Jinping.[13] In fact, Tsinghua University, dubbed the Chinese MIT for its academic reputation in science and engineering, has produced several Chinese leaders, from former president Hu Jingtao to former premier Zhu Rongji. Because of this, Tsinghua is considered the cradle of Chinese political leadership.[14]

Contemporary Chinese society has witnessed quite a bumpy disciplinary history in its behavioral and social science fields, and as a result, there is a sense of doubt and disillusionment concerning these fields among students and their parents nowadays. For example, sociology as a discipline was discredited as "bourgeois fake science" and completely shut down in 1956 when the academy reorganized its disciplines.[15] Sociology as a discipline did not reemerge as a field until 1979, after the Chinese Communist Party launched its reform and opening-up policies. Other social science fields, such as political science and anthropology, have all been weakened and suppressed intellectually.

Since China launched its reform and opening-up policies, the popularity of business fields has risen, and there has been a greater demand for business and management personnel. Figure 6.2 shows that among Chinese bachelor's degree earners, business is currently the second-largest field after engineering. About 19 percent of bachelor's degree earners are in business, which is comparable to the American statistics in Figure 6.1.

Within China, scholars have found a similar pattern of family backgrounds and college major choices. For example, in their 2017 article, sociologists Anning Hu and Xiaogang Wu, using data from the Beijing College Studies Panel Study, note that students from economically privileged families are more likely to choose a liberal arts over a STEM major.[16] They found that these differences are mediated by cultural capital, a term coined by Bourdieu and Passeron in their seminal work in 1977 that refers to the "widely shared high-status cultural signals (e.g., attitudes, preferences, formal knowledge, behaviors, goods and credentials) used for social and cultural exclusion."[17] They found that economically privileged families are more likely to possess cultural capital and that their children's access to classic literature and art drives their interest in choosing a liberal arts major over a STEM major. In my earlier work studying Asian American college major choices, I found that cultural capital also serves as a mediating factor in accounting for the disparities between the college major choices of Asian American and white students.[18] Specifically, Asian American students were found to be more likely to choose and attain a degree in a STEM field, and their lack of cultural capital helped account for their seeming success in these fields. In other words, Asian students and their families are consciously choosing STEM fields to circumvent the limitations of their cultural capital.

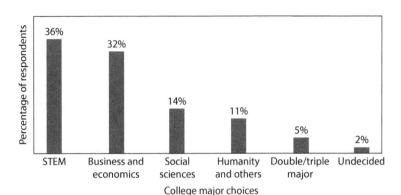

FIGURE 6.3 College major choices among Chinese international students in the United States
Source: Author's study

Contrary to the findings within China, the preference of Chinese international students—who are relatively more economically privileged than average Chinese—for lucrative STEM and business fields seems not to have faded. A comparison of figures 6.2 and 6.3 shows that the number of Chinese international students in humanities fields in the United States (11 percent) is less than half of that of their peers in China (23 percent). Disaggregating the humanities, we see that over 10 percent of bachelor's degrees in China went to literature studies alone, and 8 percent went to the arts. However, Chinese international students in the United States are much less likely to choose humanities than their peers in China. How can we understand this?

Chinese international students, in spite of socioeconomic privilege in their home country, may be constrained by their lack of Western-based cultural capital. Cultural capital in China, however, involves a set of competencies beyond those valued in the Western context. For example, a knowledge and appreciation of Chinese linguistics and literary work is a core part of cultural capital in China. However, to study literature in the United States requires additional and different types of cultural capital; so, faced with the loss of their own cultural capital, Chinese international students in America strategically gravitate towards technical fields such as STEM fields. In other words, Chinese international students experience disadvantages of Western cultural capital and the loss of their own cultural capital, which is key to understanding their avoidance of humanities majors.

As sociologist Paul DiMaggio argues, cultural capital is more relevant to students' grades in nontechnical subjects than technical ones.

> English, History, and Social Studies are subjects in which cultural capital can be expected to make a difference; standards are diffuse and evaluation is likely to be relatively subjective. By contrast, Mathematics requires the acquisition of specific skills in the classroom setting, and students are evaluated primarily on the basis of their success in generating correct answers to sets of problems.[19]

Technical fields require less cultural capital than humanistic, artistic, or other fields. The survey analysis reported in chapter 4 shows that Chinese international students experience great difficulties with history, writing, and social science courses; fewer students experience difficulties with math and science courses.[20] Their reportedly strong foundation in math and science, in conjunction with the disadvantages they confront in humanities and social sciences courses, unsurprisingly drives Chinese international students towards STEM fields.

Now the question is: Given that most Chinese international students are economically privileged, why do they still incline towards pragmatic fields such as business? In the next section, I advance the concept of pragmatic collectivism, as compared to the American creed of expressive individualism, to help us understand the rationales behind college major choices.

EXPRESSIVE INDIVIDUALISM VERSUS PRAGMATIC COLLECTIVISM

The history of development of higher education in China and the United States may influence how Chinese and American students view the purpose of a college education. Martin Trow[21] delineated his now-famous three phases of the development of higher education: The first phase is the stage of *elite higher education*, where the enrollment rate among the college-going population is less than 15 percent. The second phase is *mass higher education*, where the enrollment rate is between 15 and 50 percent. When the enrollment rate surpasses 50 percent, the system is at the *universal higher education* stage. Contemporary Chinese society has only recently passed the stage of elite higher education, with a college enrollment rate of about 40 percent.[22] The fact that China achieved a transition from the elite higher education stage to the mass higher education stage within a handful of years is unprecedented.

The recent past, when only a small number of students could access higher education in China, may orient students and their parents toward largely viewing college education as a vehicle for ramping up their skillsets and getting them a good job afterwards. On the other hand, the extended period of American mass higher education has oriented many students and their parents, particularly those from middle-class families,[23] to believe that college is just an extension of adolescence and to feel that students need to fully explore and discover who they are. This process of self-exploration entails exposure to various domains of knowledge, different types of people, and certainly to various social clubs and diversions. Because college major choices entail knowledge of self, and because such knowledge is often in flux for incoming college students, many students in the United States remain undecided about their major. New York Times columnist David Brooks once noted in a 2011 op-ed one of the most frequent messages in commencement speeches:

> Follow your passion, chart your own course, march to the beat of your own drummer, follow your dreams and find yourself. This is the litany of expressive individualism, which is still the dominant note in American culture.[24]

Expressive individualism, first made well-known in the seminal book *Habits of the Heart* (2007), still finds wide resonance in American culture—the belief that finding oneself, including discovering one's interests and abilities, serves as a guidepost for school-age children and their parents and teachers.[25] The internal search for oneself stands in sharp contrast with the external concerns for jobs and money. The differentiation often falls along the socioeconomic lines. Sometimes, with the constraints on their lives, most often socioeconomic constraints, American students have to make practical choices and incline towards lucrative college majors such as engineering and business. Due to the rising concerns of student loans and the challenging employment markets for college graduates, American college students are arguably becoming increasingly pragmatic in their views of meanings of education.[26] However, the discourse of expressive individualism is still dominant and influential, as it reflects the privileged ideology. The privileged class in America consider the meaning of college to extend far beyond skills and jobs. In their book *Paying for the Party*, Elizabeth Armstrong and Laura Hamilton identify "the party pathway."[27] College students on this pathway value college primarily on the basis of their social experiences. In such a context, they choose easy majors, such as fashion, communication, tourism, sports, recreation studies, and so forth. Armstrong and Hamilton eloquently show that American students with easy majors depend more on their family connections and resources than on their academic records and their own efforts in landing internships and job opportunities. Thus, these majors have become a reservoir for privileged students.

Expressive individualism is, however, remarkably absent from Chinese culture and its education system, which is highly standardized and collective-oriented. I argued that the differences between individualism and collectivism in the United States and China are deeply imprinted on their education systems.[28] Their impacts are manifested in the organization of everyday activities, in curricular structures, and in the college admissions process. In spite of the market economy begun in the late 1970s, which is pulling the new China towards an individualistic society in terms of its commercial sector and recreational life, the collectivist orientation of its education system has endured. Chinese students, from elementary school to high school, are expected to learn similar material at the same grade level. Individual course selections are largely unavailable, and formal tracking does not appear until the eleventh grade, when students choose science versus humanities/arts tracks as they get ready for the college entrance examination. There is little emphasis on passion or interests unique to the individual, but much value is placed on effort and the common standards that everyone can achieve, so long as there is a will.

In other words, Chinese students choose their college majors in the broad context of a collectivist-oriented society, where they are influenced by their parents, teachers, and peer networks. The shared value among these influences is pragmatism—a focus on the jobs students can get from their college majors—rather than the idealism of self-exploration and self-development through college education. The influences of pragmatic collectivism on Chinese students and the heavy coaching of parents, teachers, and peer networks lead their college major choices to be disproportionately vocational in nature.

Therefore, when Chinese students contemplate their choice of a college major, this practical orientation runs deep, and international students carry these values when they study in the United States. Job, job, job, is the primary—if not the exclusive—concern that guides their choice. At the University of Wisconsin at Madison, Chinese students host their own talk shows in Chinese on the campus TV network. They once featured the issue of career choice, and they invited two American middle-aged men who worked at the campus career services office to give advice to the Chinese students on campus. Not surprisingly, these two men conveyed advice that is all too familiar American mantra: that is, follow your passion, and let your interests guide your career choice. Many Americans do not understand why Chinese international students, with all their capacity to pay for their education, are so practical-minded and seemingly could not care less about their passions and interests. One of the talk show hosts explained his logic. He was a senior major in finance and already had a job offer from an investment bank. He made this choice because he had spent so much money here for his American undergraduate education that he felt obligated to fulfill high expectations for a return on his investment (ROI). This is straightforward economic logic not unique to Chinese culture.

Because Chinese undergraduate students have little access to scholarships, and in the case of public universities, no access to state-level tuition, their investment in higher education is even greater than that of their American peers. Coupled with their pragmatic cultural backgrounds, the pressure they feel to realize returns on their investment is aggravating. Therefore, in spite of the relative economic privileges Chinese international students have, that their college major choices tend to be technical and pragmatic fundamentally reflects their economic pressure and disadvantages in Western-based cultural capital.

SURVEY FINDINGS

The above discussion describes and explains differences in the choice of a college major among Chinese international students, their American peers, and their Chinese peers in China. In addition, there are differences in the choice of a college major among Chinese international students themselves. Several factors stand out. One is gender. Figure 6.4 presents the data for gender disparities among the Chinese international students in the online

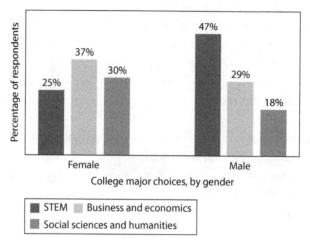

FIGURE 6.4 Gender differences of college major choices among Chinese international students in the United States
Source: Author's study

sample. As with American students, the gender gap in STEM fields in favor of male students is the most pronounced: close to half of all the men chose a STEM field compared to a quarter of the women. Chinese women make up for the gap in STEM majors through a higher share in both the social sciences and humanities. Females are also more likely than males to enter business fields.

Parental education matters, too, as shown in figure 6.5. Chinese students with college-educated parents are more likely to major in STEM fields than their first-generation counterparts who are more likely to major in business. In addition, Chinese students in selective schools are more likely than their peers in nonselective schools to major in STEM fields and less likely to major in business, as shown in Figure 6.6. Finally, future planning—the intention to stay in the United States or return to China—also matters. Those who intend to stay in the United States are more likely to study in STEM and business fields and less likely to study in the social sciences and humanities than their peers who intend to return to China, as shown in figure 6.7. This could be because American society provides more job opportunities in STEM and business fields, so that those who intend to stay in the United States make the strategic decision to enter these fields.

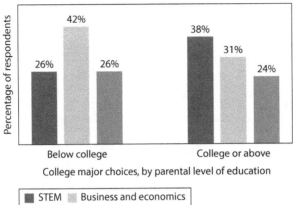

FIGURE 6.5 Parental education and college major distributions among Chinese international students in the United States
Source: Author's study

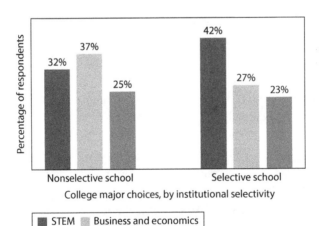

FIGURE 6.6 Institutional selectivity and college major distributions among Chinese international students in the United States
Source: Author's study

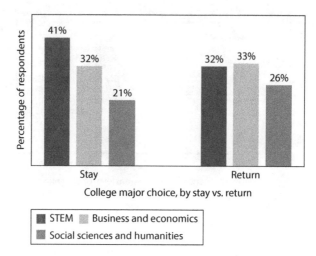

FIGURE 6.7 "Intention to stay" versus "Return," and college major distributions among Chinese international students in the United States
Source: Author's study

A good example to illustrate this is Jennifer, an applied math major at UCLA, who intentionally switched to this major from her previous humanities track in China in order to stay and work in the United States after graduation. (Jennifer's story is detailed in chapter 9.) Fields in the humanities and social sciences depend much more on language and culture, so it is more challenging to find a job in these fields in the United States.

Table 6.1 presents the results of the multivariate analysis, which took into account several key variables at once. Notably, proficiency in English, American friends, and the start time of study in the United States did not matter in the college major choices of the survey participants, so they are not included in the analysis. When all of the other factors are controlled for in model 3 (the full model), men are still over 50 percent less likely to major in the social sciences and humanities than in STEM fields, and they are over 40 percent less likely to major in business than in STEM fields. In other words, Chinese female students are much more likely to major in the social sciences and humanities and business than in STEM fields. Those who intend to return to China are over 80 percent more likely to major in the social sciences and humanities than in STEM. Students from nonselective schools are almost twice as likely to major in business as in the humanities and social sciences compared to their counterparts in selective institutions.

TABLE 6.1

Multivariate Analysis of College Major Choice among Chinese International
Undergraduates (Odds Ratios)

	MODEL I		MODEL II		MODEL III	
	Business	Social	Business	Social	Business	Social
Male	0.432***	0.342***	0.482***	0.410***	0.440***	0.398***
	(0.097)	(0.078)	(0.113)	(0.097)	(0.106)	(0.096)
Parents with college education	0.502**	0.622	0.621	0.681	0.661	0.726
	(0.157)	(0.204)	(0.207)	(0.232)	(0.229)	(0.258)
Good English	1.139	1.277	1.248	1.317	1.164	1.314
	(0.261)	(0.300)	(0.311)	(0.332)	(0.299)	(0.344)
American high schools			1.048	1.224	1.071	1.340
			(0.338)	(0.387)	(0.353)	(0.431)
Selective schools			0.567**	0.775	0.543**	0.723
			(0.137)	(0.185)	(0.135)	(0.178)
Return to China					1.386	1.815**
					(0.339)	(0.454)

*** p<0.01

** p<0.05

* p<0.1

Reference Category: STEM fields

Note: Standard errors are in parentheses. "Good English" refers to the self-perception that the student's level of English is either good or excellent, as opposed to poor and fair.

What are the deep stories behind these broad patterns? The in-depth interviews yield insights into students' rationales, dilemmas, and sometimes the tensions, both internal and intergenerational, behind their college major choices.

INTERVIEW FINDINGS

Practical, Practical, Practical

Chris, a native of Guangzhou, dreamed of being a zoologist, but instead she majored in prenursing at Georgia State. She was aware that nursing is in demand in America and that zoologists make much less than nurses. When I asked her about the American tenet to "follow your heart," she immediately dismissed it:

> Don't listen to that. It is not practical. My goal is to make an independent living. I do not want to make a lot of money, but I need to make sure that I can support myself. But it requires a lot of money to support myself in big cities, so I cannot be a zoologist.

I then asked her why she thinks a lot of money is needed to support herself.

INTERVIEWER: Some people think that they only need a little to sustain themselves, and that it doesn't require a lot of money.
CHRIS: But no. If you live in a major city, it is very expensive. I have to make sure that I can support myself.

Chris's hometown, Guangzhou, is the largest city in Southern China; it has a high cost of living and, in particular, astronomical housing prices. Circumstances like these could influence the perceptions of students on what constitutes a reasonable cost of living.

Alexa, also from Georgia State University, majored in actuarial science. She made up her mind about this college major when she was a high school student in China. She attended the international division of a high school in Guangzhou, where counselors were in place to provide information about overseas study and to help her with her college application. In addition, the international division partnered with three state universities in the United States—Georgia State, San Diego State, and Colorado State—to recommend Chinese high school students who might study there. She came to Georgia State because its actuarial science program has a high ranking. She explained her choice:

> It is a very lucrative field. I got to know this from my high school counselor in China, who suggested I go to Georgia State to study actuarial science. She told us this is a good major for Chinese students.

She went on to comment how much money her parents had spent on her education in the international division of her high school in China, which charges about 100,000 yuan per year (about $14,500). She is also paying for the out-of-state tuition at Georgia State. She harbored a strong sense of obligation to her family and wanted to reap returns from her college education to help them:

> Because my parents have spent so much money on me, I feel the need to pay them back. I also need to help my sister financially. We are ten years apart. When my sister needs money, my parents may be too old to provide assistance. I need to shoulder the responsibility.

Alexa described her family as a very ordinary household in Guangzhou. Neither of her parents had gone to college. Her mother did not work, and her father had a small business, which often faced uncertainty in the tumultuous Chinese market economy. Like many other Chinese students, she felt a strong sense of urgency to make her education useful, which often means getting a good-paying job *fast*. She had no long-term plan to stay in the United States but, as the starting salary in most jobs in the United States is still higher than in China, she wanted to get a job in the United States right after graduation and get her investment back first. When I asked her how long she thought it would take before she would be ready to return to China, she pondered a few minutes and replied, "Maybe three years?"

In spite of the overwhelmingly pragmatic orientation of Chinese international students when it comes to their college major choices, there are a few idealistic souls among them. Lei, from Shenyang, a city in North China, is such an exception. She majored in secondary education at the University of Portland. She chose this university on a friend's recommendation. Her friend had graduated from there and then returned to China and served as an educator and independent consultant. Lei chose education as her major because she had always wanted to be a teacher, and she had experienced various kinds of education, from Chinese college to American college to American summer school, as well as several types of supplementary education. She wanted to make a difference in Chinese education, and she felt that test-oriented education is a bit inhumane.

> Sometimes I felt my goal was too big and unrealistic. But I feel that even if I can just make a tiny bit of difference, I am happy. I like being a teacher and interacting with kids. They are our future.

I feel it is very meaningful to experience their growth. Life is so short. Why not pursue some meaningful goals? Life is also so long. Why not limit ourselves in our major choices? Technology develops so rapidly, and many technical jobs can be automated by machines. But humanistic education teaches me how to think. That is unique and irreplaceable.

Lei was lucky to have her parents' support. Her mother had little education; she worked as a tailor and later ran her own small business in women's clothing. Lei's mother just wanted her to be well educated and choose a field that was a good fit for her. Lei was exceptional on two fronts: one was that she had a clear sense of her interests and purpose—making a contribution to China's education—and the other was that her parents were among those who were not college-educated, so they felt that they could not provide much concrete guidance. The descriptive analysis shows that first-generation college students such as Lei are more likely to choose business as their college major above anything else. Lei is clearly an exception here. For the majority of the participants whose parents had been to college, parental influence was paramount.

Parental Influence

Parental influence is both explicit and implicit in Chinese students' college major choices. Explicitly, Chinese parents tell their children what majors they should study, what majors have a bright future, and so forth. Implicitly, some parents let their children know that they have invested a great deal and have made sacrifices for their children's education, so their children have to study something that promises good economic returns. Figure 1.3 shows that business, health, and engineering were among the top occupations of the parents of the students in the sample; parents who were professionals in their fields were often role models for their children.

Coco, a native of Nanjing, majored in neural science and behavioral studies on the premed track and minored in dance. She had been a ballet dancer since she was in first grade. She was heavily influenced by her mother's occupation in medicine. She grew up watching how her mother treated patients and saw how grateful the patients were. She felt that being a doctor would bestow a strong sense of achievement. Although she sensed great challenges ahead in getting into medical school in the United States, she tried very hard to realize that aspiration:

> I know that getting into medical school as an international student in the U.S. is extremely hard. [American medical schools] favor their domestic students and only assign a tiny number of slots for international students. But I still aimed for it. I worked dead hard. I worked even harder here in the U.S. than in China. My GPA right now is 3.9, but I want to be perfect, so that my chances of getting into a good medical school are greater.

Coco's awareness of her uphill battle to get into medical school in the United States was not unfounded. Many public institutions in the United States admit very few international students into their medical schools.

According to Datta and Miller in a 2012 article published in *Medical Education*, "in 2010, only 1,300 foreign citizens applied to US medical schools and only 171 matriculated. This 13 percent acceptance rate is much lower than that of their US citizen counterparts, whose acceptance rate hovers around 42–44 percent."[29] The long shot for international students in medical schools has deterred many, but apparently Coco was not deterred. She attributed her determination to her mother, who was a visiting scholar for a year at Emory's medical school when Coco was in kindergarten. Her mother then returned to China to work as a clinical professor at a medical university in Nanjing and has always been her role model. Coco fondly recalled her first visit to the United States and the sight of her mother at work in the Emory School of Medicine, and ever since then, she felt that she wanted to go into medicine.

In addition to serving as role models, some parents are active influencers; they steer their children away from certain majors—ones that appeal to their children's interests but are not promising in parents' eyes—and give direct advice on what their children should study. Their advice is rooted in their practical mindset, which often leads them to drive their children to study engineering, math, or economics. Alan, in spite of his original interest in design, majors in electrical engineering at the University of California at San Diego. Alan's father is the owner of an electronic device business in China. He suggested that Alan major in electrical engineering first and consider design later for graduate school. Alan explained:

> I initially wanted to design. But my dad said that I should study science and engineering and that would lay a good foundation for me, no matter what I will do in the future. My dad actually approves of my interest in design. He suggested I can combine design with engineering, so I can continue studying design for a master's degree in the future, but my undergraduate major should be in science and engineering. I thought that was a good plan, so I followed his advice. My dad runs an electronics business, so I chose electrical engineering as my major.

It is noteworthy that Alan's father approves of his son's interests in design, but suggests a STEM major instead, because a major in science and engineering "would lay a good foundation." This view that a STEM major is a foundation for any pursuit in the future echoes the pervasive belief in Chinese society that prioritizes STEM learning.

STEM fields are popular in China, so it is almost normative for parents to influence their children to major in them. But there are exceptions to this norm. In fields such as the arts and film, role modeling and the connections parents provide are especially significant. Yan, a major in film at Syracuse University, is one of the few international students in her major. Her college, the S.I. Newhouse School of Public Communications, is one of the best in the nation. Her choice to study film in America would not have been possible had it not been for her family. She has a family lineage in film directing, starting with her grandfather. Her father, who had also studied to be a director, succumbed to lucrative business opportunities in China's booming market economy and gave up his film ambitions. Her father later regretted this and encouraged her to pursue her dream. While her father did not become a professional film director, the family connections with the film industry were not severed. As soon as Yan completed her undergraduate studies at Syracuse, she went to work as an intern for the Los Angeles branch office of the Film and TV Corporation, whose headquarters are located in her hometown province—an opportunity based entirely on her family connections.

The Art of Double Majoring

Studies have shown that double majors are associated with higher returns in the labor market, and American colleges and universities have seen a rise in double majors over the years.[30] Researchers estimate that about 25 percent of college students graduate with two majors, and in some selective colleges the rate is even higher. Sometimes students utilize double majoring as a strategy for dealing with a discrepancy between their interests and their parents' wishes, trying to strike a delicate balance between utilitarian concerns and personal preferences. Chinese international students share this tendency and adopt a strategy similar to that of their American peers. Due to great parental pressure and the more pragmatic orientation Chinese international students have towards their college major choices, they tend to adopt one major that answers to pragmatic concerns and their parents' wishes, often in STEM or economics, and a second major in the humanities or arts that appeals to their personal interests.

Students have different types of double majors. Sometimes the two majors fall into similar categories, such as political science and sociology, both in the broad social sciences; sometimes they belong to different colleges, such as engineering and history. In a 2012 report from Vanderbilt University's Curb Center for Art, Enterprise and Public Policy, "Double Majors: Influences, Identities and Impacts,"[31] Richard Pitt and Steven Tepper found that only 10 percent of students in their sample of 1,760 students from nine universities had one major in a STEM field and another in the arts or humanities. Researchers call students who double major this way "spanners," as their two majors bridge the furthest intellectual distance. Spanners are rare among American students but are seen more often among Chinese international students. In this study, according to the survey, there were thirty-three double majors, twenty-seven of whom were spanners. In other words, the majority of double majors among the Chinese international students in our survey chose their two majors from distinct colleges.

Brian was such a spanner, also an exemplar of the tenet "one major for me, one major for my parents." He studied at the University of Wisconsin at Madison, double majoring in industrial engineering and psychology. His father, who had graduated from Shanghai Jiaotong University and trained as an engineer, asked him to major in engineering. His father thought that learning engineering would ensure that he could make a living, although Brian's real interest was in psychology. He ultimately followed his father's suggestion to major in industrial engineering, with an eye towards consulting for business rather than being a practicing engineer. However, unlike the Chinese students who passively follow their parents' advice, Brian stood out as someone who was intrigued by self-discovery and had a heightened curiosity about people and the outside world. He claimed that he was people-oriented and would ultimately rather work with clients than things. He graduated with his double major and went on to study for MBA, which suits his interests nicely.

Spanners are rare among American students, and even rarer among female students. In the same report, Richard Pitt and Steven Tepper showed that women are most likely to double major by adding a major in a foreign language or psychology. In other words, women tend to combine two non-STEM majors. When they do add a STEM major, that major is often biology—the most popular science major for women. In this context, Sabrina is quite exceptional. She chose physics as her college major when she entered the University of Wisconsin at Madison, and during the second semester of her first year, she added art history as a second major. She explained her interest in physics and her later encounter with art history:

> I was interested in physics when I was in high school in Guangzhou studying quantum. I was fascinated. I felt quantum is so powerful and could explain many things in life, from philosophy to psychology. At that time, I watched a film called *Secret*, using quantum physics to offer powerful explanations about various things in life. From that moment on, I decided to major in physics. After I came to Madison, I took an elective art history class during my first semester. I was again hooked. Art history gave me a new way of looking at things. So I added art history as my second major in college.

The fact that Sabrina had already studied quantum physics in her high school in Guangzhou showcases the advanced science curriculum Chinese students are exposed to. The exposure stimulated her interest in physics and directly led her to major in this notoriously underrepresented field for women in the United States. Sabrina may not have been aware of the persistent gender segregation in physics in the United States. However, her exposure to art history rekindled her interest in the arts and humanities. More important, Sabrina felt that art history brought a new way of thinking to her scientific mindset in her study of physics.

Changing Majors, Changing Heart

For many Chinese students, the decision to major in STEM fields and/or business was an a priori one. It takes intrinsic motivation, and sometimes fierce independence and tenacious grit, for them to fight against the pressure from their parents to study in the humanities and social sciences. Wei's story attests to this.

Wei's parents wanted her to study math as her undergraduate major; they considered math to be foundational and felt she could pursue various occupations with good math preparation. Her mother even asked her to write a note guaranteeing her commitment to math before she went to the United States. So, with her later change of major, she broke her promise to her mother and created a tug of war. Her mother felt that she was making a mistake and that Wei was not heeding her good advice. Her mother thought that Wei was just rebelling and not being a good daughter. Wei was persistent. When I asked her from where she derived this power to stick to her guns, she attributed it to her coursework at St. Olaf and to the way her education there had transformed her thinking:

> I think the change came during second semester when I was taking a course titled "I Want to Help People," offered in the social work department. That course awakened me and made me realize that I want to engage with the world and contribute to society. I met great American friends through that course, too. They suggested a new major to me that suits my interests well: social studies education. That major mainly prepares students to teach high school social studies, but that is not my career goal. I just like the content of the major, all the readings and discussions. It has changed my way of thinking about myself. So I persisted in my choice, and I won the battle against my mom.

Wei fought the battle to change her major and won, although the process was fraught with anxiety, and even threats from her parents, and many tears shed after the long-winding arguments with her mom. She did much soul-searching and held her ground. Apparently, the American friends she made, the open discussion of various social issues in her coursework, and all the readings she has done in her coursework had more influence on her thinking than her mother's pressure. She changed her major and her heart— American education made her into a different person.

Other students have had less dramatic, or even traumatic, experiences in changing college majors. Yiwen changed her major from physics to advertising at Syracuse University. Her decision did not meet much resistance from her parents back in China. As she noted: "They [her parents] feel that they do not understand life here (in the United States), so they trust me to make my decisions." She graduated from her high school in her hometown in Shenyang in North China and enrolled in Syracuse University as a physics major, because she was good at physics in China. She explained why she later changed her major:

> I took physics courses here and found I was one of the few girls in the classes. While I could learn the material no problem, I felt lonely. Then I took an elective course in advertising and liked it a lot. I realized that working with people is my true passion; while in China I did not know that. Smart people study science. So my teachers and parents all said that I should study physics, as I am smart and good at it. But now I feel that I am not as interested in working with things as working with people. Now my challenge is language and culture here. But it is so interesting and I am motivated to learn.

Yiwen's experience, paralleling American girls' avoidance of STEM fields along with her self-discovery that "working with people [was her] true passion," ultimately triggered her change from physics to advertising. As she said, in China "smart people study science," a belief that has driven many Chinese students to major in STEM fields. However, she was confronted with the harsh reality that there are "few girls in the (physics) classes" and felt its chilling effect.[32] Although not many Chinese students are like Yiwen in leaving science, her story provides a rare glimpse into how Chinese international students can be changed by American culture when they study in American institutions.

SUMMARY

This chapter details the choices, dilemmas, and rationales behind Chinese international students' college major choices in the United States. They have to deal with competing and sometimes irreconcilable educational needs: to appease their parents, to pursue their interests, to ensure their professional future, and so forth. Chinese students tend to be pragmatic in their college major choices, despite the fact that they are overwhelmingly from economically privileged family backgrounds. They are concentrated in business, economics, and STEM fields. This tendency is distinct from their American peers. How can we understand this?

The social contexts in China that value STEM, the fact that Chinese students have a more pragmatic orientation towards college major choices, and their lack of cultural capital in the United States, are all relevant. Overall, Chinese international students are more likely to choose business majors than both Chinese students in China and American students in the United States, and they are more likely to choose STEM majors than American students in the United States. Within these general patterns, there are important variations. Gender, parental education, institutional selectivity, and their plans regarding whether or not to stay in the United States are key differentiators within this population.

Parents play a critical role in Chinese students' college major choices in both role modeling and active influencing. The fact that business ranks among the top professions of both their mother and fathers, and that engineering ranks among the top professions of their fathers, leads to a strong role modeling effect on the students' choosing STEM and business fields. Their parents also persuade, cajole, push, and even threaten them to abandon their original interest in arts or humanities for STEM and business studies. Some students follow their parents' advice. Others resist. Still others choose to be strategic by double majoring—one major for their parents, one major to satisfy their own needs.

CHAPTER 7

Think Before Speak

I did not speak up that much in class, and neither did my Chinese classmates. I felt that everybody was waiting for everybody else to speak up.

—Christine, Georgia State University

Christine's observation was about the English language class she found herself in because her TOEFL score was 76, which is less than the required minimum score at Georgia State. This is an increasingly common practice adopted by American colleges and universities across the nation: for those whose English scores do not meet the admissions requirement, the institution will first admit them into an English language class. So these students pay tuition before earning college credits. The language class consisted of most of Christine's Chinese peers. Her observation that "everybody was waiting for everybody else to speak up" vividly highlights the dynamics of a classroom dominated by Chinese international students.

Active participation in class discussions is integral to a liberal arts education, and it is one of the key vehicles for exchanging ideas and contributing to understanding among diverse groups of students. With the skyrocketing increase of Chinese students, who are not inclined to engage in verbal exchanges with faculty and other students, the value of diversity and American liberal education could be compromised, ultimately damaging the education of both Chinese and American students.

American faculty and students are often puzzled as to why Chinese students do not speak up. An understanding of why Chinese students behave this way can inform American college faculty and academic advisors and help them appropriately teach students how to make positive changes. In addition, this understanding may propel American faculty to make adjustments in their pedagogy, especially in their class participation activities, so that Chinese students, too, can adjust and develop their own pace in speaking up and participating.

A quick yet superficial understanding of barriers inhibiting classroom participation for international students involves language barriers. The findings of the survey analysis in this study reveal that close to 60 percent of the participants thought their English was good or excellent, but only a little more than 30 percent of the survey participants often spoke up in class. So language barriers are far from a sufficient explanation. Chinese international students are not a homogeneous group. The analysis further revealed that factors such as institutional selectivity and interest in one's program of study give rise to significant differences among the respondents. Our in-depth interviews provide key insights into two additional sources of influence: one concerns the cultural differences between China and the United States relating to speaking, and the other concerns the exam-based education system in China that is not amenable to open-ended classroom participation.

LANGUAGE BARRIERS

Language barriers constitute one of the fundamental and enduring challenges for international students whose native language is not English. Almost all colleges and universities in the United States require Chinese international students to take English language tests such as the TOEFL, the IELTS, or the PTE (Pearson Test of English), submit the test results,[1] and meet a minimum score requirement for admission. The most commonly accepted English test is the TOEFL; its i-BT (internet-based version) has a maximum score of 120, and it encompasses four areas: speaking, writing, reading, and listening. There is no generally regarded passing or failing score, as individual higher education institutions set their own standards, and some institutions have different thresholds for admission into different majors.

For example, at Syracuse University, the TOEFL score requirements vary quite a bit across the different academic units. The preferred score is 85 for the college of arts and sciences, 90 for the Whitman School of Management, and 102 for the Newhouse School of Communications; the remaining colleges, including those for engineering and education, have the lowest preferred score of 80. Before 2011, Syracuse University preferred TOEFL scores of 80 for all of its colleges, except for the Newhouse School of Communications, which required 100. The higher thresholds and proliferating tier system at Syracuse for TOEFL score requirements in recent years are readily seen in many other colleges and universities in the United States.[2] This trend mirrors the perception among Chinese international students that institutions are ramping up their requirements as the selection process grows increasingly competitive. Chapter 2 shows that some Chinese students took the TOEFL several times to increase their scores.

However, in spite of the increasingly higher TOEFL score requirements for Chinese international students, American faculty members and university administrators still complain about these students' lack of language proficiency and their reticence in the classroom. Chinese students themselves are often anxious about this as well. In fact, reticence and anxiety are very common among English as a second language (ESL) learners. There have been extensive studies of ESL learners, and reticence and anxiety are common themes explored in the literature.[3] ESL learners are typically found not to respond to questions from their teachers, not to seek clarification or ask questions, and not to initiate discussion in the classroom. This pattern has been observed in the home country classrooms of ESL learners as well. For example, in a 2009 study[4] in a renowned university in Beijing, Liu and Jackson found that Chinese ESL students tend not to respond to their teachers' questions. This study consisted of 500 first-year, non-English majors and grouped students into three levels of English proficiency. The study found that the more proficient group was more active in classroom discussions. Also, the Chinese ESL students were more willing to engage in pair work and speak in English than to respond to a teacher's questions in English, regardless of their proficiency level.

Chinese international students studying in the United States confront English barriers that are more complicated than those of ESL learners in China. These occur on both objective and subjective levels. Objectively, a lack of vocabulary and a lack of familiarity with the English language learning environment make reading and writing challenging and pose additional barriers to class participation. Subjectively, situations where the majority of students are native English speakers increase the sensitivity of Chinese students to the language barriers they face. Often, sensitivity turns into anxiety, especially in courses that depend more on the use of English.[5] That could help explain in part the difficulties Chinese students feel in those language and cultural courses. According to our survey, Chinese students find courses such as history and writing more challenging than math and science courses (see figure 4.5).

Figure 7.1 shows that even though close to 60 percent of the students surveyed thought their English was good or excellent, only a little more than 30 percent of them often spoke up in class. Notice that what they attribute this to is not their objective English proficiency but their self-evaluation of their English abilities. Subjectively, Chinese students' awareness of and sensitivity to their imperfect English often thwarts their initial courage and optimism in learning, which further slows them down. This is shown in the following comment by Wen, an economics and education double major at Beloit College.

My professor told me that my English is good, but somehow in my mind I am more critical of myself: I am always alert to grammar mistakes or any inappropriate language use or wrong word when I speak.

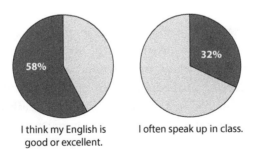

I think my English is   I often speak up in class.
good or excellent.

FIGURE 7.1 Self-evaluation of English proficiency of survey respondents versus their tendency to speak up in class
Source: Author's study

These sentiments resonated with those of many other Chinese students, such as Kaisy, who is an accounting major at Lehigh University:

> In class when the professor throws out a question, my American class-mates can provide spontaneous responses. But I feel that I am often drafting the response in my mind, then, when I feel that I am almost ready, the conversation has shifted to the next topic. So I am always trying to catch up. I am exhausted, but I am still unable to join the conversation.

Complaints about Chinese students' English are often heard from faculty and other students, but the cruelest critics are often Chinese students themselves. They are alert to their grammar mistakes and incorrect language use before any listener has the chance to catch them. They are often reluctant to speak up in class because they are quietly fretting and "drafting responses in their minds" but are not able to catch up with the quick conversational flow in the classroom, where their American peers can speak in a spontaneous manner.

This subjective barrier can be more lucidly understood through W. E. B. Du Bois's concept of double consciousness. Du Bois originally conceived of this concept to describe the experience of black males in the United States, and then it was widely applied to other marginalized groups who are the targets of discrimination and racism. I argue that this concept can fruitfully help us understand Chinese international students' language barriers and the impact these barriers have on students' communication and interpersonal relationship building. In *The Souls of Black Folk*, Du Bois explains:

> It is a peculiar sensation, this double-consciousness, this sense of always looking at one's self through the eyes of others, of measuring one's soul by the tape of a world that looks on in amused contempt and pity. One ever feels his twoness, an American, a Negro; two souls, two thoughts, two unreconciled strivings; two warring ideals in one dark body, whose dogged strength alone keeps it from being torn asunder.[6]

Du Bois uses double consciousness to conceptualize the troubled times endured by African Americans at the hands of white supremacists, as they struggled with being American and black, and were subjected to inequality and the racist dehumanization.[7] I extend this concept of double consciousness to Chinese international students as they negotiate their language and cultural otherness in American society. This perspective from the outside marks their twoness, their double consciousness in the host society as they look at themselves from the perspective of native speakers. This tendency to always look at oneself through the eyes of native speakers, be it their professors or their American classmates, or through the eyes of an imagined speaker of "standard English," leads Chinese international students to develop double consciousness. They are at once conscious of one voice of the native speaker—the standard English in their minds—and another voice of the ESL speaker like themselves—marked by its brokenness and accents they are so eager to shed. The native speaker is critical of the ESL speaker, and the latter is always trying to measure up to the former in terms of correct word choice, grammar, pronunciation, and intonation; and more often than not the effort is futile, because English is not their native language, and they cannot speak it impeccably, as they imagine their American evaluators expect them to. In other words, the double consciousness results in two voices, one critical of the other, and Chinese students are torn by their own internal critic, sometimes more than by their external ones.

It should be noted that parents' educational attainment plays a critical role in Chinese international students' English proficiency. In the survey, about 18 percent of respondents were first-generation college students. Apparently, the respondents were disproportionately from college-educated families, which is not really surprising, as their parents' education often contributed to the privileged family economic resources that underwrote their American college experience. Figure 7.2 shows that about 64 percent of the

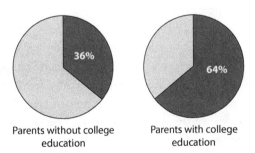

Parents without college
education

Parents with college
education

FIGURE 7.2 Survey responents who self-evaluate their English skills as "good or excellent," by level of parental education
Source: Author's study

students whose parents were college-educated thought their English was good, whereas only 36 percent of the first-generation students thought so.

The interviews yielded a consistent insight that the students felt that language was a key barrier to their academic and social experiences in American universities. In this respect, first-generation college students lag significantly behind their counterparts. Parents often play a key role in helping their children to learn English and establish their children's comfort level with speaking the language. During the interviews, students often mentioned that their parents pushed them to learn English and provided learning materials, such as videos and tapes purchased abroad. Han, an information management and economics double major at Syracuse University, clearly benefited from his dad, who worked as a manager in a state-owned enterprise in Beijing. When he was young, his dad often travelled abroad to English-speaking countries and brought back original CDs or DVDs of English music and films. Han always enjoyed listening to and watching them, and his English, especially his spoken English, had been the envy of his peers since grade school. However, he struggled with math, so much so that he was marginalized and felt a loss of self-esteem because of it. Then his parents switched him to the international track of his school, where he went from being stymied in the regular division to being full of enthusiasm and pride about himself because the priority shifted from math to English. He described the change:

> I feel that I've picked up all the loss of self-esteem in the international division, as English was again emphasized and valorized. I've had great relationships with all my teachers, and my classmates admired my abilities and elected me head of the class.

Han's English was so good that his American professors and friends often mistook him as someone who was born in the United States. He was active in classroom discussions and was able to make quite a few American friends. English played a critical role in Han's academic success later on, and he attributed a great deal of this success to parental support, much of which hinges upon resources.

In spite of the critical role of language proficiency, the question of speaking up in the classroom cannot be fully addressed through the idea of language competency alone. For example, the children of Asian immigrants have English as their first language, but they are still less likely to speak up in class. Although they grow up in the United States, studies have shown that they also tend to be quiet in school.[8] In fact, East Asian learners in general have been widely noted not to participate as actively as their white counterparts in American classrooms. Therefore, something more than language proficiency may be at work. The following section discusses cultural difference in speaking between China and the United States.

CULTURAL NORMS IN SPEAKING

China: Actions Speak Louder than Words

Education researcher Jin Li has written a comprehensive book on learning differences between the East and West, *Cultural Foundations of Learning*. She devoted one chapter of the book to attempts to understand the phenomenon of the "reluctant speaker," which is broadly seen in East Asian societies and even among East Asian immigrants' children who have grown up in the West.[9] She argues that the three major spiritual traditions in East Asian culture—Taoism, Buddhism, and Confucianism—place little to no emphasis on speaking. Taoism values harmony between human beings and nature, without much need for talk, as is exemplified by Lao Tzu's well-known saying "those who understand are not talkers; talkers don't understand." Buddhism emphasizes quiet meditation to gain a peaceful mind and achieve personal enlightenment, and little human communication is needed to this end. The most influential spiritual tradition in China—Confucianism—categorically distrusts words and discourages speaking while putting a premium on actions. For example, in *Analects*, Confucius writes, "The exemplary person wants to be slow to speak yet quick to act."[10] More important, Confucius links speaking with moral cultivation and more often than not casts suspicion on speech in judging one's moral being. For example, Confucius identifies three kinds of problems with speaking: (1) a glib tongue, arguing that "glib words corrupt virtue," (2) flattering speech, which leads to vanity and loss of sincerity, and (3) boastful speech, which violates the key Confucian virtue of modesty.[11] Although some traditional Chinese cultural practices have been heavily critiqued and then jettisoned by contemporary Chinese, the cultural norms relating to speaking have endured. This impact can still be felt in democratic Japan and Korea.[12] Jin Li argues that the reason lies in

> Confucian persuasion for personal moral development. Even when eloquent speakers emerge as they do, people may not admire and trust them as much as they do in the West, resulting in less power granted to such speakers. Consequently, political, social, business, and education leaders may not be eager to develop or to display oratory skills either. None of the current Asian political leaders are distinguished speakers. Instead, they project an image of speaking cautiously, slowly, softly, and hesitantly, as exemplified by UN Secretary-General Ban Ki-moon.[13]

Tsinghua University, the preeminent Chinese university, which has graduated several top political leaders, including former president Hu Jintao and former premier Zhu Rongji, has this aphorism—"Action is better than words." All of this indicates that Chinese teaching and learning value rumination and contemplation, not elaborate verbal exchange.

Confucius's distrust and discouragement of speaking go hand in hand with his emphasis on speaking appropriately.[14] This means that speakers should be attuned to social contexts and social relations, such as when speaking with authority figures like teachers, professors, doctors, and family elders. There is a robust body of research on the East Asian trait of deference and respect to authority and the elderly, which stands in sharp contrast to the Western cultural value of individual assertiveness and willingness to challenge authority.[15] This contrast is evident even after Chinese immigrate to the United States. For example, a study examining assertiveness found that Chinese American students are less likely to ask a professor to clarify a lecture than their European American peers.[16] Chinese American students consider challenging their professors directly in class inappropriate; they believe they should seek out their professors after class and discuss issues privately, rather than making a public scene.[17]

In other words, it is not that Chinese students do not want to ask questions, but they want to ask them in an appropriate way. It has to be noted that Chinese culture's emphasis on respect for authority and the elderly is often misunderstood in the West as depriving individuals of agency and independent opinion. Quite the contrary, even traditional Confucian culture recognizes the need to question authority; it just ought to be done in a culturally appropriate way. For example, the Confucian scholar Han Yu once said, "*Shi bu bi xian yu di zi*" ("Teachers are not always more knowledgeable than students, and students do not necessarily know less than teachers"). This saying reflects the spirit of encouraging students to challenge teachers. Therefore, it is important to recognize that the normative expectation of speaking appropriately often means "think before you speak" and minimizes random and spontaneous speech.

However, Chinese culture is changing. The traditional notion of discouraging and distrusting oratorical skills has been slowly eroded as China has become increasingly integrated into the global economy, and the significance of communication and oratorical skills, very much emphasized in the West, has started to influence Chinese society, too. This is evident in the media, where several prime-time TV shows, such as *I Am the Speaker*, which feature speech and oratory contests, have scored high ratings. Charismatic leaders like Barack Obama and Jack Ma (the Chinese homegrown entrepreneur, CEO, and founder of the Alibaba group) are admired not only for their professional success but also for their eloquence, an integral part of their personal charisma. Chinese education systems are, however, less responsive to the changing reality. Schools still primarily teach to the test and prepare students for the Gaokao, which is an entirely written test. Although Chinese youth are heavily exposed to the media, it is in school that they spend most of their formative years.

The United States: A Tradition of Oral Eloquence

The American society and its education system put a premium on oral eloquence, which has its long tradition as well. According to Jin Li, "there is a long tradition of oral eloquence that dates back to Greek antiquity through the Roman era and Christian tradition of delivering sermons to congregations."[18] She argues that speaking matters in four areas in the West: a distinct personal quality, a basic human right, a coveted leadership trait, and last as art.

As a personal quality, verbal fluency is highly regarded and closely associated with intelligence in the United States. Research shows that there is a positive bias towards eloquent, talkative people over shy and quiet people.[19] Talkative and eloquent people are often considered more intelligent and creative than those who are quiet and shy, even though objectively there are no such differences. Speaking one's mind is valorized in Western culture as a good personal quality, denoting integrity and forthrightness. It indicates the courage to stick to one's true thoughts without fear or intimidation of external authority. There are many heroic figures in American history, including whistleblowers, who have spoken up against authority. This sharply contrasts with the principle of speaking appropriately emphasized in Chinese culture. The societal norm and expectation to speak appropriately in China often requires one to be sensitive and attuned to the roles, status, and situations of speakers and listeners, which often makes speaking one's mind awfully difficult.

Jin Li has traced speech in the West as a right to the ancient Greek democratic system, which used verbal argumentation to settle disputes in court. The central role of speech, to articulate reason verbally, has been given legitimacy and institutionalized judicially. The United States further protects and institutionalizes freedom of speech through the First Amendment to its Constitution. In this case, "speaking is not only a granted legal right, but, more importantly, a political right that all people enjoy."[20] This is almost the opposite of the traditional Chinese saying that "disaster originates from speaking up." This caution against speech still has currency today in China, manifesting in its pervasive censorship of the media and academic research.[21] In the age of the internet, there are more venues where one can speak up now in China, but censorship and self-censorship are still in force, so that the cultural norms pertaining to speaking have not been fundamentally challenged.[22]

From ancient Greece to the modern American political system, delivering speech is a necessary and vital skill for any political leader. Charisma, an intangible leadership attribute, is almost always linked to verbal fluency and eloquence. This is true not only in politics but also in religion (consider how a congregation is managed through sermons) and in secular life. The central role of speech in personal and professional success has driven American education to include training in speaking as an integral part of its curriculum. It can take various forms. From grade school, American students engage in group discussions and individual presentations. From middle school onwards, schools often have debating teams, and students participate in debating contests at various levels. Talented debaters can win city, state, or national competitions, and these accolades help win the hearts of college admissions officers at selective institutions. In colleges and universities, classes in public speaking are routinely offered and sometimes required. Communication and rhetoric studies have become one of the major fields of study for American students. Presentations, individual or group-based, have been adopted as one of the major means of evaluation adopted by American professors in all domains, ranging from engineering to business to English.

In my interviews with foreign teachers in Chinese public high schools, one of the recurring themes was the feeling on the part of the teachers that their students were too quiet in the classroom. This was not just in the humanities or social science but also in math, where there would seem to be little need for open-ended debate, yet the expectation gap in communication still emerged for the Chinese teachers and their students. In contrast, Western learning emphasizes the role of communicating, articulating, and debating in its teaching and learning spaces.

During my fieldwork in the international division of Wuxi No. 1 High School, Andrew, a math teacher from the UK, told me about his experiences teaching math in China. He effusively praised Chinese students' math abilities and their good learning habits in general; the only area where he felt they fell short of his expectations was communication.

INTERVIEWER: What do you mean by lack of communication in math?
ANDREW: I mean these kids can solve the math problems magically and methodically, yet they cannot articulate their thinking to others. I think articulating and debating various approaches to solving math problems are equally or more important than merely solving them.
INTERVIEWER: Do your Chinese students understand the importance of communicating in math?
ANDREW: I am not sure. I try to convey that to them, but I can see it is hard for them to act on it. They are used to quietly working on math. I guess that is because their previous teachers didn't emphasize communication in math learning.

Andrew recognized that it was hard for Chinese students to meet his expectations in communicating about math. He attributed this to the long-standing practice of Chinese teachers to expect quiet work when solving math problems. Interviews with the students showed that they did not at all understand their British math teacher's expectations for them to communicate. They felt quite strange that their British math teacher had such an expectation. So the exposure to Western teachers and Western curriculum cannot automatically change the long-standing practices and learning habits among Chinese students when it comes to the role of speaking and communicating in learning.

"I DO NOT WANT TO RAISE SILLY QUESTIONS"

Once Chinese students arrive in America, surrounded by teachers and peers expecting and engaging in oral communication and discussion as an essential way of learning, they have a heightened awareness of the importance of speaking up. However, this awareness can hardly be put into action. Many Chinese students often find great barriers, both internal and external, to acting upon this awareness. Zhong, a psychology major at Vanderbilt University, understood that speaking up would improve his grade, so he made great efforts to do so in the face of great barriers. He gave a vivid description of those barriers:

> I tried to increase my frequency of speaking up, but this turned out to be a big challenge. I have to constantly think about what to ask, as I do not want to raise silly questions. I want to ask valuable and thoughtful questions. I have to think really hard, but sometimes my thinking slows me down, and then I find that the professor has already moved on to the next topic. Sometimes the professor talks really fast, and English is my second language, so it takes me more time to respond and think in English than my American peers. I know this is important for my grade, so it is quite stressful.

Zhong's remarks show that the cultural norm of thinking before speaking he was accustomed to in China, on top of the language barrier, posed enormous challenges to his speaking up, despite his strong motivation and awareness of the importance of doing so. The dilemma of knowing its importance, yet being unable to do it, was defeating and stressful.

THE TEST-ORIENTED EDUCATION
SYSTEM IN CHINA

This discouragement of verbal exchange, coupled with the hierarchical relationship between teachers and students, leads to a relative lack of questioning and classroom participation in China. Other East Asian societies, such as Japan and South Korea, deeply influenced by Confucian culture, also exhibit similar characteristics in their classrooms: quiet learners, fewer verbal exchange between teachers and students, and so forth.[23] What these societies share in common, besides reticent learners, is another key feature of their education systems: high-stakes standardized testing. I argue that high-stakes standardized testing also plays a critical role in making students reticent and anxious learners.

Contemporary Chinese education systems are geared towards the ultimate college entrance examination (the Gaokao). A famous saying in China goes: "The Gaokao is like a baton," which means that this most important test directs teachers, students, and parents. Whatever is tested is important and is relentlessly practiced. However, oral communication is not part of the test, so it is not a priority among educational goals. Up to now, in spite of curriculum reforms, presentation and debate have rarely been incorporated into the standard curricular structure at the elementary and secondary school levels.

Testing as the exclusive mechanism for identifying talent in China has deep historical and cultural origins. China boasts the world's oldest standardized test, the Imperial Examination System, which lasted about 1,300 years (605–1905 CE). The Imperial Examination System gradually developed and solidified into a civil service exam for selecting government officials.[24] The exam was based on how much and how deeply a candidate understood the Confucian classics.[25] Societies that are influenced by Confucian culture share this commonality of the importance of testing.[26] For example, Japan and South Korea also have the tradition of relying exclusively on test scores in selecting talents. The Imperial Examination System has deeply influenced contemporary East Asian societies and resulted in the notorious examination hell facing students in these societies, as a preponderance of research has shown.[27] Research has not only described and decried the hellish experiences of East Asian students, but more importantly, it has investigated the reasons for the enduring use of the test-oriented system. Researchers such as Samuel Peng have argued that a merit-based examination system is the only way to satisfy the distinct needs of East Asian societies: the central role of family in light of the moral principles of Confucian teaching and equality of education for all regardless of their background. These two needs are inherently in conflict when the gatekeepers of educational resources, such as admissions officers, confront their family members' requests for preferential treatment. This also helps explain why the American method of evaluating candidates, such as through interviews and recommendation letters, cannot gain traction in China. Recent reforms that have tried to incorporate just a few alternative means of evaluation like these, borrowed from the American college admissions process, have aroused widespread public skepticism concerning corruption and injustices in China.[28]

As reasonable and realistic as the examination hell is in China, it has nonetheless created some unintended consequences for students, one of which, I argue, is their being reluctant speakers. Students are accustomed and expected to give right or wrong answers to prescribed questions, and the high stakes of testing have wired students to be afraid of making mistakes. Western-style, open-ended discussion questions aimed at getting students to speak up in class, thus, totally disorient Chinese students. Peng, majoring in applied math, finance, and information management at Syracuse University, spoke of his observation of Chinese students in American classrooms, including himself:

PENG: Often in my class, some American students would talk and talk, from the start to the end of the course, and the Chinese students would just watch them talk. . . . I forced myself to interject occasionally, to express my opinion, but I was afraid to make mistakes. Then later I realized that this was not a question with a clear right or wrong answer.

INTERVIEWER: So why were you afraid? What did you fear?

PENG: I guess we [Chinese students like him] fear mistakes, fear to give wrong answers. But there is not always a right answer to the question.

INTERVIEWER: Yes, but what held you back?

PENG: I think it was the test-oriented education in China that we get so used to. There is always a right answer [in that system]. But there is not in the American system. American students are taught in their system that many questions are open-ended, so they dare to offer their answers. . . . But we [Chinese students] were wired by our system to believe that there is a right answer, so we are afraid to make mistakes.

Peng's reflection is illuminating in that it points out the legacy of high-stakes standardized testing for Chinese international students—a mindset of searching for the answers and lingering insecurity over being judged right or wrong. This mindset is present even in the absence of testing—students are wired to judge themselves and others—and it hijacks Chinese students from freely expressing themselves.

WHAT MAKES A DIFFERENCE?

There are systematic variations among Chinese international students in their tendency to speak up in class. The results of the survey analysis reveal significant patterns. First, parental education matters. Figure 7.3 shows that among the first-generation college students, about 18 percent often spoke up in class, while among the Chinese students with college-educated parents, about 34 percent often spoke up. At the same time, parental education matters for children's self-assessed English proficiency. Figure 7.4 shows that institutional selectivity can matter as well. Among those in nonselective institutions, only about 24 percent often spoke up in class. The corresponding

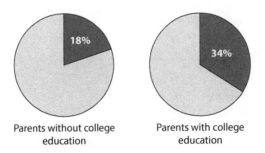

Parents without college
education

Parents with college
education

FIGURE 7.3 Survey respondents' tendency to speak up in class, by level of parental education
Source: Author's study

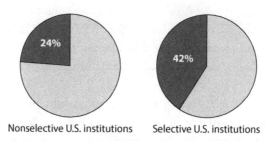

Nonselective U.S. institutions   Selective U.S. institutions

FIGURE 7.4 Survey respondents' tendency to speak up in class, by U.S. institutional selectivity
Source: Author's study

number in selective institutions was 41 percent. Figure 7.5 displays the data for the role of interest in the program as an important reason for college choice. Among those who chose their current college based on interest (rather than on ranking, parental advice, etc.), 42 percent often spoke up in class. Among those who did not come to American colleges motivated by program interest, only 24 percent often spoke up in class.

To further test the relationships among the above potentially significant variables, multivariate regression analysis was used. For example, given that English proficiency is highly relevant to speaking up in class, it is possible that parental education exerts influence on speaking up in class through its impact on English language. Table 7.1, indeed, supports this hypothesis. It includes parental education in the first model. Students whose parents were college-educated were over two times as likely to speak up often in

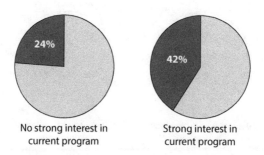

No strong interest in   Strong interest in
current program   current program

FIGURE 7.5 Survey respondents' tendency to speak up in class, by degree of program interest
Source: Author's study

class as first-generation college students. However, after students' English proficiency was included in Model II, parental education lost its statistical significance. This means that parental education impacts speaking up in class through its role in promoting English proficiency.

Table 7.1 shows that two other factors make a statistically significant difference: interest in a program as a key consideration for college choice and institutional selectivity. As for interest in the program, this factor captures motivation to study in a field before coming to the United States. That is to say, those who came to study at American institutions because of an interest in a particular program were significantly more likely to speak up in class than those who did not. This makes sense, because those who are

TABLE 7.1

Multivariate Analysis on Students Actively Speaking up in Class (Odds Ratios)

	MODEL I	MODEL II	MODEL III
Male	1.172	1.251	1.109
	(0.232)	(0.264)	(0.252)
Parents with college education	2.301***	1.612	1.677
	(0.702)	(0.526)	(0.612)
Good English		3.913***	3.905***
		(0.948)	(1.029)
American high school		1.170	1.161
		(0.312)	(0.334)
Interest in program		1.550**	1.801***
		(0.328)	(0.405)
Selective institutions			1.791***
			(0.398)
Research institutions			0.967
			(0.340)

*** $p<0.01$

** $p<0.05$

* $p<0.1$

Note: Standard errors are in parentheses. "Good English" refers to the perception that the student's level of English is either good or excellent, as opposed to poor and fair. "Interest in Program" refers to being interested in a program as a reason for college choice.

178 ✦ Think Before Speak

intrinsically motivated and find substantive interest in a program may be more likely to overcome their internal and external barriers—namely, the barriers embedded in a test-oriented education system and in societal norms that do not emphasize oral eloquence—to speak up in American classrooms. Another factor that makes a difference is institutional selectivity. Students enrolled in selective institutions, including both major research universities and small liberal arts colleges, were more likely to speak up than those who were enrolled in nonselective institutions. Interestingly, the model also tried to capture institutional diversity by differentiating major research universities from small liberal arts colleges, but that difference turned out to be nonsignificant. The model also included other factors that could potentially make a difference, such as whether to attend American high schools, but statistically they were not significant. That does not mean that time in the United States was irrelevant for any single student over time. The in-depth interviews provide a crucial complement in this respect.

LEI'S AND JOLINA'S STORIES

Lei is a vivacious and chatty sophomore at the University of Portland. In spite of her enthusiasm and strong desire to participate, she finds it very challenging to speak up in her class. She said: "I found it very hard to chime in, so I tended to step back. I listened most of the time during class, or after class, during my team discussion." But she feels that she has made quite a bit of progress over the past year. During the first semester of her sophomore year, she took a class in public speaking, which made a lot of difference. She also reached out to campus staff in counseling centers and international student centers, and they counseled her to reduce her anxiety about speaking and participating. She feels those conversations were very helpful for unlocking her energy, and the more she felt free to express herself, the more confident she felt in speaking up, and the more she was able to speak up. Owing to her very strong desire to participate and express herself, she took less than a year to do so. Other people take longer, if they manage to do it at all.

Jolina is a self-described introvert studying at Emory University. She started in ninth grade at an all-girls private high school in Virginia. Unlike Lei, Jolina was indeed not chatty during the interview. However, she said that she had no problems speaking up in her classes at Emory. She said that compared to her Chinese peers who finished high school in China, she felt that she had more confidence in her spoken English, which helped her to speak up in American classrooms. She felt that is probably one of the advantages she got from her American high school experience. She somehow got used to the classroom expectation that she needed to participate, which was important to her grades. She compared herself to a boy in her class who had graduated from a top high school in China. She said that her participation grade was always higher than that boy's, even though he could write so well that his essays always got higher grades than hers.

WHAT CAN BE DONE?

Not only do Chinese international students experience growth over time in their comfort with English and their confidence toward speaking up, but they are also attuned to different contexts. Key contexts are small versus large groups. Most people feel more comfortable speaking up in small rather than large groups. As for Chinese international students, their anxiety about speaking is only escalated when it comes to large groups. This was echoed in many of the student interviews.

Wei was majoring in social science education at St. Olaf College. She was very motivated to learn about social issues, such as inequality and educational equity, and those issues prompted her to get into a big fight with her family to change her major from math to social science and education. She acknowledged that she learned a lot from group discussion and relished exchanging ideas and views with her American classmates. Although she had not participated much in group discussions during her first year, she started to become active during her second year. She differentiated the small group context from the large group one:

> I was more comfortable speaking up in small group discussions. I found myself very engaged and motivated to participate in a small group. But in large groups, I was still not able to speak as much as I wanted to. I certainly could not speak up in a big lecture hall when professors would throw out a random question, but almost always American students could seize the opportunity. They could speak up much more freely and speak as they think. I still felt anxious in a large group setting, and had to think first and then speak.

Wei's greater anxiety in a large group than in a small one is broadly shared by others. Small groups are more intimate and less intimidating, especially for Chinese international students who do not speak English as their first language and who have been trained not to speak up in classroom settings in their prior schooling in China. An intimate small group can help alleviate students' speaking anxiety and enable them to become more spontaneous in responding; as Wei put it to "speak as they think" rather than to have to think first, draft a response in their mind, and then speak. The latter process often results in a heightened sensitivity about the appropriateness of their language and its content, delaying their ability to respond and lowering their chances of speaking up altogether.

Given the above findings, American faculty can adjust and adopt certain practices to enable Chinese international students to speak up in class more frequently and comfortably. As Chinese students are more likely to speak after they think than their American counterparts, due to their language barriers and their cultural concerns about speaking appropriately, American professors could help by giving all students, both domestic and international, three to five minutes to write down their thoughts about the discussion question before they jump-start the discussion. I call this technique quick-write sessions and employ them in my own classes. Depending on the length of the class period, professors could adjust this quick-write time accordingly. The purpose is not only to help international students who need some extra time collect their thoughts and get up to speed but also to give domestic students additional time to prepare a more well-thought-out response. The latter can also help bridge personality differences. Those who used to be reserved are more likely to open up because they feel more confident with their thoughts written down, and students who are vocal and spontaneous in speaking in public will learn to formulate more articulate ideas, thus improving the quality of their discussion. Overall, this technique not only more equitably distributes discussion opportunities among students with diverse backgrounds, but it also enhances the quality of classroom discussion for all students.

American professors need to be aware of the examination system Chinese students came from and the impact it has had on their learning habits and mindset. Professors can help alleviate their students' stress over making mistakes by stating explicitly that "there is no right or wrong answer" to some of the questions they ask. They can also motivate Chinese students to speak up by linking speaking to classroom participation and grades. While some professors are explicit about this, it is often merely assumed by other students and professors. By recognizing that Chinese students are from a test-oriented education system where speaking is rarely taken to be part of formal evaluation, American professors can help Chinese students shift from a cramming-for-the-test mindset to a mindset of multidimensional evaluation in which speaking and classroom participation often play a critical role. Slowly, Chinese students can shift their stance and change their behavior by speaking up more often and more confidently once they understand that it is rewarded and rewarding.

SUMMARY

This chapter addresses the question of why Chinese students tend not to speak up in American college classrooms. The first and most obvious reason is the English language barrier. It is a challenge for many students to communicate in English in the classroom. Parental education plays an important role in boosting students' English proficiency, which in turn increases students' chances of speaking up in class. However, the English language barrier is an apparent but insufficient explanation for their reticence. This study found that both premigration characteristics and the type of institution matter as microcontexts, and that cultural differences in speaking and the test-oriented education system in China are relevant as macrocontexts to understanding Chinese students' avoidance of speaking up in American classrooms.

When English proficiency was controlled for, those who chose their American institutions based on program interest, as opposed to other factors such as ranking and financial aid, were more likely to speak up in classes; and those who attended selective institutions were more likely to speak up than their counterparts in nonselective institutions. In addition, the test-oriented education system in China and profound cultural factors relating to speech behavior are central to an understanding of why these students tend not to speak up. Traditional Chinese culture, which values actions over words and emphasizes speaking appropriately, has left deep imprints on Chinese education and society, influencing how Chinese students are taught—namely, to keep their heads down and their mouths shut. Last, the contemporary test-oriented education system also contributes to Chinese students' reluctance to speak up in class. Students are accustomed to giving right or wrong answers to prescribed questions. The Western open-ended discussion questions intended to prompt students to speak up in class disorient Chinese students. Chinese students are simply afraid to make mistakes, preventing them from actively speaking up in class.

CHAPTER 8

Changes and Reflections

I feel that studying abroad has humanized me. In my Chinese high school, we felt like test-taking robots, with intensive knowledge input every day, and our output was test scores. Now I realize that academics are important, but there is other equally important stuff in life, such as family, inter-personal relationships, self-care, and human connections.

—Lei, an education major at the University of Portland

Lei, a native of Nanchang, a provincial city in Jiangxi Province in the southeastern part of China, was admitted into a local college in Nanchang, which is not among the top colleges in China, and she became dissatisfied with her studies there. She didn't like the test-oriented education of her middle school and high school years, and her disappointment in the Chinese education system persisted in college. Her college experience in China echoes a theme in chapter 4 on the disconnect between high school and college in China—most of her peers are not motivated to learn and her professors are not keen on teaching them well. Lei enrolled at the University of Portland to restart her college career in 2014 with the help of her friend who used to be an international student in America herself.

In the United States, she became driven and eager to learn. She wanted to realize her childhood dream of becoming an educator. According to

Lei, she changed from a passive, "test-taking robot" to an active human being with her own thoughts and emotions. She worked as a campus connector in the international students' office. She supported new international students, providing them with information about resources available on campus. Through this process, she came to know about various kinds of resources, such as advising and counseling, which she utilized to her benefit. Studying in the United States is a humanizing experience for her.

When asked how their study in the United States changed them, Chinese students frequently responded that they felt they had become more independent and proactive in their lives. They tended to compare their situation with their previous life in China, where their parents and teachers made almost all of their decisions for them. In the United States, they felt that they were regaining their lost autonomy.

The changes they went through were multifaceted. Eric Liu, a second-generation Chinese American, once wrote in his book *The Accidental Asian*, "Freedom, well nurtured, can grow to fidelity."[1] In the context of his book, Liu refers to the idea that if immigrants were to grant more freedom to their American-born children to explore their identities and cultural heritages, the children might ultimately find solace in, and become loyal to, their parents' culture. This meaningful line resonates with many Chinese international students—their newfound freedom in America also intensifies their feelings of being Chinese.

These students often cherish their freedom after they arrive in the United States: the freedom of being away from parents, the freedom to explore new places, to manage their spare time, to take courses, to participate in extracurricular activities on campus, and so on. However, after a while, a number of these students found a renewed interest in their own culture—Chinese culture and society—something they thought they were eager to dump. This renewed interest, and ultimately their rediscovery of being Chinese while abroad from China, could be an unintended—but valuable and profound—consequence of their overseas experience.[2]

In this chapter, I let the students speak for themselves to elaborate on how these changes manifest. The changes fall under three themes: new experiences in global citizenship, new attitudes towards China and the United States, and personal transformation.

GLOBAL CITIZENSHIP

Scholars debate the value of studying abroad for cultivating global citizenship. On the one hand, they recognize that the world is increasingly interconnected and that the ability to understand, engage, and interact with unknown territory is an integral part of an education in global citizenship.[3] For example, Cheng and Yang demonstrate that studying abroad could serve as an effective pathway to global citizenship because it helps develop relevant knowledge and skills as well as values and attitudes.[4] On the other hand, critics point out history and power dynamics among nation states are at work when it comes to study abroad. The colonial fantasies and desires of white students who study abroad in former colonies of their home countries highlight this point.[5] Whether and to what extent international education is the process of growth for students or the manifestation and mechanism leading to increasing social inequality among groups and countries is an issue of the unsettled scholarly debate.[6]

The students of the new wave of Chinese international students in America, however, explicitly mention global citizenship in their motivation for studying abroad. This is in part due to their career ambitions to have a global platform; it is also due to suppressed citizenship education in China and the lack of opportunities to engage in global citizenship practices, which will be elaborated in the following sections. They are appreciative of the opportunities to understand and practice global citizenship in the United States.

The Promise and Perils of Global Citizenship in China

The scholarly discussion of global citizenship varies from a general sense of belonging to a global community to specific competencies and capacities that are key to cultivating global citizenship.[7] Philosopher Martha Nussbaum proposes three capacities that global citizenship entails: the capacity for critical examination of oneself and one's backgrounds; the capacity to recognize oneself as a human being bound to all other human beings in the world; and the capacity to see the world from the perspective of others.[8]

Education scholars Laura Oxley and Paul Morris help elucidate the ambiguity surrounding the concept of global citizenship by distinguishing two forms: namely, cosmopolitan-based and advocacy-based.[9] For Chinese international students, their desire and engagement with global citizenship fall primarily within the realm of the cosmopolitan-based. Chapter 2 shows that for some students and their parents, global competencies and global awareness are part of cosmopolitan capital, which is one of their integral goals in studying in the United States. They believe that studying abroad entails and promotes an understanding of different cultures and increasing interdependence between peoples and societies, and American higher education can help them gain cosmopolitan capital. They find that Chinese education is lacking on these fronts, and even international education in China cannot deliver what it promises.

Some students went through the International Baccalaureate (IB) curriculum before they started college in the United States. The IB's curriculum explicitly points to "international-mindedness" and advocates for "students to engage with multiple perspectives."[10] This is very appealing to Chinese students, who are steeped in their test-oriented education sector, drowning in sameness, with the same curriculum, same standards, and same goal of high test scores. They are at once hungry for and bewildered by new opportunities to learn about global citizenship.

The students I interviewed from the international division of a high school in Nantong talked about how they were able to participate in a model United Nations, which is a popular activity adopted by most of the international classes in Chinese schools. They gave oral presentations and debated issues ranging from the AIDS epidemic to the education of girls around the world. The students exuded curiosity and excitement. They were nonetheless discontented with what they called an incomplete global education. As Xue, an eleventh-grade student, observed:

> Although we are in the international division, we do not have enough courses that are about international issues. Most of our courses are in natural science and math, or business and economics. There are very few options in social science and humanities courses, so our global education is very incomplete.

During the past decade, Chinese educators have joined educators in other countries in trying to add global contents in curricula. These global contents broadly fall within what scholars term as global citizenship education, which is "widely held to be a revolutionary paradigm shift in our schooling practices."[11] The international divisions of many public high schools in China have touted the value that they place on global education, sometimes explicitly framing this value in terms of global citizenship. A high school teacher in Beijing whom I interviewed taught a course called Citizenship Education. He started teaching this course around 2010, and when I interviewed him around 2017, he felt it increasingly difficult to continue offering this course. His principal supported his course with great enthusiasm initially until several years later, after increasing pressure from the municipal government. The Chinese government apparently is concerned about the content of citizenship education due to its close affinity with Western democracy and its potential to be devoid of national identity. Ultimately the school leadership revised their approach to this course, changing its slogan from "global citizenship" to "global outlook, Chinese heart."

The Chinese government's sensitivity to citizenship education and global citizenship is not surprising. The concepts of citizenship and global citizenship are rooted in the discourse of Western democratic institutions.[12] In her widely cited article "Global Citizenship: Abstraction or Framework for Action?,"[13] international education scholar Lynn Davies focuses on three key aspects of global citizenship: social justice, rights and culture, and cultural conflict. Davies draws on previous models of global education and defines a global citizen as someone who "knows how the world works, is outraged by injustice and who is both willing and enabled to take action to meet this global challenge."[14] Based on this idea, global citizenship entails outrage and action, not just international-mindedness and empathy. In other words, the advocacy-based form of global citizenship is hard to enact among Chinese students who for the most part engage in cosmopolitan-based global citizenship. The Chinese government, conversely, has been pursuing and promoting social harmony and stability in the face of various kinds of social tensions and injustices in its fast-changing society. The last thing it wants is to nurture a form of education that promotes outrage and, thus, potential instability.

Experiencing and Embracing Global Citizenship in the United States

Given the various limitations on citizenship education in China, Chinese students seem to have more opportunities to engage in global citizenship *after* they come to the United States. These experiences involve both the cosmopolitan-based and the advocacy-based work, using the helpful typology developed by education scholars Laura Oxley and Paul Morris.[15]

For many Chinese students, navigating American race relations is their first experience in an ethno-racially diverse society, and they become more reflective about multiracial and multicultural life. Prior to their arrival in the American education system, their impressions of racial minorities in the United States are heavily influenced by the media—American TV shows and Hollywood films in particular—where implicit bias and stereotypical images abound. As such, Chinese students, who are minority students themselves, often hold biases against other minorities, particularly African-Americans.

Keeanga-yamahtta Taylor, the author of *From #BlackLivesMatter to Black Liberation*, has written about this phenomenon, whereby minority groups maintain biases, and sometimes racist notions, about other minority groups:

> Why do many Black workers accept racist anti-immigrant rhetoric? Why do many Black Caribbean and African immigrant workers think that Black Americans are lazy? . . . [I]n short, if most people agree that it would be in the interest of any group of workers to be more united than divided, then why do workers hold reactionary ideas that are an obstacle to unity? There are two primary reasons: competition and the prevalence of ruling-class ideology.[16]

Interviews with Chinese students show that this bias is rooted in the ruling-class ideology spread by the mass media. June was a global and French studies major at Colby College. She talked about how she previously held biases about African Americans:

> I had biases and stereotypes before about Afro Americans. I thought they were lazy. I thought they were not interested in education. But my roommate has totally changed my attitudes. I have learnt so much from her, I mean, like, about life in general. She is Afro American from the South, and she is very smart and hard working.

I went further to ask where her previous bias came from. June replied: "I guess from TV. Blacks are not shown in a good way. I really did not know any in person until now."

It is striking that Chinese students are so quickly influenced by the ruling class ideology of racism through media representations even prior to their arrival in the United States. However, lived experiences can chip away the not-so-deeply-rooted racist ideas that these young students harbor. Like June, they can be transformed quite rapidly.

Sometimes, Chinese students recognize their minority status in American universities, and the identification not only helps them change the implicit biases formed earlier but also brings them closer to other minorities and facilitates friendships among them.[17] Zhong's experience at Vanderbilt University illustrates this well. Zhong, a psychology major, talked about the dynamics of his friendships on campus:

> Before I came to the U.S., I thought blacks were rude and dangerous. But my first-year roommate at Vanderbilt is a black student. He is extremely polite, and he is a football player. I find him very easy to get along with. But the white kids on our campus, they are filthy rich and dumb. I initially thought white people were civil, but gosh, these kids are so immature they don't even flush the toilet. . . . I find them hard to get along with.

Zhong's previous positive bias towards whites and negative bias towards blacks was apparently influenced by an ideology of racial hierarchy and white supremacy. The fact that he had never been to the United States but was still influenced by this ideology shows that such an ideology has global appeal. His lived experiences at American universities quickly dispelled his negative stereotypes of blacks.

In addition to changing implicit bias, many students are active in various kinds of volunteer activities that not only connect them with people from a wide range of backgrounds but also provide advocacy platforms. Alisa, a math major at Bryn Mawr, has derived great satisfaction from her volunteer work in the United States, which was closely tied to her involvement in churches. She volunteered to help people in low-income neighborhoods with their tax returns. As a math major, she wanted to put her knowledge to good use, thinking tax preparation would require math. However, she realized that what she was expected to do had little to do with math. She took the initiative to provide free tutoring in math for kids in those low-income neighborhoods and organized her fellow students from Bryn Mawr to provide more free tutoring and advocate the importance of studying math for these low-income kids. She found the work to be very meaningful:

> I found the work really helpful. I got to know diverse kinds of people. I learned how to effectively communicate with many different people, who I do not have chance to meet otherwise. Knowing about their lives and being able to help them makes me feel very meaningful. I especially like my work in organizing other volunteers for free-tutoring of math. I can see that low-income kids here are already left behind, and I feel obligated to do what I can to level the playing field for them.

Alisa went on to explain how her school, Bryn Mawr College, a liberal arts women's college, stimulated her mind for advocacy work and equality:

> As a women's college, we embrace the goals of diversity and equality. This is not just lip service; we really practice it. Before, it was for minority women, and there are many black female students in our school. Now with the increasing number of international students, we extend the principle of inclusion. People here are global citizens.

Alisa was proud to be in an environment that values global citizenship. She spoke highly of the remarkable support provided by her school's international student office, where she has a part-time job. The office staff work as a conduit for international students on campus to provide guidance and direction for various kinds of support, ranging from visa paperwork to tea-time social events. Stimulated by the international mindset of her college environment, Alisa also actively contributes to the inclusive international community in her school.

Kathy, from Eastern Tennessee State University, which has a couple of hundred international students, is one of the cofounders of her campus's first-ever International Student Association. By founding and leading the organization, she hopes to build a bridge to connect domestic and international students, and she has organized activities in partnership with domestic American student organizations to this effect.

Kathy was not socially engaged during her early days in the United States as a transfer student to a Catholic high school in Tennessee when she started eleventh grade. She described the lonely and withdrawn lifestyle she had during the two years of her high school in Tennessee:

KATHY: It was really bad and I cried many times.
INTERVIEWER: So what have you learned?
KATHY: I learned much about American culture. From readings to TV to music. . . . I tried to absorb everything around me.
INTERVIEWER: This was done while you felt lonely and had difficultly integrating into your environment?
KATHY: Yes, but I did not give up. After a while, especially in college, I can see that I've really improved. So I am ready to engage in college, much more so than in high school.

Kathy exhibited a growth mindset during her journey to study abroad in the United States, developing beyond her early days of alienation to become a leader who is inspired by, and engaged with, her campus and the community. As a public health major, Kathy has joined advocacy groups on campus to march on the street in support of breast cancer research. She has gained new experiences in advocacy that she had little experience with in China. She aspires to work in a nonprofit organization like Doctors Without Borders or Mercy Ships, and she wants to provide health services to people from all over the world.

CHANGES IN ATTITUDE TOWARDS THE UNITED STATES AND CHINA

A Renewed Interest and Strengthened Affinity with China

Chinese students' increased engagement with global citizenship during their time in the United States does not come at the expense of a loss of affinity with China. Absence makes the heart grow fonder. Being away from China rejuvenates an interest in Chinese culture and society.[18] This often happens through coursework, particularly in humanities courses at American universities.

Yue started her college career as an economics major at Syracuse University, and after taking a course titled Religion in Chinese Society, she added religion as a second major. She described how taking this course made her recognize her ignorance of Chinese culture, which she had taken for granted. She reflected on the profound influence it had on her in an application for an award at Syracuse University:

> The course was titled Religion in Chinese Society, which I was excited about, given my familiarity with the subject matter. It turned out, however, that I had entirely misjudged the true nature of religion courses. Even though I was superficially familiar with almost every topic on the syllabus, I soon realized I did not know any of them deeply. There was a chapter discussing the Chinese tradition of paper burning, which my prior education had convinced me was "pure superstition," so I began to question the practicality of studying superstition in a college-level religion class. My preconceived notions prevented me from keeping my mind open. However, after I learned about the profound cultural meaning paper burning has for my people, I began to realize my ignorance. I was trying to deny the value of paper burning just because I had been taught in China that it represented superstition and an absence of progress. Beginning with that Chinese religions class, I slowly embraced the cultural insights that studying religion provides.

Yue not only acknowledged that this class changed her outlook on and understanding of Chinese traditional culture, but she also described how it changed her approach towards her family foundation work in China's remote Yunnan Province. Yue's parents are successful business entrepreneurs, and they started a family foundation to help build schools in Yunnan Province in southwestern China, where ethnic minorities are concentrated. Yue was involved in helping to improve the local schools. As someone of Han ethnicity from the wealthy areas of Shanghai, Yue initially thought having the minority students in Yunnan learn what students in Shanghai usually learn, such as computer science and ballet, would be helpful to them. With that rationale, the family foundation spent a great deal of money to import such a curriculum into the local schools in Yunnan. However, Yue realized there was a problem, as she wrote in her application statement:

> After living with them (the local students in Yunnan) for almost six months, I realized that our attempts to help these students were in

fact only hurting them. We were teaching them computer science, despite the fact that many of them would never own a computer and would never have that option, because they had to work on their farms to make sure their families had enough to eat. This strategy was crippling the students, who were not focusing on useful skills like reading and who began to devalue their local culture as they saw themselves fall behind their Han Chinese countrymen. Although it was a tough decision, we have now removed from the curriculum courses that are irrelevant to the local children's daily lives. I realized that our ignorance of the real situation had caused us to try to apply unrealistic and damaging standards. In exchange, we invited local artists and artisans to teach the students about local traditional handicrafts. Our students have learned to appreciate and value themselves and their culture and have learned how to fight against unfair disparagement from outsiders. They are proud of themselves, and I am proud of them, too.

What Yue gained from an American liberal arts education was not only a new understanding of the cultures and societies she had previously taken for granted but also empathy and respect for the community and people she was trying to serve.

Diana, an economics major at Johns Hopkins University, enrolled in a Chinese history course and became totally absorbed. Before she left China, she could not have cared less about Chinese history and culture; all she desired to know about was American culture. Notwithstanding the heavily technical studies in her majors, she took advantage of a liberal arts education requirement in her university and took several humanities courses, one of which was titled Modern Chinese History.

You know, we [Chinese students] took history throughout our middle-school and high-school years in China, but I was especially fascinated by the analysis of modern Chinese history by my American professor—a white man in his middle age who can speak very good Mandarin. I think highly of my professor's ability to provide a neutral interpretation of modern Chinese history. Most of my professors are very good teachers. They make me want to learn, especially about my own background, culture, and history.

Diana admitted that she became an insatiable reader about Chinese history and about history in general. She confessed that she never used to be into reading at all, and she attributed her fresh interest to her stimulating American professors. At the same time, she felt that her time away from China gave her an increased sense of, affinity to, and pride in China. Her parents, business owners of a factory in Shanghai, had toured all over Europe and North America for either business trips or leisure. Their conclusion was that "Shanghai is the best place on earth." Diana now concurs with her parents, saying that Shanghai is indeed the best, and she returned to Shanghai after getting her master's degree in the United States.

Even those who care more about mundane aspects of life, such as eating and entertainment, find that they are interested in Chinese food and Chinese forms of entertainment, like karaoke and poker, while they are away from China. In other words, their fondness for the Chinese way of life has been renewed and reinforced since they landed in the United States.

Criticisms of American Government and Institutions

Chinese students tended to have a rosy picture of the American system before their arrival in the United States. Sabrina described her romanticized view of America prior to coming, saying, "Everything about the U.S. was ideal to me," but her experiences in the United States made her realize that things are a lot more complicated than she had originally thought. She specifically talked about her disillusionment with democracy:

SABRINA: I realize that "one person, one vote" is not necessarily a good system at all. It might work sometimes, but it will not work for China. Even here [in America], such a system has not worked so effectively. Now Americans have to live with the Trump presidency. Everybody around me is complaining. I thought, "Hey, Trump was elected by the American people. What is wrong with you?"

INTERVIEWER: So you desired democracy before you came to the U.S.?

SABRINA: Certainly I did. I felt it was an equal and effective system. But now I do not think it will work for China.

INTERVIEWER: Why not?

SABRINA: Because people are not as informed, and may not make good
judgments. Look at Trump voters. Now they have to suffer from the
bad choices they made and all the bad policies. Chinese leaders are not
elected through a democratic system, but that does not mean they cannot govern well. Even some Western scholars, like my professors, consider
Chinese society to be well governed.

Sabrina is right in pointing out that some Western thinkers believe that
Chinese leaders have done a decent job of governing, and indeed some
have argued that good governance has constituted an important part of state
legitimacy.[19] Her sojourn in the United States bore witness to the chaotic
election process and to the American people's dissatisfaction with their own
political choices. Her view that democratic elections are not necessarily keys
to good governance has actually been under active discussion and debate
among political scientists.[20] Recent empirical studies have shown that the
Chinese state has actively improved governance, paying particular attention
to providing public goods to improve quality of life, which in turn has generated higher levels of public support for the regime.[21]

In addition to being critical of the American democratic election system, some students were critical of American society's foreign policies and
domestic inequality. In raising these criticisms, they are sometimes quite
aware of their critical thinking skills and readily attribute them to their
American education. Wei, a social studies education major at St. Olaf College, credited American college education with giving birth to her critical
thinking skills. She became a new person in the United States (her personal
transformation is elaborated in the next section). Nonetheless, her personal
growth in the United States did not draw her closer to the American political
system. She became very critical, and her opinions were largely informed by
the courses she took at her American college.

I took many courses in college and they have transformed my thinking. For example, I am taking American history and ethics courses
this semester. These courses have made me think a lot and question
many of my previously held assumptions. For one thing, I started to
be critical about American government intervention policies abroad,
spreading their version of freedom and democracy. I feel that is not

right. I am quite cynical about American government. My study of American history has exposed me to much wrongdoing the American government has done in the past.

In other words, due to courses taken in her American college, Wei developed a critical view about American history and government. She went further to analyze her growth due to the liberal arts education she received in the United States:

The liberal arts education I've gotten has not instilled in me Western and American values, but has taught me how to think about and analyze the real world. I feel that four years of undergraduate education have helped me develop a whole system of thinking about the world.

Wei was also critical of the American education system, particularly K–12 education in America. Ironically, through studying American education, she realized that the American K–12 education is fraught with problems, far from what she thought before she came to America. She conducted a research project in her independent study course on American standardized testing and gained some in-depth understanding about issues of race and achievement gaps, and inequality among schools.

Students like Sabrina and Wei were liberal arts majors, and Sabrina went on to study law at the University of California at San Diego. Wei, after graduating from St. Olaf College, worked in a series of nonprofit international organizational jobs. Their concerns focus on America's political systems and international relations, but many other students have concerns that are more about their everyday life experiences.

Jolina, a premed major at Emory, voiced her concern that Chinese students cannot take excused absences during the Chinese New Year, but other students, such as Jewish and Muslim students, can take days off during their religious holidays. She thought it unfair that the most important Chinese holiday does not qualify as excusable. Other students voiced similar complaints. They particularly felt bad when they could not go back home to celebrate Spring Festival—the lunar Chinese New Year—with their families in China, as their schools did not recognize it. It is the most important holiday in China, a time when family members typically are expected to return home for a reunion. Joy, a fashion design major from New York City's prestigious Parsons College of Design, was very upset with this, especially given the high percentage of Chinese students at her school:

> I find it unfair that we cannot take time off during the Chinese New Year, while Jewish holidays are recognized here. But we have many Chinese students in our school, like, in any course with a dozen students there will be two to six Chinese students. America preaches equality, but does not practice it.

To get a better sense of the impact of this unexcused absence policy on her, the interviewer further asked:

INTERVIEWER: How did that affect you, the fact that you cannot take time off during Chinese holidays?

JOY: I feel that I've lost much quality time spent with my family and friends in China. I feel that this is a loss and the cost of my study abroad experience.

Joy's reflection on the cost of her study abroad experience has both a tinge of sadness and a critical analysis of inequality in America. Ironically, the very thing that American education helps them cultivate—the pursuit of equality and critical thinking skills—enables them to challenge the realities they perceive as unfair treatment in America and leads them to conclude that "America just preaches equality, but does not practice it."

America Is More Family-Oriented Than China

While these students lamented their loss of family time while they were abroad, they often recognized that American society offers a more family-oriented environment than today's China, where people are busy chasing fortunes and neglecting their families.[22] In particular, they mentioned the relatively more slow-paced and laid-back lifestyle they had witnessed in ordinary Americans' lives, compared to the fast-paced and stressful lifestyle that they had seen in their parents' and others' lives in China.

Justin, a student on UCLA's premed track, aimed to follow his parents' footsteps to become a doctor. His parents were doctors in Shantou, Guangdong, and he described them as too busy to spare any quality family time. He felt his parents' lifestyle in China is unappealing. "They are too busy. Most of their time is at work, not just in the hospital treating patients, but outside, having meals, lots of drinking." Phyllis, studying at North Carolina State University, concurred. She often complained about her parents' not having dinner with her. So her dad offered to bring her along to the dinner events he usually went to with his clients. She went once and pledged never to go again:

> I went there with my dad, thinking to have some family time. But my dad and his guests—his clients—smoked and drank a lot of wine and talked about things I did not understand. I was so bored that I just played with my cell phone. Then my dad asked me to stop using my cell phone and join their conversation. I refused. How did I know what to say on those occasions? Very awkward. My dad was mad at me, and I was mad at him. It did not go well.

In spite of this, Phyllis never questioned her dad's love for her. In fact, she readily acknowledged that she has a doting father who endured many struggles in his own youth during the Cultural Revolution, and he did not have children until middle age. Phyllis is his only child. He did not go to college until the end of the Cultural Revolution, when the college entrance examination was reinstated. Then the market economy presented him with many opportunities that improved his and his family's lives to a considerable extent. Eighty percent of the parents of the Chinese international students in the sample were college-educated. The market economy opened up many opportunities, especially for those with college degrees. These opportunities brought them the streams of extra cash that enable their children to study at American universities.

As it is often portrayed in the West, family historically takes a central place in Chinese culture and society.[23] However, today's Chinese families, in embracing the market economy, are too busy and too work-oriented to have time for their children. The students in my study rejected this kind of lifestyle, which, ironically, led to the success in China that financed their educations in the United States. Nonetheless, through their education and study-abroad experiences, they realized that life could be different, more leisurely and meaningful. This desire for a life with leisure time, and the wish not to repeat their parents' experiences, set some of them on a path to stay in the United States and not return to China, a theme to be elaborated on in chapter 9.

PERSONAL TRANSFORMATION

The personal transformation that Chinese international students undergo shares some commonalities with that of typical college students in America—they become more independent and proactive.[24] However, their prior socialization in China casts their transformation in a new light; some of the changes these Chinese students go through are unique. They become more rebellious, and intergenerational tensions in family relations emerge transnationally.

From Passive to Proactive

Fang, an accounting major at Syracuse University, transferred from a Chinese college after a two-year, unsatisfying experience there. She described herself as being passive interpersonally, although not really introverted. Her change from being passive to proactive manifested in two ways: in her approaching teachers and participating in campus organizations.

> I would not turn to teachers when I needed help in China. Perhaps when I had major issues I'd go to my teachers. But here I have formed a new habit of talking with professors. Whenever I want some advice, I know that I can make appointments with my professors, as I see my American peers do that all the time. Here, professors also encourage you to do that. But not in China. Because it's only when you are in trouble that teachers will approach you or your parents. So I always tried to stay away from my teachers in China.

Fang changed from being passive to proactive in approaching teachers, and she attributed this change to observing her American peers, who always take the initiative, and she wanted to learn from them.

She also talked about the tepid life she had in China during college:

> College life in China has no stress, and what you do makes little difference. Most of my Chinese classmates rely on their parents to find jobs for them after graduation. Here, it is different. I have to plan for myself, and my efforts will make a huge difference. That gets me excited and motivated.

This belief in effort is shared widely by Chinese students, as seen in chapter 4. But studying hard and a strong work ethic are not equivalent to strong interest in academics. What was new after they came to study in the United States was a renewed academic interest.

Sunny was an accounting senior at Syracuse University. She felt unmotivated in China, as she did not know what she was interested in. She said that her father's generation had to work hard to have a good life, but she already had a good life, so she lost drive in China. After coming to the United States, she became very driven and motivated. She described the change:

> I was not interested in what I learned in China. It was all about test scores. I am not good at tests, and at best I'm a B student. Teachers did not like me because I am not an A student. But here, test scores matter, but other things matter too. I am very active in my accounting club. I've made many good friends there, and we help each other in learning and professional development. I feel that I am now the owner of my life, and I am very motivated.

Sunny, a self-described B student in China, became a straight-A student in the United States. She gained confidence, motivation, and drive in learning and, more broadly, in life. Sunny's increased motivation to learn is an example of a learning mindset changed from passive to active.

However, this restored sense of self and the feeling that "I am the owner of my life" may sometimes turn into students' rebelling, primarily against their parents in China, leading to intergenerational tensions across the Pacific.

From Obedient to Rebellious

Wei, a social studies education major at St. Olaf College, underwent a transformation from being an obedient, student in China, where her life was pretty much determined by her parents and teachers, to being reflective and rebellious in the United States, where she made decisions that generated much fury and tension with her parents. I discussed her choice of a college major, from her initial plan to major in math to her final decision to major in social studies and education, in chapter 7. She went against her mother's wish that she go to graduate school, and her mother was so furious that she threatened her.

> My mom has a dominant personality. She believes in credentials and advanced degrees and desperately wanted me to go to graduate school. She also thinks that as a girl, I need to get married and have children after my studies. So I must make good use of my time now to obtain my degrees, as if I will not have time to do so in the future. I tried to convince her that in the U.S., many people wait until later to go to graduate school so they know what they really want to do. But she did not believe me, thinking I am just lazy and want to avoid school.

The interviewer went further to ask:

INTERVIEWER: So how did she feel when you did not listen to her?
WEI: She felt very disappointed. She said repeatedly that she had sent me to study in the U.S. not just to get a bachelor's degree. She felt she was right, and she was trying to make the right choices for me. . . .
INTERVIEWER: Do you mind sharing why you want to delay your applying to graduate school, which your mom wants you to do?
WEI: I have a wide range of interests and that is the reason that I want to explore before going to graduate school . . . she insisted that I should go to graduate school right after college, at a better-ranked school than my undergraduate college. But I have my own plan and will stick to it.

Indeed she did not listen to her mom. After college, she chose to work for the Women's Bean Project—a nonprofit organization in Denver—which helps marginalized women to gain independent life and work skills by making food and hand-made jewelry. Eighty percent of the participants in the Women's Bean Project are women of color, and many are single moms who have experienced substance abuse or domestic abuse. After the year she spent at the Women's Bean Project, Wei went to Cambodia for another community development project and is still there at the time of this writing.

Jennifer, an applied math major at UCLA, also acknowledged that after several years in the United States she has changed quite a bit and often disagrees with her parents. She used to be a good girl by Chinese standards, listening to her parents and doing what they asked. Now, she often dares to voice her disagreements to her parents, and they are understandably frustrated and confused.

> My dad would say, "How have you changed so quickly? You have been living in China for seventeen years. You are not a daddy's girl anymore." . . . But now I think always listening to parents is not necessarily good. Because sometimes parents are wrong.

Jennifer then gave an example of how she differed with her parents. Her parents could not understand the "going Dutch" approach she adopts in dining with her friends. Her parents think she should pay for her friends, and in return, the next time, her friends should pay for her. Her parents often attempted to pay for their friends after a meal; they believed this is an effective way to maintain interpersonal relationships. Her parents' approach is quite customary in China, where social networks are paramount in people's status attainment.[25] However, Jennifer felt that paying her friends' bills only makes them indebted to her. She does not want that. She wants economic independence from her friends, and should they ever need help, she will extend it.

SUMMARY

Chinese undergraduates not only study in the United States but also live, interact, and engage with Americans and others from all over the world, on and off campus. This has changed the students significantly, especially given that these are formative years of their lives.

This chapter has discussed these changes through students' own voices and experiences; they fall under three themes: global citizenship, attitudes towards China and the United States, and personal transformation. Chinese students' engagement with global citizenship is enriched in the United States compared to their limited and curtailed access to citizenship education in China. They also find that American education transforms them personally, helping them to become more active and engaged citizens, reflective and reflexive about the social worlds they live in. This heightened awareness inevitably leads them to question their previous ideas and biases, which sometimes result in rebellion and conflicts with their parents. These changes have not alienated or estranged them from China, however. Quite the contrary, many Chinese students have felt a renewed interest in and awareness of being Chinese while they are abroad.

Some have argued that American higher education has become a key source of American soft power.[26] The findings of this chapter offer mixed evidence to support the claim that American higher education transmits American cultures and values and that Chinese students find them attractive and carry them back to China. Partly as the result of American liberal arts education and its prized critical thinking skills, Chinese students have learned to analyze and think for themselves about the complex world they live in. For some, this meant that their attitudes towards the United States changed from a romanticized perception to a critical and realistic one.

CHAPTER 9

Stay versus Return

THAT IS THE QUESTION

*I am really torn: whether to stay in the U.S. or return to China? It is so hard to get
a job here, but I do not want to return empty-handed. I do not want to waste my
parents' hard-earned money.*

—Cheng, international relations major at Boston University

A s an international relations major, Cheng found her career
opportunities are scarce in the United States—many are
beyond her reach as they have a citizenship requirement, so
she wanted to return to China after completing her studies at Boston University, but she felt guilty about not being able to reap returns on her parents' investment in her studies abroad. Her parents, according to her, are
"just ordinary doctors from Nanjing. They are not wealthy at all." Doctors
in China, according to Cheng, are not nearly as prestigious and lucrative
as in the United States. Her parents were stretched thin due to her education in the United States. Her ideal plan was to work for a couple years in
the United States, accumulate some savings, and then return to China; this
plan is hardly attainable as it is really challenging to find a job in her field
in America.

The question of whether to stay in the United States or return to China
is more complicated than it seems. Not only because the nature of decision-
making process is vexing, but also because a binary of stay vs. return is not
sufficient in understanding the more dynamic and open migration plans in

today's interconnected world.[1] In addition, current research largely focuses on postgraduate plans for graduate students, and we know little about the migratory intentions of Chinese undergraduate students. Does this new wave of students aspire to stay in the United States as new immigrants, to return to China, or to travel back and forth and join the league of transnational residents? Given that they are a relatively new cohort and are from a rapidly changing China, where business opportunities have mushroomed and the entrepreneurial spirit is palpable, the intentions of these undergraduates from China toward their future aspirations and plans are especially uncertain. The complexities surrounding visa policies and the unwelcoming messages sent by the Trump administration to international students have exacerbated the uncertainties about their postgraduate plans.

VISA POLICY CONTEXTS

In general, international students can stay in the United States after graduation for one year under the program termed Optional Practical Training (OPT). This program initially allowed international students to work on a student visa for up to twelve months. In 2008, President George W. Bush extended the period to twenty-nine months for those in science, technology, engineering, and mathematics (STEM) fields. The Obama administration increased the extension to thirty-six months in total, effective May 10, 2016.[2] The OPT program offers international students an opportunity to work in the United States temporarily during or soon after completing their studies in American higher education. The Trump administration has put on their agenda to place new restrictions on the OPT program, to "improve protections of U.S workers who may be negatively impacted by" foreign students on OPT.[3] No changes have yet to be made.

If students get job offers, their prospective employers can choose to sponsor their H1-B working visas, which usually provide six years of legal stay in the United States. An H1-B visa offers a pathway to permanent residency and citizenship. According to U.S. Citizenship and Immigration Services (USCIS), "The H-1B program allows companies in the United States to temporarily employ foreign workers in occupations that require the theoretical and practical application of a body of highly specialized knowledge and a bachelor's degree or higher in the specific specialty, or its equivalent."[4]

However, the exponential growth of international students does not match the limited slots for H-1B visas, which provide the only way to work for an extended period of time after the OPT term expires. In fiscal year 2017, international candidates submitted 236,000 H-1B applications, but there were only 85,000 slots available. Only 36 percent of applicants would be successful. Among the 85,000 slots, 20,000 were reserved applicants with a master's degrees or higher. In other words, just 65,000 slots were available for applicants with bachelor's degrees. As one article in *Forbes* stated, "The chance of getting a H-1B work visa is the same as getting into a top 50 university in the United States, except that H-1B is 'purely' based on a lottery system."[5] That means opportunities for Chinese students to accumulate work experience or work on the path to permanent residence are gradually diminishing.

The Trump administration has been very critical of the lottery system and has promised to curtail the H-1B program, arguing it is rife with loopholes and displaces American job opportunities. In January 2017, the Protect and Grow American Jobs Act was introduced in Congress. This bill raises the minimum salary for H-1B holders from $60,000 to $90,000. It also requires companies to send detailed reports to the Department of Labor about efforts to recruit American workers, including how many other candidates apply for jobs and the reasons they are not chosen. On November 15, 2017, the bill passed the House Judiciary Committee, the first step towards making it into law. President Trump also signed the "Buy America, Hire American" executive order in April 2017.[6] Since then, the number of H-1B visa denials has increased.[7] In light of all this, the odds are increasingly against Chinese international students who intend to stay in the United States after completing their studies.

Not all policy changes have been bad for Chinese international students, though. In 2014, President Obama announced a new reciprocal ten-year visa policy for tourists and business people traveling between the United States and China.[8] That is to say, Chinese citizens can apply for an American visa if they are tourists or on a business trip, and it will remain valid for ten years. This policy is mutual; American citizens can apply for a Chinese visa that will be good for ten years, too. This visa policy has enabled Chinese and Americans to travel more freely between the two countries without the hassle and cost of applying for a visa before each trip. So far President Trump has largely kept this policy intact, except for a few cases where some Chinese researchers' ten-year visas were voided by the American embassy.[9]

The ten-year visa policy has great potential to benefit Chinese international students who are still able to travel to the United States for conferences, business meetings, and social networking, even if they leave the country. This can empower Chinese students who want to traverse transnational spaces even after they return to China.

Visa policies aside, existing studies often draw from brain drain, brain gain, or more recent theoretical framing in terms of brain circulation to understand international students' post-graduation plans.

BRAIN DRAIN, BRAIN GAIN, OR BRAIN CIRCULATION?

George Borjas, an economist in migration and immigration studies, claims that many international students choose to study in the United States as a pathway to immigration.[10] This rationale of studying to migrate is bolstered by demographer Michael Finn's findings that the stay rate of international doctoral students from certain countries, notably China and India, is phenomenally high.[11] In 2005, the stay rate of Chinese doctoral students was 92 percent and it remains the highest among all countries, followed by Indian students at 85 percent. In the most recent report in 2018, Finn reports a declining stay rate of 85 percent among Chinese doctoral graduates in the United States.[12] Although Chinese doctoral graduates still have one of the highest stay rates, it is noteworthy that the rate is declining, indicating that more graduates are returning to China. Stay rates are higher among natural science and engineering students than among humanities and social science students. Note that the high stay rates that Finn has reported are those of doctoral students, who are often lured by the better research environments in the United States compared to China.

The tendency of Chinese international doctoral graduates to stay in the United States upon graduation and eventually become legal immigrants can be explained via the so-called brain drain and brain gain literature, which describes and explains the movement of skilled migrants from developing countries to developed countries. The term *brain drain* characterizes the negative consequences of movement from the country of origin, while *brain gain* points to the benefit to the host country.[13] The World-System Theory, developed by sociologist Immanuel Wallenstein, describes how individuals from peripheral nations tend to move toward core nations.[14] Countries on the periphery tend to produce labor-intensive and low-technology goods, while higher education is considered a high-end good of higher value if it is produced in a core country. Globalization has brought more countries to the integrated world market and has sped up the process of societies' transitioning from the periphery to the core. The most notable example is China, which used to be on the periphery but is now taking on an increasingly important role in the world system.[15]

The problem with the brain gain and brain drain framework is that it assumes this type of migration is static and permanent while neglecting the dynamic development of nations and their status in the world system. One of the consequences of China's transitioning to the league of core nations in the world system is that it is capable of attracting its sojourners back home, including its students overseas. When home country government policies are put in place to lure students back home, this serves as a strong pull for international students abroad to leave their host countries and return to their country of origin. Over the past decade, the Chinese government has adopted new policy initiatives to recruit Chinese students with foreign credentials so as to boost national competitiveness.[16] Alberts and Hazen, in their study of international students' intentions to stay rather than return to their home country, found that Chinese students are the only group that cited government incentives as a reason for returning home.[17]

In addition to government incentives, the private sector also embraces returnees. The New Oriental Education and Technology Group, a company that used to specialize in test preparation for the TOEFL and the GRE and in helping Chinese students to study abroad, recently opened a new specialty branch to help returning overseas students to either look for a job or start a new business in China. Now the company has specific branches specializing in consulting on international study as well as career services for overseas returnees. This dual mission is aptly reflected in the new talent recruitment firm Haiwei Career, part of the New Oriental Group. The firm has recently adopted the slogan: "A bridge to study abroad, a rainbow to return to China." Haiwei Career in China has specialized in providing internship and other job opportunities for overseas Chinese students.[18]

What was once a clear pattern of brain gain benefiting the United States is being reversed now by return migration. The Chinese Ministry of Education reports that in 2016, the number of overseas Chinese who returned to

China with a foreign credential reached 432,500, compared to 9,121 in the year 2000.[19] That is close to a fifty-fold increase.

However, these returnees do not necessarily return to China permanently and cut off their relations with their host countries. As the notion of brain circulation indicates, some of these returnees often keep their transnational networks and develop their careers or businesses in both their home country and host country. As AnnaLee Saxenian showed in her influential paper on brain circulation,[20] returnees are traveling back and forth between their motherland and the host country, transferring technologies, developing business relationships, and promoting local entrepreneurship in their home country. Saxenian focused on Taiwanese immigrants who travel back and forth from Silicon Valley to Taiwan for business and technology transfer. In recent years, studies have examined how Chinese returnees in Beijing utilize their transnational business and technology networks across the Pacific.[21]

In the following sections, I discuss findings from both survey and in-depth interviews, with the former presenting the broad patterns about students' stay versus return intentions and the latter going beyond the binary decisions and providing nuanced stories.

SURVEY RESULTS

Figure 9.1 presents the decision tree of students' intentions regarding whether to stay in the United States or return to China. More than 60 percent intend to return to China after graduation. Most plan to return after accumulating some experience through their one- to three-year Optional Practical Training program. What is notable is that over three quarters of Chinese students plan to attend graduate school in the United States. The return rate[22] is slightly higher among those who plan to attend graduate school than those who have no such plan. The reason became apparent during the interviews: many students consider a graduate education in the United States a conduit to returning to China, as they can garner more prestigious academic credentials so as to be more competitive in the Chinese job market. Often, parents will push their children to pursue advanced degrees. Wei's story, covered in chapter 8, exemplifies how Chinese parents have pushed their children towards graduate school and emphasized immediate entry to graduate school as the most efficient route to landing a competitive job in China.

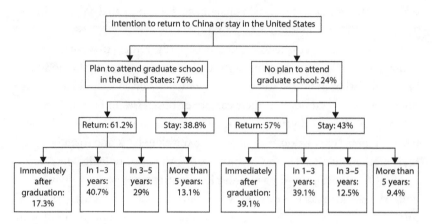

FIGURE 9.1 Intentions to return to China or stay in the United States, of survey respondents
Source: Author's study

So who intends to stay and who plans to return to China? The bivariate analysis shows some broad patterns. Figure 9.2 shows that perceived English proficiency matters. Specifically, 39 percent of those who considered their English to be excellent planned to return to China, compared to over 60 percent of those whose self-perceived use of English was not excellent. Figure 9.3 shows that college major choices are relevant. Fifty-four percent of the STEM majors planned to return to China, while about 64 percent of the social science majors and 65 percent of the humanities majors planned to do so. This is consistent with the literature, which shows that the American labor market

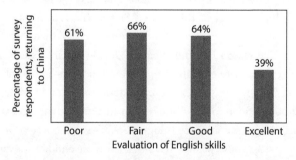

FIGURE 9.2 Percentage of survey respondents intending to return to China, by self-evaluation of English skills
Source: Author's study

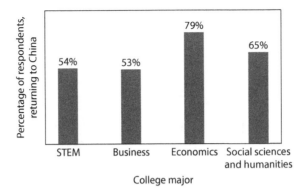

FIGURE 9.3 Percentage of survey respondents intending to return to China, by college major
Source: Author's study

suffers from a shortage of domestic STEM graduates and a disproportionate number of foreign students and workers fill in.[23] Given that humanities and social science fields depend more on host country language and culture, it makes sense that those students are more likely planning to return to China.

The next set of bivariate analyses focuses on social integration measures. Figure 9.4 examines the relationship between the students' number of American close friends and their intention to return to China. Only half of those with three or more close American friends intended to return to China, compared to 65 percent of their peers who had such an intention.

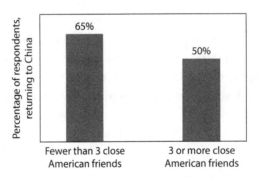

FIGURE 9.4 Percentage of survey respondents intending to return to China, by number of close American friends
Source: Author's study

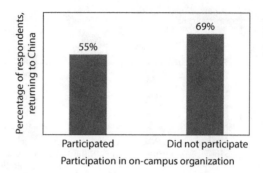

FIGURE 9.5 Percentage of students intending to return to china, by their participation in an on-campus organization
Source: Author's study

Figure 9.5 shows that participation in a campus organization made a difference as well. Sixty-nine percent of those who had never participated in a campus organization intended to return to China, compared to 55 percent of their return-minded peers who had participated. This indicates that campus social integration is positively related with the intention to stay in the United States among Chinese students.

Table 9.1 presents the multivariate analysis of the intention to return to China. College majors, American high school attendance, and participation in campus organizations stand out as significant factors affecting the intention to return to China. Specifically, Chinese students majoring in social science and humanities are more than 90 percent (in model III) more likely than their peers majoring in STEM to intend to return. Those who attend American high schools are over 30 percent less likely than their counterparts to intend to return. Those who participate in campus organizations are about 50 percent less likely to intend to return. In other words, STEM fields, attending American high schools (thus studying in the United States for longer periods of time), and campus organization participations boost the probability of staying in the United States.

INTERVIEW FINDINGS

Interview findings present nuanced rationales that go beyond the binary stay versus return options. They fall along the four major lines: returning

TABLE 9.1
Multivariate Analysis of the Intention to Return to China (Odds Ratios)

	MODEL I	MODEL II	MODEL III
Male	1.036	1.103	1.000
	(0.194)	(0.218)	(0.205)
Parents with college education	0.989	1.067	1.024
	(0.247)	(0.291)	(0.287)
Good English		0.722	0.842
		(0.147)	(0.185)
American high schools		0.658*	0.652*
		(0.164)	(0.169)
Business		1.369	1.314
		(0.320)	(0.320)
Social/humanities		1.802**	1.925***
		(0.436)	(0.485)
Participation in campus organization			0.490***
			(0.108)
Close American friends			0.858

*** p<0.01

** p<0.05

* p<0.1

Note: Standard Errors are in parentheses. "Good English" refers to the perception that the student's level of English is either good or excellent, as opposed to poor or fair.

to China, staying in the United States, traversing transnational spaces, and wavering hearts and changing plans.

Return to China

The America First rhetoric touted by the Trump administration and the ongoing policy moves towards raising the H-1B wage premium have had a chilling effect on international students, who feel they are being discouraged from staying in the United States. Some have tried to stay, while others have not even bothered trying and simply returned to China. Guo is such an example. He started his education in the United States as a high school student in New Hampshire before enrolling at Syracuse University. He graduated with a major in Information Studies and went on to earn a master's degree in a related field from Boston University. He went back to China immediately after completing his master's degree. As he explained, "I was just scared away by the H-1B lottery policy." He now works in Shanghai.

Some students want to return to China, regardless. This study reveals several rationales for why Chinese international students might intend to return to China, independent of the increased difficulty in obtaining work visas that prevent them from staying in the United States.

THE LURE OF FAMILY AND HOMETOWN

Almost all of the study participants were among China's one-child generation, and many reported that they were homesick and missed their parents while studying in the United States. Many mentioned that family was the ultimate lure when it came to planning their futures. For example, Dan, a girl from Zhongshan in Guangdong Province, followed in her father's footsteps by studying aerospace engineering at the University of Saint Louis. When she talked about how her parents missed her, tears welled in her eyes. She was firm about returning to China because for her "the most important thing is to be close with my family."

Some students are also deeply attached to their hometowns. Most of our study participants were from China's developed regions and cities. Diana, a Shanghai native, was an undergraduate in economics at Johns Hopkins University. When I interviewed her at Hopkins in 2015, she already made up her mind:

INTERVIEWER: Do you plan to stay in the U.S. or return to China after completing your study here?
DIANA: I plan to return to China. Actually, I want to work in Shanghai.
INTERVIEWER: Why? You like Shanghai?
DIANA: Yes, Shanghai is the best. It's my hometown.

After completing her BA degree at Hopkins, she went on to get a master's degree in quantitative finance at Washington University in St. Louis. She indeed went back to Shanghai immediately after she got her master's degree in 2017. Even though she worked as an intern in China's financial sector during two summers of her undergraduate years, her credentials in the United States were not enough to land her a permanent job in the competitive financial sector in China. She was still an intern at the time of this writing.

GRADUATE SCHOOL IN THE UNITED STATES AS A CONDUIT TO RETURNING TO CHINA

The survey data show that more than half of the participating students expressed an intention to return to China eventually, but most of them planned to return within one to three years after completing their bachelor's degree. During that interim, more than three quarters of the survey respondents planned to attend graduate school in the United States, and of these, more than 61 percent intended to return to China for permanent employment. This was slightly higher than the percentage who intended to return to China with no plan to first get an advanced degree. It seems that for Chinese students, graduate school serves more of a conduit for returning to China than for staying in the United States.

Many students who plan to attend graduate school in the United States aim to boost their credentials and prestige by attending a graduate school with a better ranking than their undergraduate institution. This can be seen in Ping's educational trajectory, which led to a career in journalism in China.

The first interview I conducted with Ping was in 2013, back when she was a junior majoring in newspaper and online journalism at the Newhouse School of Communications at Syracuse University. As a fairly demure and low-key student, she was confident in her job prospects in the United States, because her school is reputable enough that all of her Chinese friends who wanted to stay were able to find a job in the United States during that time. However, she did not intend to look for a job in the United States; she wanted to return to China.

INTERVIEWER: Could you please tell me why you want to return to China for work?

PING: I am determined to go back to China, because I think China provides better opportunities for my future career advancement. But I need to go to graduate school first before I can go back.

INTERVIEWER: Why graduate school?

PING: . . . [Although] my college is well known in the U.S., it is not nearly as famous in China. Chinese employers only recognize the Ivy Leagues and a handful of big-name schools. My current school is not on their list. I have to get into a graduate school that is famous in China, so that I can get a good job there.

INTERVIEWER: So what are the famous schools you plan to apply to for graduate school?

PING: I am considering Columbia, NYU, and the University of Chicago now.

Ping has achieved her goal and later enrolled at NYU. She now works as a journalist in Shanghai for a local TV station.

That Chinese students use graduate school in the United States to elevate their competitive advantage in the Chinese labor market can be viewed from two distinct angles: vertical educational attainment and horizontal institutional prestige. The theoretical discussions in chapter 2 centered on how parents from upper-middle-class backgrounds try to transmit their class advantages to their children by advancing their children's education, both quantitatively and qualitatively. Quantitatively, pushing on to graduate school is a critical step in their children's vertical educational attainment. In China, college expansion started around the turn of the twenty-first century, but the job market for average college graduates in China has spiraled downward, and Chinese students need to acquire additional distinctions to stand out in the increasingly competitive job market.[24] Initially this served as a push factor for many students to study abroad, as shown in chapter 2; but now, an American bachelor's degree seems not to be enough, and Chinese students have to keep moving up to American graduate schools. Consequently, many college students in China have delayed their entry into the job market by enrolling in graduate programs in China and overseas.

Qualitatively, institutional prestige carries more weight than ever. Rankings have always been a determining factor in Chinese students' college choices.[25] However, getting into a top-ranked college as an undergraduate is competitive for domestic Americans and perhaps even more so for Chinese international students. For students like Ping, graduate school provides a chance to get into a higher-ranked institution, and Ping was keenly aware that the Chinese labor market would not recognize Syracuse as much as NYU. Most of the study participants managed to go to a graduate school that is better-ranked and more prestigious than their undergraduate institution. For example, to name just a few, Brian went from the University of Wisconsin at Madison as an undergraduate to the Wharton School of Business at the University of Pennsylvania for his MBA; Wen went from Beloit College as an undergraduate to Columbia University Teachers College to study in its graduate program for economics of education; Kathy went from Eastern Tennessee State University as an undergraduate to study in Columbia's Master of Public Health program.

Better Opportunities in China versus the Glass Ceiling in the United States

Like Ping, most other respondents cited better opportunities as the primary factor luring them back to China, although some returned to China with no job offers or offers with unattractive salaries. However, they remain optimistic. They chose to return to China because they have faith that in the long run, they will slingshot forward. When probed about what they meant by "better opportunities," the Chinese students always compared the relative advantages and disadvantages of the American and Chinese job markets.

Joey, a computer engineering major from Johns Hopkins, focuses on the language barriers most Chinese students face and argued that Chinese students can rarely reach leadership positions in the United States as a result of various barriers. He explains:

> The workplace is different from school. Communication, interpersonal relationships, and all these soft skills are very important. All of this depends on language. This is similar in both U.S. and China. But in the U.S., English is not our native language, and Chinese students will always be at a disadvantage in the workplace because of that. My friends and I can barely understand American jokes. How can a leader in a workplace not understand a joke? But in China, my friends and I are full of personality, and we can be charismatic leaders. English for us can be an advantage, not a barrier, in China.

Joey focuses on the language and cultural barriers that impede the advancement of Chinese students like him in the American labor market. Other students' observations show a remarkable understanding of the status of Chinese immigrants and Asian Americans in general in the United States labor market. This often comes from the intimate knowledge they have gathered from friends and relatives. Peng is an example. He has an uncle who immigrated to the United States about twenty years ago and now works as a senior engineer in Silicon Valley. When describing his uncle's experiences, Peng spoke with a tinge of sarcasm and sadness:

> My uncle is a typical Chinese immigrant of his generation. He is smart, hardworking, and works as an engineer. He has a big house, two cars, and two kids. When I was a small kid, my family admired his life in the U.S. But now it is different. My family has an exciting life in China, and they do not admire my uncle's life in the U.S. any longer. My uncle is still an engineer, and he told me that his aspirations to become senior management staff are not going to be realized in America, because he is Chinese, and language and culture pose challenges. I have ambitions beyond just a comfortable material life. I think my future is in China.

What's behind his uncle's thwarted career aspirations is a typical story of a glass ceiling—or bamboo ceiling—the invisible barrier facing Asian Americans advancing toward managerial and leadership positions beyond the technical track they are often stuck in.[26] This is a longstanding social problem confronting Asian Americans; though now the younger generation of Chinese students has come to know this well before they decide to enter the American labor market. This is due in part to the critical mass of Chinese Americans resulting from contemporary Chinese immigration to the United States post-1965,[27] as in the case of Peng's uncle. The life of the earlier generation of Chinese immigrants is not particularly appealing to the younger generation who desire career advancement and leadership opportunities beyond material comfort. The awareness of the disadvantages Chinese immigrants confront in the American labor market acts as a disincentive to Chinese students, discouraging them from staying in the United States.

Peng returned to China in early 2016 after completing both his bachelor's and master's degrees in finance. Now, in Shenzhen in South China, he has started a fund focusing on quantitative trading. This is a domestic fund, and his long-term goal is to set up an overseas fund based in Hong Kong. He has indeed realized his dream of becoming a financial entrepreneur, which he thought was unlikely to be achieved had he stayed in the United States.

Staying in the United States

WANTING A DIFFERENT LIFESTYLE

Those who wanted to stay in the United States cited factors such as pollution and corruption in China as deterrents to returning. They also talked about certain characteristics of the urban lifestyle in China—its fast pace, long working hours, lack of time with family—as key factors prompting them to stay in the United States. Jennifer, an applied math major at UCLA, was sent to boarding school in China starting in elementary school, which, ironically, was only five minutes from her home, just because her parents had no time to take care of her. She complained to me, "I do not want to repeat my parents' lives. They hardly stayed home to have dinner with me."

Jennifer's parents, like the parents of most of the study participants, are college-educated. They have reaped the benefits of the vast opportunities presented to their generation in China, which the previous generation could never have imagined. However, they have to work extremely long hours, endure much stress from their work, and often continue to spend time with their clients after work for meals and other social engagements. The career success of these children's parents enabled them to study in American universities. Yet these children are keenly aware of the costs, not just the financial costs but the social and emotional costs their parents have paid in order to afford their education.

When Jennifer came to Los Angeles and stayed with her one-year home-stay family before she enrolled at UCLA, she was impressed by the quality family time her host family enjoyed. The wife, a nurse, and her husband, a technician, were able to have dinner at home every day and engage in various fun activities during the weekend. She compared their life to the lives of her parents and her parents' friends:

> I find the life my parents have in China is not desirable: they are very busy and tired. I do not want to repeat it, and I do not want

my own children to grow up with absent parents. My host family here in America were very ordinary people, yet they lived a fun-filled and comfortable life. That is the life that I want: slow-paced, family-oriented, and just relaxed and easy. . . . But it is so hard to live this kind of life in urban China now.

Jennifer took a job as a statistician in Los Angeles after graduating from UCLA. This is the lifestyle choice for her—she likes America and considers its calm and relaxed lifestyle appealing.

ENVIRONMENTAL CONCERNS

Chinese students refer to the environment in China in two distinct ways: one refers to the natural environment, for instance China's air, water, and soil pollution; the other pertains to the social environment and refers to corruption, food safety, and a general lack of trust in this fast-changing society.[28]

Alan arrived in the United States feeling that it was like rural areas in China, and he was quite disappointed; however, over the past few years, his feelings started to change, and now he prefers life in the United States to life in China. When asked how he changed, he responded:

My parents influenced me a lot. They have their own business, and they often fret about the challenges of doing business in China: people do not follow rules, and they can do anything to make money. They are also concerned about food safety, pollution, and other issues in China. So now I am more inclined towards life in the U.S. No matter what choices I make, I want more options for myself and my family.

Alan later added that his parents want him to be able to settle down in the United States so that he can ultimately sponsor them to immigrate to the United States. They do not want to immigrate immediately, as they still need to run their business in China.

However, Alan's parents are an exception to the norm in terms of wanting to follow Alan to the United States. Most of the parents who want their children to stay in the United States want to stay in China themselves, largely due to language and cultural barriers. Jane, an accounting major at

Ohio State University, mentioned that her parents encouraged her to stay in the United States because "the sky is so blue, and people are so nice." But her parents plan to stay in China.

INTERVIEWER: So what is your parents' plan for themselves if you are going to stay in the U.S.?

JANE: They said they will retire and move in with their siblings, and they plan to take care of each other, but I feel quite guilty when thinking about this. . . . I do not know what I should do. . . . I want to stay in the U.S., but how can I take care of my parents?

INTERVIEWER: So what do your parents think about the future separation between you and them?

JANE: They say that it is okay. They want a better environment for me. As long as I have a better life, they are okay. But I feel guilty. I already feel guilty now.

Wanting a better life for their children is common to all parents, but the extent to which Chinese parents are willing to go and the sacrifices they are willing to bear is nothing short of extraordinary. This is a fundamental drive for an increasing number of Chinese parents—to send their children to study in the United States, and at increasingly younger ages, and for some, to encourage their children to stay in the United States despite their long-term separation from each other.

The social environment is particularly challenging for those in some occupations in China, such as doctors. Compared to the respectful and prestigious status American doctors enjoy, being a doctor in China is considered one of the most resented, and even dangerous, jobs, as the doctor-patient relationship is fraught with tension. It is not uncommon for patients to have to bribe doctors to get treated in China, and there is a lack of trust that the relationship can work without bribery. Then, if a treatment goes awry, patients may resort to retaliation or violence. Violence against doctors has escalated and made multiple news headlines.[29] This problem of corruption is rampant since China has embraced the market economy and social services began commercialized, and the problem is particularly acute in medical fields.[30]

For example, both Phyllis and Justin are premed majors and want to become doctors. Justin is from a family of doctors in China. Even though his parents made it clear that they did not want him to study medicine—as according to them, "it is dangerous to be a doctor in China"—Justin is still on track wanting to be a doctor. He said it is in his genes. Still, his parents vehemently oppose his plans. So Justin concluded: "The doctor-patient relationship is too corrupt and dangerous in China. I will not return to China if I want to become a doctor." They study very hard to try to get into medical schools in the United States and their goals are to practice medicine in the United States, not China.

RETURN ON INVESTMENT

Chinese students are keenly aware of the costs and sacrifices their parents have made in sending them to the United States. While they rarely have to shoulder financial debts, the very fact that the cost of their American education cut deeply into their parents' savings has made them feel they owe a great emotional and fiscal debt to their parents. This sentiment of emotional debts is commonly found among international students, not just from China.[31]

Samantha was an accounting major at Indiana University at Bloomington. She said that she wanted to get a job here in the United States to make some money so that she could recoup her investment in her education. She voiced her thoughts:

SAMANTHA: Here, the average job is still higher than what I can get in China for an average job. I really need to make some money here to make my investment worth it. Otherwise, I would feel so bad to face my parents.

INTERVIEWER: So are you under pressure to pay them back?

SAMANTHA: Not really. They didn't say that. I just feel that they worked so hard. This is their hard-earned money, and I would feel so bad if I wasted it.

INTERVIEWER: Have you talked about this, their expectation for you to pay back?

SAMANTHA: We haven't really talked about it. I do not even know the exact amount of money I have spent to study and live here. My parents always comforted me and said not to worry. I know that they also expect me to get a good job with high pay. So I study accounting here, hoping to get a job. I am often uncertain whether studying here is worth it.

Samantha did not express any desire to settle in the United States permanently; all she was concerned about was her parents' investment in her and whether she would be able to pay them back.

While Samantha's parents remained silent about their expectations regarding their educational investment, Alfred's parents were explicit and upfront about it. Alfred, a computer science major at Boston University, came from a working-class family in Shanghai. The only reason he could afford an education in the United States was the rising value of real estate in Shanghai; his mother was able to take advantage of the opportunity to cash in. He described the situation as follows:

> My mom sold our apartment in the downtown district and bought two smaller units far away from the city. Our family lives in one small unit and rents the other one. After the recent surge in property values, she sold her other property. So I can study at BU. My mom said my education in the U.S. is like her stock investments. I need to get a job here to reap her returns.

Could Alfred recoup his mother's investment in his education? He was pretty optimistic in regard to his job prospects in the United States. He studied computer science. Actually, foreign workers, particularly from China and India, constitute the backbone of the industry.[32] Alfred was positive that he could get a job in the United States and pay back his mother's investment. In 2015, he indeed graduated and got a job in an IT company in the Boston area. He wants to move to the West Coast and try his luck in Silicon Valley, because the pay there would be even higher, and given that many Asians are on the West Coast, the food and other features of the lifestyle there would suit him better than Boston. He is now still in the Optional Practical Training (OPT) program, and because he is in a STEM field, he can remain here in the United States under the OPT program for three years. While he is optimistic about his job prospects, he is not so optimistic about his visa prospects. He is not at all sure that he can get one of the coveted H-1B visas through the lottery system. If he cannot get one when his OPT term expires, he will have to return to China. He said: "I am not resistant to that, either. Shanghai now has many opportunities for me. After three years, I could earn enough money to pay back my mom. So I think

I should be fine." All in all, he is optimistic, whether he stays in the United States or returns to China.

Alfred could find a job in the United States and start to pay back his mother's investment due to his major in computer science. Cheng, also enrolled in Boston University, is not so fortunate. She majored in international relations. Originally from Nanjing, she was also highly concerned about the enormous financial burden her parents incurred for her study in the United States. However, international students like her have few job opportunities in the United States in the field of international relations. Cheng complained:

> Many government jobs and national organization jobs require citizenship, or at least a green card, for someone even to be eligible. As a Chinese international student, I find it extremely difficult to get a job in my field. My parents want me to get a job in the U.S. and stay here, as they have already spent so much money on me. If I just return to China without any job experience, I could not get their money back. But it is so hard.

Students from nonwealthy families often share the intention to land a job in the United States to earn tuition dollars back. For students like Cheng who study in fields that do not present many job opportunities for international students, they face an uphill battle if they want to work in the United States. The process is fraught with anxiety, guilt, and stress.

Traversing Transnational Spaces

Chinese students' career aspirations often extend beyond either their home or host countries. For some, these aspirations started as early as high school, particularly among those with exposure to international education. In my fieldwork in the Chinese high schools, I encountered students who were preparing to study abroad but whose career aspirations reached beyond national borders. Many sought to work in multinational companies, many of which have moved some of their key functions to China. They hoped to utilize their bilingual and bicultural knowledge and business know-how to operate on a global platform but primarily and physically from China.

These young students intend to combine the best parts of the two worlds in China and the United States.

Kathy, for example, majored in public health and wanted to work in American government, but she knew that she couldn't due to her lack of American citizenship.

> Many jobs in America list "U.S. citizenship," so I might work in Hong Kong. I really want to work in those major nonprofit organizations such as Doctors without Borders and Mercy Ships. Mercy Ships, particularly, is of interest to me. It operates a hospital ship providing health care at port cities, often in Africa. It is a very large nongovernmental organization providing services to many people all over the world. I really want to work in those settings. I may return to China or settle somewhere someday, but I want to travel to the U.S. and other countries often and develop my old and new relationships, as today's world is really connected.

Restricted by her citizenship status, Kathy is not thwarted and intends to engage in brain circulation—by traveling to the United States and other countries often, developing relationships, and serving "many people all over the world." As a public health major, she intends to work in settings that can provide health care services to people internationally. She considers Hong Kong a likely place to launch her career, and she wants her career services to reach people in Africa.

Brian provides another example of students participating in brain circulation. He majored in industrial engineering and psychology at the University of Wisconsin at Madison before going on to earn his MBA from the Wharton School of Business at the University of Pennsylvania. During his undergraduate study at Madison, he returned to China every summer to spend time with his parents. He also worked part-time as an English instructor in the office of the New Oriental School in Guangzhou, his hometown, to help students prepare for the TOEFL. He was once a student at this center, and he wanted to give back by contributing the skills and knowledge of English that he gained in America.

During his time in the United States, Brian set up an education consulting business in China, helping Chinese students like himself apply to American colleges and universities. The business was so successful that he could support himself financially during his graduate studies at Wharton.

After graduating at the end of 2016, he went back to China to work full-time on his education consulting business. In March 2017, he wrote on his social media account: "I just graduated from Penn, and now one of my students got an offer from Penn. How magical life is!"

Brian was clearly engaged in brain circulation, both during his time studying in the United States and after his return to China as an education entrepreneur there. As an undergraduate in the United States, he was transferring knowledge he gained in the United States to students in China during his summer teaching there. During his time at Wharton, he was part of the initial leadership that launched the US-China Forum at Penn. That forum has become an annual event, to which he regularly returned. Now he directly connects local Chinese students with educational resources in the United States, leveraging connections he built up at American universities. The new visa policy that allows Chinese citizens like Brian to apply for an American visa for business meetings and remains valid for ten years eases the process of traveling between China and the United States. Brian regularly visits the United States to attend meetings and forums to make business connections. He also serves his alma mater from afar by becoming one of the Penn alumni interviewers in East Asia.

Wavering Hearts and Changing Plans

In spring 2016, when I first interviewed Stefanie, a finance and applied math major at Notre Dame, she had already landed an internship opportunity at one of the big Wall Street banks. She was confident that this internship stood a good chance of leading to a permanent job, based on her friends' prior experiences. With an applied math degree in a STEM field, she can work under the OPT program for three years in the United States. A degree in finance would not qualify her for an extended OPT term, which, in part, is why she picked up applied math as a second major. She seemed to have her plans to stay in the United States laid out quite clearly for the next three to four years. She explained that she wanted to stay in the United States in the long run:

> I am thinking from the perspective of the next generation. I want my kids to grow up with little peer pressure. I feel that not just in China, but countries in Asia, such as Japan and South Korea, all have a very

strong social pressure. I've studied abroad in Japan (while at Notre Dame) before, and I've also been to South Korea. People living in these countries are not as free as those in the U.S. American people live as individuals. Everybody is unique. I like this culture and I want my kids to grow up in American society where they can be who they want to be, rather than what the society expects them to be.

Stefanie's intention to stay in the United States in the long run seemed to arise from long-term considerations. She had already thought out where she wanted to raise her children. The fact that she had traveled and lived not just in the United States and China but also in Japan and South Korea made her realize that East Asian societies share some broad cultural and societal features that she felt are not as amenable to what she perceived as respecting children's individual development as compared to the American society.

However, American culture is complex, and at times contradictory. What she didn't see as a student on the idyllic college campus of Notre Dame quickly hit her when she started working on Wall Street, and her desire to settle in the United States began to waver. A year or so later, I interviewed her again, this time in New York, when she had already been working full-time at the bank she interned for. She felt that she could not achieve her full potential here. Recently, she had met several Asian friends living in the United States, and the encounter had shaken her quite a bit:

These are all Asian Americans, I mean, they were born here, and they have an identity issue. They grow up feeling that certain things they cannot do, just because they are Asians. I feel shocked because I grew up feeling that I could achieve anything I want if I work hard in China. Now in the workplace, I also feel that I have certain limitations in presentations and in interacting with others, but I feel more at ease interpersonally in China. So now I am not as committed to staying in the U.S. as before.

I reminded her of how she had previously thought about this and of her interest in having her future children educated here, and she replied:

China has changed so fast. Last summer, I went back there, and I found that there are many other education options than what I had previously thought. I feel that my children can have many more education choices in China than my generation did. There are many schools in Shanghai that have both Chinese and Western curriculums. I may try those schools. They can get the good part of Western education without having the negatives that my Asian friends growing up in the U.S. have had.

It remains to be seen what Stefanie will ultimately do as she follows her wavering heart and changing plans. One thing is certain: as she came to know more, she changed her original expectations and plans, and more important, as she put it, "China has changed so fast"—the changing reality of China also affects Chinese students' expectations and plans like a moving target.

SUMMARY

This chapter examines the postgraduate plans of Chinese undergraduates. The survey data discussed in this study reveal broad patterns in students' intentions and show that college major, social integration, and English proficiency all matter in their decision making. Undergraduates from China who are STEM majors, have more than three close American friends, and think their English is good are more likely to intend to stay in the United States than those who lack these characteristics. Overall, approximately 60 percent of Chinese students intend to return to China.

In-depth interviews contextualized the decision-making processes and revealed additional complexity in the students' thought processes and the rationales for their decisions. The ten-year business/travel visa policy ushered in by the Obama administration has eased travel between the United States and China and expedited the "brain circulation" in which many Chinese students desire to engage. However, new policy changes regarding the H-1B visa have scared many Chinese students away from their desire to work in the United States, and the increasingly unfriendly attitude of the Trump administration towards immigrants and foreigners has had a chilling effect overall on Chinese international students and their perception of their prospects in America.

CHAPTER 10

What American Higher Education Needs to Know about Chinese Undergraduates

O ver the past decade, a new wave of Chinese international undergraduates has swept into American higher education institutions. Their stories are of coming of age in the two most powerful countries in the world; they tell of how a privileged yet diverse group of young people from a changing China navigates the complications and confusions of life in the United States during their formative years. The multifaceted analysis explicates the complex and often conflicting desires and behaviors of Chinese students and sheds light on the class-based experiences of this relatively privileged population.

Drawing from research in Chinese high schools and American higher education institutions, I have let Chinese students speak for themselves about their expectations, imaginings, and educational journeys before arriving in the United States, and their current experiences, challenges, and reflections in the United States. However, this is certainly not a comprehensive study of all aspects of their American experiences. Due to the voluntary participation of our sample, such social problems as mental health issues and academic plagiarism by these students have not been engaged deeply in this book, although they are important in their own right.

This book has covered a wide range of academic and social aspects of this new wave of Chinese international undergraduates' time in America, contextualizing their ambitions and anxieties in relation to their social, cultural, and educational backgrounds in fast-changing China. Transformative social changes in China have opened the minds of millions of

Chinese and kindled their desire to travel, study abroad, and migrate, and they have enabled the Chinese middle class to accumulate enough wealth to finance an American education, which was beyond their reach just a decade ago. The rise of China also gives the younger generation of Chinese a new pride in their country, and they find America is not as developed as they used to perceive; Social changes have also created exciting new opportunities to entice these young sojourners to come back home, so that they face a more vexing decision than their predecessors of whether or not to return to China.

CONTRADICTIONS AND COMPLEXITIES

The very complicated and sometimes contradictory desires and behaviors of Chinese international undergraduates in America emerge from this research. They desire a liberal arts college education in the United States that is not test-oriented, yet they still work their hearts out to take the SAT and TOEFL multiple times, as if these tests were the only thing that matters to get them into their dream schools. They complain about their previous education in China as running the risk of suppressing their creativity, yet credit their solid math and science training and tenacity in learning to the Chinese education system. They appear to like hanging out among themselves, yet dislike the fact that there are so many Chinese students in their American universities. They wonder out loud what the point is of studying in the United States if they are surrounded by Chinese peers. Many of them are silent in the classroom but quietly fret about their silence and its potential damage to their grades.

The above contradictions bring light to the fact that the United States and China are very different societies with distinct education systems, cultural values, and norms. This new wave of Chinese international students and their parents have the ambition to navigate two very different systems and combine the best of both worlds, which are intricate enough to generate much of the anxiety that is integral to their journey to study in the United States—from applying to colleges before arriving to looking ahead upon graduation. For this reason, it is impossible to have a profound understanding about their experiences without connecting their experiences in China and the United States.

Ambitious and Anxious: Connecting China and the United States

To a great extent, their ambition and anxiety, developed in China, bear upon their experiences in the United States. This book has shown this connection in the following ways.

First, Chinese students and their parents bring their test-oriented mind-sets to the process of applying to colleges overseas. I argue that a culture of studying in the United States has emerged in urban China and has become the new education gospel, challenging the old gospel of the Gaokao,[1] which determines college access and placement in China. These students' early ambition is to crack the various levels of high-stakes testing that culminate in the Gaokao; and subsequently this ambition shifts to cracking the American college application process and getting into a top-ranked American university. If their prior anxiety was over testing in China, now it is to decipher the elusive codes of the American holistic admissions standards, but they feel the sure-fire course to success is still to achieve the highest test scores possible. The other elements of the process—personal statements, recommendation letters, and extracurricular activities—are too new and intangible for them to grasp. That is why, even if students choose the international curriculum designed to steer them away from the test-oriented track of the Gaokao, they still enroll themselves in after-school TOEFL and SAT cram classes. They even skip their regular classes altogether to make it to these cram sessions, surprising and frustrating the foreign teachers who work in the international divisions of Chinese public schools. Ultimately, their understanding of merit is rooted in the test-oriented Chinese education—merit can be measured in a single dimension of test scores, which is fundamentally different from the fluid and multidimensional conception of merit in the United States as reflected in the holistic admissions standards.[2]

Second, years of Chinese education have cultivated certain modes of learning and interacting with teachers, and they have left an indelible mark on the studies of these students in the United States. They complain about their previous schooling in China, which in their view suppresses critical thinking and wires them into a dichotomous mindset of looking for right or wrong answers. Their dissatisfaction with the Chinese education system in part drives them to the United States, and their study in the United

States has not let them down: they are impressed by their American peers' creative ideas and American teachers' openness to questions and challenges. However, what they do not anticipate is the discussion-oriented American classroom, where they feel both excited and anxious—excited because the classroom is so active and the professor so approachable, and anxious because they feel unable to fully participate. Speaking up turns out to be much more than a matter of English proficiency. Chapter 7 uncovers the inhibiting factors: the cultural values inculcated in them in China, which emphasize actions over words, and the effects of the Chinese education system, which taught them to look for one single right answer. As much as Chinese international students desire and value the critical thinking skills American liberal arts education can cultivate, they are steeped in their previous dualistic thinking mode expecting right or wrong results and struggling to come to terms with multiple perspectives/interpretations.[3]

The positive impact of students' prior Chinese schooling on their college education in the United States pertains to an effort-based mindset. Chinese students feel that they can "eat bitter" in the face of academic challenges and frustrations—what American educators call resilience[4]— much more than their American peers. This generation of only child in China is often portrayed as a bunch of "little emperors."[5] However, while there is some truth to this, the gruesome academic training of their pre-college education instilled in them a sense of endurance when it comes to learning. Chinese students in various fields, ranging from humanities to business to engineering, reported that their effort-based learning style benefited their studies in the United States. Chapter 4 reveals that more than half of our study participants reported that they study harder than their American peers, and only a small share of Chinese students reported in the opposite direction.

In addition to recognizing the value of their effort-based learning mindset, the participants felt that they had a more positive attitude towards math, mainly due to the national emphasis on math-related subjects in China. Many students felt that they sailed through math and science courses here in the United States, even though some of them were not especially strong in those subjects in China. This has much to do with an ability-based attitude toward learning in the United States,[6] the belief that only the talented few are fit for math and science, so that average Americans shun those fields.

Chinese students credit their strength and solid foundations in math to their prior schooling in China and consider math skills to be essential in paving the way for technological innovation. With good preparation and a strong foundation in math-related subjects on the one hand and a lack of Western-based cultural capital on the other, when it comes to the choice of a college major, most Chinese international students in the United States choose STEM and business fields and avoid the humanities and social sciences. Some students are torn between the pragmatic values towards higher education in China and the expressive emphasis on passion and interest in the United States. The disproportionate number of Chinese students graduating from STEM fields and business helps prepare for the innovation success China has had recently in such areas as artificial intelligence, mobile payments, electrical cars, etc.

Third, Chinese students' cultural background and prior socialization in China have a bearing on their social relations in the United States. American faculty and students often notice Chinese students tend to hang out amongst themselves. How to understand this seemingly voluntary segregation? As international students, they are vulnerable to neoracism based on language and culture.[7] The rise of China and its perceived threat has added additional layers of neoracism. The Trump administration's explicit labeling of Chinese students as spies and a national security threat is a new and intensified version of neoracism.[8] From the privileged to the marginalized,[9] many Chinese international students experience a sense of loss, disillusionment, and disappointment. Their loss is aggravated if their American college is located in a small town or rural area. The new wave of Chinese students almost all come from urban areas and large cosmopolitan cities. As chapter 2 has shown, they came to study in the United States in part to increase their cosmopolitan capital in this presumably epic center of globalization—American society—or at least that is how they imagined it.[10] However, many of them arrive in small towns and rural communities in America, which are nothing like the cosmopolitan places they imagined. Moreover, although they had been exposed through American media to the ways American students entertain themselves, by partying and drinking, they are still shocked and shaken by the party scene once they are actually in it. The collectivist Chinese society socializes them to be group-oriented,[11] and when access to American friends is limited or undesirable, they resort to their own groups of Chinese friends.

Social Class and Social Reproduction

Previous studies and public understanding tend to portray Chinese international students as a homogeneous group. This book delineates their class differences. This can be readily seen in the different educational trajectories they follow in their move from China to America. Chapter 3 examines these trajectories, stratified by the resources needed to come to America. The most cost-demanding trajectory is to start one's American education in a private secondary school and then move on to tertiary education in the United States. The least expensive trajectory is to start college in China and then transfer to the United States.

In addition, parental education figures prominently in shaping Chinese students' academic and social experiences. First-generation college students from China are at a distinct disadvantage in several ways: they are less likely to enroll in selective institutions, speak up in class, or have close American friends. I consider speaking up in class a critical indicator of academic integration, and friendship formation with American students a critical indicator of social integration. On both counts, first-generation Chinese college students fall short compared to their college-educated peers.

The impact of parental education on Chinese students' academic and social outcomes in the United States is sometimes manifested through students' English language proficiency. First-generation college students are more likely to have poor or fair English, which impedes their academic learning and social integration. Chapter 7 shows that first-generation college students are less likely to speak up, but after taking English-speaking ability into account, they are as likely to speak up as their peers with college-educated parents. Chapters 2 and 3 show that college-educated parents not only have broad and intimate knowledge about college education but also in some cases have first-hand knowledge about studying in the United States, which they acquired from their own international travels, training, or study overseas. They recognize English proficiency as involving more than testable grammar and see language as something to be used authentically in everyday life. When they traveled abroad, they returned home with digital materials in English for their children's learning, which give them a leg up in their English proficiency.

When it comes to social outcomes, the role of parental education is more enduring. Chapter 5 explains how the status of first-generation college students is still a barrier to their forming close American friendships after their English proficiency is at comparable level with their peers. How do we understand the lingering impact of parental education on Chinese students' social outcomes? The interviews show that college-educated parents often pushed their children to make a conscious effort to reach beyond their comfort zone and socialize with Americans. These parents are often well-travelled and well-heeled, with their own personal and professional global networks. They were versed in the liberal educational ideal of embracing diverse experiences and people.[12] However, first-generation college students from China do not have this support from their parents who are new to higher education, let alone of global nature.

Institutional Differences

This book considers two dimensions of institutional characteristics in American higher education. One dimension captures institutional types—namely, major research universities versus liberal arts colleges; the other dimension concerns the institution's degrees of selectivity, based on the rankings of the *U.S. News and World Report*. Chapters 2 and 3 demonstrate that Chinese students and their parents muster their resources in their efforts to gain admission to selective institutions. The question is: How do institutional differences play out in these students' experiences in America?

Overall, Chinese students in selective institutions have better academic records than those in nonselective institutions, as indicated by their higher GPAs. The Chinese students in selective institutions are also more likely to major in STEM fields than their peers in nonselective institutions. Perhaps related to their academic records, the likelihood that students in selective institutions will speak up in class is greater than that of their Chinese peers in less selective institutions. The positive association of attending a selective institution and speaking up endures after the explanatory model takes parental education and students' English proficiency into account. In other words, if two Chinese students have college-educated parents and similar English-speaking ability, the one in the selective institution is still more likely to speak up in class than the one in a nonselective institution. Note that this is only association, not causation, as there is a positive selection process of getting admitted into selective institution, and our explanatory model cannot fully capture every relevant factor in the process.

The survey analysis shows that there is no statistical association between institutional types and indicators of social integration; however, the interviews show that institutional differences are relevant. The data in chapter 7 reveal that students feel more comfortable speaking up in classrooms with smaller class sizes, and institutions do differ in class size. Although no statistical significance is evident, the interviews do show that students in liberal arts colleges often report relatively positive social and academic integration.

THEORETICAL IMPLICATIONS

The findings in this book have four theoretical implications. First, they contribute to the literature on college choice and admission and the meaning of ranking to international students. The dominant college choice model in America hinges upon gathering information about different schools, and for domestic students, gathering information from routine college recruiting, college counselors, and college visits.[13] This model does not work well for Chinese students, as these information venues are largely unavailable to them. Direct recruiting by American universities in China is rare; college counselors represent a new profession in China and are not quite institutionalized in schools; and college visits are beyond reach of a large majority of Chinese students. Overall, this book has shown that Chinese students lack information—about American college admissions process in general and specific colleges and universities—and the information gap drives them to resort to the third-party agencies for help.

The differences between the college admissions systems in China and the United States are salient and profound. As education scholar Mitchell Stevens has pithily summarized: the holistic admissions criteria that characterize the American college admissions process are "demanding and broad."[14] I would further argue that holistic admissions create cultural binds for Chinese students who are steeped in the test-based admissions system in China. The broad requirements of holistic admissions in the United States are not only distinct from the test-based college admissions in China but also are disconnected from everyday realities of Chinese schooling. Few people in a typical student's social network in China can write recommendation letters in English, and school counselors are beyond reach for many. As a result, the "demanding and broad" college admissions requirements on the part of American higher education necessitate and incentivize Chinese students to turn to for-profit agencies for guidance.

Chinese students turn to accessible but insufficient information on institutional ranking.[15] I argue that rankings—stated in straightforward numbers—lay bare the hierarchical nature of the American college and university system and provide an oversimplified understanding for Chinese students eager for information about American higher education. The hierarchical scores of rankings present the mirror image of the Gaokao scoring system—the Chinese college admissions system—so this parallel lends convenience and comfort to anxious Chinese students and their parents striving in the dark to grapple with the unknown and unpredictability of the American holistic college admissions system. As a result, students' and parents' overreliance on rankings in the college choice process feeds into the hectic race to get into the best-ranked institution, which, combined with a test-oriented mindset, leads to more testing and anxiety; many students take the qualifying tests multiple times to achieve the highest scores possible. This helps to account for the paradoxical nature of Chinese students' educational desires[16]—the desire to get the highest test scores possible and the antithetical desire to escape from the high-stakes testing, the hallmark of Chinese education system, to American liberal arts education that presumably does not fixate on test scores.

Second, this book contributes to the literature on college major choices, which reports robust evidence across different national contexts for the impact of social class: economically privileged students are more likely to be able to pursue an interest in liberal arts and humanities than their less privileged peers, who tend to gravitate towards lucrative technical and business fields.[17] Privileged families may enable their children to perceive college education in a less pragmatic manner than the less privileged, who may want to make sure that their college education leads to a good job and high pay. However, this does not ring true for Chinese international students, in spite of their privileged backgrounds. I advance the concept of pragmatic collectivism to describe the national ethos in China, characterized by a collective inclination towards pragmatic fields of study in college as compared with the expressive individualism ideal advocated by the dominant discourse in the United States. This book has identified a strong economic pressure and urge among these Chinese students to realize the returns on their higher education investment in the United States, which drives them to high-earning fields of study. In addition, I contend that these students suffer from the loss of cultural capital in the United States compared to their peers in China. Their linguistic and literary knowledge in Chinese culture can rarely gain traction amidst the Western-based cultural capital in American higher education.[18] This helps elucidate their lower likelihood in majoring in humanities than both their American counterparts and their peers in China. It is vital to understand the economic pressure and cultural marginalization of Chinese international students, despite their seeming economic privilege.

Third, this book contributes to the literature on the social integration of international students. Social relations are vital for any college student,[19] and they are indispensable for Chinese international students, who are tens of thousands of miles away from their families and old friends. Drawing from the theory of neoracism as it applies to international students and the theory of protective segregation among disadvantaged domestic students,[20] I advance a framework of interrelated processes of external exclusion and internal withdrawal to explain the social behaviors of these Chinese students. They feel marginalized and excluded from the social scenes on American campuses, which are often dominated by excessive partying and drinking. This is similar to what the research reports about disadvantaged domestic students in the United States,[21] despite the fact that from a socioeconomic perspective the two are quite distinct student groups. Chinese international students also feel a certain sense of loss for their imagined America, a loss that has both economic and cultural origins. The rise of the Chinese economy has led this wave of Chinese youth—growing up in the most prosperous era of China over the past century—to be quite disillusioned with the declining prosperity they witness in the United States, especially in rural and small-town America where many colleges and universities are located. The individualistic cultural orientation also disorients collective-minded Chinese students[22] because their imagined warm friendships with Americans do not materialize. This all contributes to a process of withdrawal into their Chinese peer groups for comfort and support.

Last, this book sheds new light on the international migration literature and challenges the conventional understanding of the study-to-migrate path.[23] Previous studies have focused on the high stay rates of international students, often graduate students, in the host country.[24] Except for some students who want to stay in America for good, due to economic opportunities and lifestyle choices, this study found that a majority of Chinese undergraduate students intend to return to China. The increasingly stringent work visa policy in the United States coupled with the promising career opportunities in China—with family and friends close by—are key to understanding their intentions. This represents a marked change from the previous scholarship on Chinese students, who often missed their family and friends yet still chose to stay overseas to take advantage of better opportunities.[25] In addition, the perceived glass ceiling confronting Chinese immigrants, and Asian Americans in general, serves as a disincentive to the current wave's prospects of staying in the United States in the long run, and the chilling immigration environment deters them from staying in the short run. Many Chinese students are interested in engaging in brain circulation—keeping and developing their networks and careers in both home country and host country—and returning to China does not prevent them from achieving that goal. This speaks volumes about the increasing interconnectedness of the world and, as Chinese citizens, how empowered they feel in this globalized world.[26]

POLICY IMPLICATIONS

Due to a decrease in the college-going population and the cooling of China's economy, a slow-down in Chinese international students' coming to America was inevitable.[27] Furthermore, as other major countries such as Australia, Canada, and the UK ramp up their efforts to attract international students, American colleges and universities face the risk of losing their appeal to Chinese students.[28] The Trump administration's platform of America First has further discouraged foreign students from moving to the United States, although leaders of American higher education and the technology sector have made a strong case that international students strengthen American leadership rather than threaten it.[29] On the other hand, there seems to be an insatiable hunger for international education on the part of Chinese students and their parents, as indicated by the booming international education industry there. In this state of flux, the findings from this book have policy implications for American higher education institutions to continue attracting Chinese international students and improve their support in the following administrative and instructional units.

The first is admissions. Admissions leaders and officers do not fully recognize that there is a mismatch between the holistic admissions system in the United States and the test-based system in China, which creates a massive void for third-party brokers to fill and to profit from. The American higher education system needs to invest more in direct recruiting in China. They can do this by collaborating with local schools in China, disseminating information, and sharing knowledge about how to navigate the application process. If the goal is to recruit high-quality students, a good strategy is to directly recruit from local magnet schools, where students are drawn from local areas through highly selective processes already. These students are much more likely to be motivated and have high academic abilities. This strategy requires networking and partnering with these schools. In the process, Chinese students and their parents can gain opportunities to learn about American universities and colleges in a more authentic and complex way than by relying solely on rankings. Chinese students' lack of knowledge drives them to resort to agencies that specialize in study-abroad consulting, which often push them to take tests multiple times and consider those admitted by the high ranking schools as their bragging rights, fueling a rat race of testing. A proactive effort on the part of American universities would help Chinese applicants, who are otherwise in the dark and at the mercy of their for-profit agents, to identify those schools that really fit with their abilities and interests. In return, the institutional effort would result in the recruitment of better prepared and qualified students. This could be a win-win situation for both Chinese students and American institutions.

The second unit is student affairs. Many American higher education institutions provide orientations to Chinese students right after their arrival at campus, which is far from sufficient. Sustained services that are culturally specific need to be offered throughout their time at the university. Increasing the Chinese speaking staff in key student service functions, such as residence halls, international student centers, and counseling services, are vital to improving Chinese students' campus experiences. I find that the seemingly voluntary self-segregation by many Chinese students is, in fact, involuntary. Chinese students are in need of intentional support from American higher education to mix them with domestic students. American institutions need to provide institutional platforms to provide diverse networking opportunities between international and domestic students for optimal global learning for all. International student offices in particular need to have a better vision in terms of providing a social home for international students and bridging international students and domestic students, rather than serving as a rubber-stamp office for immigration paperwork. For example, many Chinese students do not appreciate the party culture on American college campuses, but they are not connected with those American peers who do not party—some actually find it as distasteful as their Chinese peers do. American institutions can help bridge these disparate communities on campus. If united, they could form an alternative coalition to counter the dominant party community and diversify American college culture. As for first-generation Chinese college students, their social marginalization and disadvantages are sometimes masked by their economic resources. American higher education needs to provide extra support to help them make friends. This study found that joining campus organizations had a strong and positive effect on Chinese international students' forming friendships with their American peers. This is an area where American institutions can help by making intentional efforts to encourage Chinese international students to join campus organizations.

A third area is faculty support. American higher education needs to provide resources and support, such as forums and seminars, for faculty to understand and learn to manage classrooms with Chinese international students. Faculty with deep knowledge and experience about China and/or Chinese language skills can be an important asset to provide peer mentoring and support. Leveraging faculty with Chinese expertise and experience needs to be rewarded and resourced on an institutionalized platform rather than in a haphazard manner. For example, university-wide committees consisting of faculty and student representatives with Chinese expertise can be charged to host speakers and discussion forums about a wide variety of issues pertaining to Chinese international students. The institutionalized platform can give legitimacy and regularity to faculty support in gaining a deep understanding about Chinese international students' learning needs and styles and engaging in a sustained dialogue with them. For example, chapter 7, on Chinese students' reluctance to speak up in class, points to significant cultural differences related to speaking and to students' test-oriented background as profound factors that inhibit them from fully participating. American institutions need to learn more about these differences and provide support to faculty to promote culturally appropriate pedagogies. In particular, Chinese students feel more comfortable speaking in small-group rather than large-group settings. Although speaking in front of a large group is a valuable ability that needs to be inculcated, content course instructors might prioritize the exchange of ideas rather than public speaking skills and organize small group discussions as much as possible. Faculty may make intentional efforts to assign Chinese international students to diverse groups, particularly in classrooms where Chinese students already form a critical mass. In this way, they do not have to form groups on their own, which more often than not results in homogeneous Chinese peer groups in class.

The last area is career services. Although this book has challenged the conventional wisdom that international students "study to migrate," many Chinese students still want to gain some work experience in the United States before they return to China. The recent H-1B visa shortage highlights the desire for international students to work in the United States, at least on a temporary basis. However, the challenges of securing a work visa and finding employment opportunities in the American labor market ultimately jeopardize American universities' efforts to recruit international students. Career services on college campuses in the United States are largely designed for domestic students. The question is: How can a domestically oriented career service provide support for international students?

One potentially effective strategy for career services is to collaborate closely with alumni engagement offices focusing on building a stronger global alumni network. This book shows that many Chinese international students aspire to work at multinational companies or international organizations in and outside China. In other words, they seek global career platforms—which is entirely consistent with their initial motivation to study in the United States—to become globally competitive. Many multinational companies and international organizations have operations in China, from human resources to finance to technology, and they look for Chinese nationals with intercultural competence to fill those positions. American higher education career services can serve as bridges between those companies and Chinese students, just as they have always done for domestic students. The challenge is to identify those employment opportunities in multinational companies and international organizations that employ Chinese nationals. The Chinese alumni network can be leveraged to meet the challenge. Many Chinese alumni have established successful careers in greater China and around the world, but they often remain untapped resources in American institutions whose alumni offices are largely if not exclusively domestic-oriented. It is vital for American higher education to reach out to international alumni and help them stay connected with their alma mater and engaged with campus communities, and particularly current Chinese students. This connection can potentially open up career opportunities outside the United States.

SUMMARY

This concluding chapter addresses the question of what American higher education needs to know about Chinese international undergraduates—their experiences fraught with contradictions and complexities, which can only be understood in the context of their social, cultural, and educational backgrounds in fast-changing China. Based on the deepened understanding of this new wave of Chinese students, this chapter also delineates what American higher education needs to do from admissions to student experiences to faculty support and career services if they want to continue attracting Chinese students and provide better support to them.

Chinese international undergraduates aspire to a high-quality college education and a bright future in today's global world. Their ambition to rise to the top among the excessive competition within the Chinese education system drives them to cross the Pacific Ocean. Their parents, who want them to succeed at all costs, tread with them through the muddy waters of the college application process and sometimes place the entire family assets behind their only child's educational future. Studying in the United States represents broader life aspirations—with a global platform. What enables these aspirations and ambitions is the increasing affluence of Chinese nationals and their movement from the periphery to the core of transnational privilege.

What remains masked by their economic privilege and transnational mobility is the relative loss of social status and cultural capital after arriving in the United States. From academic studies to social integration, their marginalization is palpable, leading to much anxiety. The disadvantages associated with the first generation Chinese students whose parents have never been to college are more severe. However, leaving their protective parents and living independently thousands of miles away, Chinese students often begin a journey of self-discovery in the United States. Some are caught amidst the cultural clashes between China and the United States, which leads to tensions with their parents and further fuels their anxiety. This is exacerbated with the Trump administration's increasingly restrictive visa policies and the overall unwelcoming attitudes towards foreign students.

What marks this generation of Chinese international students from earlier generations is how natural it feels for them to study in the United States. The very term *natural* speaks to the pervasive and dominant study abroad culture in urban China; studying abroad is no longer reserved for a few academic or economic elites. This change embodies the change of the social structure in China—namely, the rise of the middle and upper-middle classes.[30] The desire to send their children abroad is rooted in the desire of emerging middle- and upper-class families to pass their social statuses on to the next generation. Increasingly ambitious and cosmopolitan, this generation of Chinese parents and their children are also anxious and insecure about their future. The duality of ambition and anxiety embodied in this new wave of international undergraduates may be part and parcel of today's China—a rising empire changing too fast to know itself.

Appendix on Methodology

My research assistants and I utilized the snowball sampling method to conduct an online survey of Chinese students in the United States, from which we selected those who showed willingness to participate in in-depth interviews. We recruited participants for the online survey by reaching out to our personal and professional networks, including international student offices and Chinese student organizations at over one hundred colleges and universities. Recruitment channels included emails and posts on social media including Facebook and Chinese WeChat. The survey was in English, and it was open from June 2013 to May 2014. Over two thousand students started our surveys; we received 507 complete usable surveys from fifty institutions. The response rate seems to be consistent with typical online surveys. At the end of the survey, those who were willing to be interviewed were asked to provide their contact information (email or phone number), and we were able to conduct interviews with sixty-five undergraduate students enrolling in American higher education from 2013 to 2016.

I tried my best to conduct interviews face-to-face, through my conference travel to colleges and universities, and through my summer trip back to China to meet with those participants who also spend summers in China. My identity as a Chinese scholar who had studied in the United States and now a faculty member in a respectable American institution not only enhanced the credibility of my research but attracted interest from Chinese students who were eager to share with me their experiences and sometimes confusions and anxieties. All the interviews were one-on-one semistructured interviews. The sessions took place in a private setting of the student's choice and lasted one to two hours each. I met students at their workplaces, at my workplace, and in coffee shops and school libraries. I let participants choose English or Chinese to speak during the interview, and almost everyone spoke Chinese. Interviews were transcribed verbatim in Chinese and then translated into English.

It is through in-depth interviews with Chinese students already enrolling in American higher education that I realized that some of them were from specialized high schools where they largely train students to opt out of the Gaokao and study overseas. Some of my interviewees in America have become my contacts and led me to their alma mater high school to conduct fieldwork. I conducted fieldwork over the summers of 2013 and 2014, and during the spring of 2015 in nine high schools in China in six cities: Beijing, Shanghai, Guangzhou, Chengdu, Wuxi, and Nantong. Given rapid development and changes in these high schools, I visited three of the nine high schools again during the summer of 2017. I attended classes and social events, made observations, and conducted one-on-one interviews with twenty high school students who were all on track to apply to colleges in the United States. I also interviewed ten school counselors, eight school principals or division heads of international classes, and five foreign teachers. The following table lists all the interviews conducted with various parties from 2013 to 2017.

Chinese college students in America	65
Chinese high school students	20
High School counselors in China	10
High school principals/heads in China	8
Foreign teachers in China	5
Total	108

Admittedly, we were not in total control of the process of selecting participants—the students made the choice of whether or not to participate in the survey and interviews. Self-selection bias is often inevitable in web surveys.[1] In this context, chances are that students who are academically and socially motivated were more likely to participate. In other words, there could be some positive selection in the sample of voluntary participants. If positive-selected students expressed academic and social anxiety, chances are that other Chinese students might experience even more issues. On the flip side, chances are that students who were on academic probation or had mental health issues were less likely to participate. Therefore, this book is limited in understanding these issues.

We did make efforts to offset the above limitations. First, we achieved a gender-balanced group. Survey researchers have found that females are more likely than males to volunteer in survey research, and this kind of gender bias is consequential in academic outcomes, as research indicates that females tend to study harder and get higher grades than males.[2] To make up for this gender bias, I hired a male Chinese undergraduate research assistant to recruit through his personal and professional networks. Through his efforts, we were able to reach more males to achieve a gender-balanced sample.

Second, we recognize the role of institutional type in shaping student experiences. We aimed to reach a diverse set of institutions. These fifty institutions are widely dispersed, not only on the East and West Coasts but also throughout the Midwest and the South. Moreover, the types of institutions were diverse; they included small private liberal arts colleges, major public land-grant institutions, major private research universities, and women's colleges.

I tried to maintain contact with the participants via social media and managed to stay in touch with two-thirds of the interviewees. While I have not conducted formal longitudinal interviews, I do gather follow-up information as much as possible, such as their internship experiences, their graduation and graduate school enrollment, and if possible their job placements in China and the United States.

INTEGRATING QUANTITATIVE AND QUALITATIVE DATA

The survey was useful for gathering information about the frequency and magnitude of the group's behaviors. For example, the survey asked students whether they planned to stay in the United States or return to China after graduation. The survey results cast light on the patterns of these students' plans and on the factors associated with their decisions—for example, whether their choice of a college major or their family background was driving their decision. However, the survey falls short of revealing how the students were thinking about this and the nuances behind their intentions. In the interviews, they were asked not only about their decisions but also about the rationales behind them. The interviews gave space to the respondents to provide their thoughts and reflections and to explain their dilemmas. For those who were unsure of their intentions, the interviews provided them with a platform for probing further into their thoughts about the future and deepened their understandings of the process of formulating their stay-versus-return intentions.

Another area best addressed by a mixed-methods approach is that of the social experiences of Chinese international students. The survey questions ask whether an undergraduate from China has close American friends, and how many. Such information will help assess the percentage of Chinese students who have no close American friends, and examine what factors (institutional type, college major, family background, etc.) affect their social experiences. However, survey questions cannot tackle why some students do not have any close friends, which can be probed during the in-depth interviews. This will not only address the question of barriers to forming close friendships with Americans but also explore the meanings of what these students might regard as a close relationship.

Sometimes survey data and interview data speak to each other in both complementary and contradictory ways, and together they provide a fuller, richer, and more nuanced picture. For example, an increasing number of Chinese parents send their children to study in American high schools, believing that this will provide better access to selective higher education institutions and help their children to have better experiences in American colleges. However, our survey analysis (in chapter 3) finds no evidence for any systematic advantages in college placements for students with American secondary school experiences. If anything, the longer Chinese students stay in the United States, the less likely they will work harder than their American peers in academic studies (chapter 4 shows this). However, the lack of significant advantages in getting into selective institutions does not mean that there is no educational benefit to attending American high schools. Our in-depth interview data provides evidence that for some students, American high school attendance helps improve their English, adjust to American learning culture and environment, and boost their overall college experiences in the United States. Taking both quantitative and qualitative data into account, the understanding of what roles American high schools play in Chinese international students' experiences and outcomes is multi-dimensional, and it would be over-simplified to conclude it in a definitive way.

Notes

1. AMBITIOUS AND ANXIOUS: CHINESE UNDERGRADUATES IN THE UNITED STATES

All student names in the book are pseudonyms, for the sake of confidentiality. Some students adopt English names in America, and other students use their original Chinese names. Whether the pseudonyms are English or Chinese is consistent with students' own choice in how they want to be identified in the United States. More than half of Chinese students I interviewed go by their English names.

1. Peck 2014.
2. The annual tuition for undergraduate education in China is approximately $1,000 or less, including elite universities such as Peking University.
3. Redden 2018a.
4. Redden 2018b.
5. Fan 2016.
6. Feng, Gu, and Cai 2016.
7. Cameron et al. 2013; Fong 2004.
8. Lareau 2011.
9. *Times Higher Education* 2018.
10. For details of Chinese higher education and stratification, please see Liu 2016.
11. Osnos 2014.
12. Bourdieu 1998.
13. Ong 1999; Brooks and Waters 2011; Waters 2005.
14. Haugh 2016.
15. Abelmann and Kang 2014.
16. Lyman 2000.

17. Johanson 2016.
18. Liu 2015.
19. Associated Press 2015.
20. Al-Sharideh and Goe 1998; Bevis and Lucas 2007; Zhao, Kuh, and Carini 2005.
21. Ruble and Zhang 2013.
22. Zhao and Bourne 2011.
23. Dolby and Rahman 2008; Lee and Rice 2007; Lee 2010.
24. Marginson 2014.
25. Hung 2015.
26. BBC News 2016.
27. Hedrick-Wong 2018.
28. For China's emerging middle class and its social implications, please see Li ed 2010; Babones 2018; Lu 2010; Hung 2015; Guthie 2012.
29. Lu 2010.
30. UNESCO 2017.
31. Hung 2015.
32. Ministry of Education 2018.
33. Fong 2011.
34. Guthrie 2012.
35. Guthrie 2012.
36. Soong 2016.
37. Burton 2007.
38. For details, see U.S. Department of State 2005.
39. Kujawa, Anthony 2006.
40. Fischer 2019.
41. Redden 2018b.
42. Institute of Internal Education 2017.
43. Institute of International Education, "Open Doors: International Students in the U.S.—2017 Fast Facts," https://www.iie.org/en/Research-and-Insights/Open-Doors/Fact-Sheets-and-Infographics/Fast-Facts.
44. Pokorney 2018.
45. Bound et al. 2016.
46. Ruiz 2016.
47. Drash 2015.
48. Ma and Garcia-Murillo 2017; Brooks and Waters 2011.
49. Briggs 2017.
50. Altbach and Knight 2007.
51. Gareis 2012.
52. Author compilation of data retrieved from the Institute of International Education.
53. Loo 2017.
54. Xu 2006; Yan and Berliner 2011.
55. Heng 2016; 2017; Purdue 2018, https://www.purdue.edu/crcs/wp-content/uploads/2018/10/2018-Purdue-Survey-Report_Rev.pdf.

56. Wang 2008.
57. Bellah et al. 2007.
58. Nye 2005b.
59. Borjas 2002; Finn 2003.

2. A LOVE FOR SEPARATION: STUDY ABROAD AS THE NEW EDUCATION GOSPEL IN URBAN CHINA

1. Shavit and Blossfeld 1993; Lucas 2001.
2. Zhao 2007; Stevens 2009.
3. Brooks and Waters 2011; Ong 1999.
4. Hossler and Gallagher 1987; Perna 2006.
5. Yeung 2013; Wu and Zhuoni Zhang 2010.
6. Times Higher Education 2018.
7. Loyalka 2009; Xinchen 2018; Ma and Wang 2016.
8. Loyalka 2009; Li, Morgan, and Ding 2008; Mooney 2006.
9. Altbach 1999; Chen 2007.
10. Liu 2013; Liu 2016.
11. Ma and Wang 2016; Zhang, Zhao, and Lei 2012.
12. Rui 2014, 12–13; Fu 2018.
13. Yeung 2013; Mooney 2006
14. Bodycott 2009
15. Weenink 2008; Chiang 2018
16. Hout, Raftery, and Bell 1993; Davies and Guppy 1997.
17. Oakes and Guiton 1995; Gerber and Cheung 2008.
18. Lucas 2001, 1652.
19. Guthrie 2012; Hung 2015.
20. Fong 2004.
21. Kipnis 2011.
22. Osnos 2014; Osburg 2013.
23. Waters 2005.
24. Noddings 2005, 8; Zhao 2007.
25. Abelmann 2009.
26. Weenink 2008, 1092; Huang and Yeoh 2005; Waters 2005.
27. Weenink 2008, 1092; Ma and Garcia-Murillo 2017.
28. Fong 2011.
29. Espeland and Sauder 2007.
30. Cebolla-Boado, Hu, and Soysal 2018.
31. Hu 1944; Chung 2016.
32. Espenshade and Radford 2009; Chambliss and Takacs 2014.
33. Liu 2013; Li 2010.
34. Chen 2007; Waters 2005; Hoover-Dempsey and Sandler 1997.

3. "FROM HELLO TO HARVARD": THE PATHWAYS TO AMERICAN HIGHER EDUCATION

1. Some universities have SAT-optional admissions policies; the most recent case is Northwestern University, where the SAT is not part of the requirements for application. Other universities have adopted the policy of accepting the Chinese *Gaokao* scores in lieu of SAT scores. But the majority of elite universities still require the SAT.
2. Deschamps and Lee 2015; Liang 2018; Young 2017.
3. Farrugia 2017a.
4. Farrugia 2017a.
5. Fong 2011; Lan 2019; Cheng and Yang 2019.
6. Li 2010; Ma and Wang 2016.
7. Young 2017.
8. Zanten 2015; Waters 2007.
9. Chao 1994; Lin and Fu 1990; Porter et al. 2005.
10. Kaufman and Gabler 2004; Lareau, Annette 2011.
11. Suen and Yu 2006.
12. Chua 2017; Lan 2019.
13. Joseph 2013; Hoover-Dempsey and Sandler 1997.
14. Zhao 2009; Ma and Wang 2016; Liu 2016, Black, Cortes, and Lincove 2015.
15. Stevens 2009; Bastedo et al. 2018; Hossler et al. 2019.
16. Farrugia 2017a.
17. Farrugia 2017b.
18. Ling 2015; Wu 2012.
19. Schulte 2017.
20. Schulte 2017.

4. NAVIGATING AND COMPARING CHINESE AND AMERICAN EDUCATION SYSTEMS

1. Tucker 2011.
2. Aik-Kwang 2001; Morris and Leung 2010. Aik-Kwang and Smith 2004; Lin 2011.
3. Ma 2015; Li 2012; Stevenson and Stigler 1994.
4. Hofstede and Hofstede 1991.
5. Wu 2015; Ma 2015.
6. Oakes 1995; 2005; Ma and Wang 2016; Liu 2016.
7. Kim 2005. LeTendre 1999; Chu 2017.
8. Hong and Kang 2010.
9. Park 2013.
10. Weisberg 1993, 92.

11. Weisberg 1993, 73.
12. Zhao 2009, 91.
13. Bradsher 2017.
14. Storer 1972; Zuckerman and Merton 1971.
15. Kuhn 2012; Storer 1967.
16. Friedman 2005, 365.
17. Riegle-Crumb and King 2010; Ma and Liu 2015.
18. Perry 1970; Perry 1981.
19. Li 2012, 118.
20. Kim 2005; Li 2012.
21. Turner 2006; Gu 2008.
22. Stevenson and Stigler 1994.
23. Hong et al. 1999, 588; Dweck 2006.
24. Duckworth 2016.
25. Lee and Zhou 2015.
26. DiPrete and Buchmann 2013; *The Economist* 2015.
27. Gordon 1964; Chiswick 1978; Alba and Nee 1997.
28. Loveless 2006.
29. Xie and Killewald 2012.
30. Eagan et al. 2014.
31. Scott-Clayton, Crosta, and Belfield 2012.
32. Ma and Wang 2016.
33. Liu 2016; Liu 2018.
34. Li et al. 2012; Wu 2010.
35. Redden 2015; Qing et al. 2016.
36. The University of Iowa cheating scandal is a clear case of intentional violations aided by a cheating ring in the for-profit business sector. Please see Qing et al. 2016.
37. Russikof et al. 2013.

5. PROTECTIVE SEGREGATION: CHINESE STUDENTS HANGING OUT AMONG THEMSELVES

1. McPherson, Smith-Lovin, and Cook 2001.
2. Gareis 2012; Tian 2019.
3. Ogbu and Simons 1998.
4. Sawir et al. 2008.
5. Ma and Garcia-Murillo 2017.
6. Kudo and Simkin 2003; Marginson et al. 2010.
7. Wei et al. 2007, 385; Glass et al. 2014.
8. Ruble and Zhang 2013.
9. Ting-Toomey 1989; Trice 2007; Kim 1991.
10. Armstrong and Hamilton 2013.

11. Yuan 2011; Will 2016.
12. Rose-Redwood and Rose-Redwood 2013; Heng 2017.
13. Stevenson and Stigler 1994.
14. Heng 2016b; Glass et al. 2014; Hail 2015.
15. Lee and Rice 2007.
16. Ruble and Zhang 2013.
17. Hail 2015, 319.
18. Tuan 1998.
19. Hail 2015.
20. Anderson 2006.
21. Fong 2011, 6.
22. Beoku-Betts 2004; Lee and Rice 2007.
23. Whyte 2010; Ma 2011a.
24. Hofstede 2001; Heng 2017.
25. Gareis 2012; Kim 1991; Searle and Ward 1990.
26. Bellah et al. 2007, xiv.
27. Hofstede, Hofstede, and Minkov 2010; Hofstede and Geert 2001.
28. Steele and Lynch 2013.
29. Ma 2015.
30. Gareis 2012, 321.
31. Ostrove 2003.
32. Kariuki 2016.
33. Matheson 2016.
34. Bista and Foster 2011; Choudaha 2017.
35. Matheson 2016.

6. COLLEGE MAJOR CHOICES, RATIONALES, AND DILEMMAS

1. Humanities Indicators 2017.
2. Davies and Guppy 1997; Ma 2009; Gerber and Cheung 2008.
3. Eccles 1994; Ma 2011b; Charles and Bradley 2009.
4. Loyalka 2009; Liu 2016.
5. Lowell 2010.
6. Hira 2010; Ma 2011c, 1169–90.
7. Yu and Killewald 2012.
8. Tang 2000.
9. Rimer 2008.
10. Ma and Lutz 2018.
11. Hao, Long, and Zhang 2011.
12. Author compilation from the Statistical Yearbook of 1985 in China, 591.
13. Li 2001.

14. Andreas 2009.
15. Yan 2010.
16. Hu and Wu 2017.
17. Bourdieu and Passeron 1977, 156; Lamont and Lareau 1988.
18. Ma 2010.
19. DiMaggio 1982, 194.
20. See figures 5a to 5d in chapter 4.
21. Trow 1973.
22. Jeung 2013; Li et al. 2012.
23. Armstrong and Hamilton 2013; Marginson 2006.
24. Brooks 2011.
25. Bellah et al. 2007.
26. Deresiewicz 2015; Gerber and Cheung 2008; Li 2010.
27. Armstrong and Hamilton 2013.
28. Loyalka 2009; Ma 2015.
29. Datta and Miller 2012.
30. Del Rossi and Hersch 2008.
31. Pitt and Tepper 2012.
32. Seymour 2000.

7. THINK BEFORE SPEAK: A REAL CONUNDRUM FOR CLASSROOM PARTICIPATION?

1. Some schools waive students' TOEFL scores if they have obtained credentials, either high school degrees or college degrees in English-speaking countries.
2. Tyre 2016.
3. Tsui 1996; Liu 2006.
4. Liu and Jackson 2008.
5. Cheng and Erben 2012.
6. Du Bois [1903] 1982, 45.
7. Falcon 2008.
8. Sue, Diane, and Ino 1990; Zane et al. 1991.
9. Li 2012.
10. Ames and Rosemont 2010, 93.
11. Li 2012.
12. Yum 1988; Lyon 2004, 137.
13. Li 2012, 302.
14. Gao 1998; Chang 1999.
15. Liberman 1994. Liu 2002.
16. Zane et al. 1991, 63.
17. Cortazzi and Jin 1996; Li and Han 2010.

18. Li 2012, 120.
19. Cain 2013.
20. Li 2012, 281.
21. King, Pan, and Roberts 2013; King, Pan, and Roberts 2014.
22. Xu, Mao, Halderman 2011; Wacker 2003; Guo and Feng 2012.
23. Paulhus, Duncan, and Yik 2002; Aristotle 1992.
24. Suen and Lan 2006.
25. Grigorenko et al. 2008.
26. Miyazaki 1981; Niu 2007.
27. Lee and Larson 2000.
28. Ma and Wang 2016.

8. CHANGES AND REFLECTIONS

1. Liu 1998, 197.
2. Ma 2014.
3. Levin 2009; Salisbury, An, and Pascarella 2013; Gacel-Ávila 2005.
4. Cheng and Yang 2019.
5. Zemach-Bersin 2007; Jorgenson and Shultz 2012.
6. Soong, Stahl, and Shan 2018; Maxwell and Aggleton 2016; Cheng and Yang 2019.
7. Ibrahim 2005; Nussbaum 2002.
8. Nussbaum 1997; Nussbaum 2002.
9. Oxley and Morris 2013.
10. Resnik 2012; Bunnell 2009.
11. Dill 2013, 5.
12. Banks 2004; Armstrong 2006.
13. Davies 2006.
14. Richardson 1979, 1.
15. Oxley and Morris 2013.
16. Taylor 2016, 212.
17. Amir 1976.
18. Hail 2015.
19. Ang 2016; Shen and Tsai 2016.
20. Tong 2011; Gilley 2006.
21. Dickson et al. 2016; Kweon and Choi 2018.
22. Osnos 2014.
23. Thornton and Fricke 1987; Fuligni and Zhang 2004.
24. Baxter Magolda 2009; Baxter Magolda 2004.
25. Bian 1997.
26. Nye 2005b.

9. STAY VERSUS RETURN: THAT IS THE QUESTION

1. Wu and Wilkes 2017; Arthur and Nunes 2014.
2. Costa and Hira 2015.
3. Reginfo.gov 2018.
4. U.S. Citizenship and Immigration Services 2019.
5. Wang 2016.
6. U.S. Citizenship and Immigration Services 2017.
7. Semotiuk 2019.
8. Diamond 2014.
9. Wu 2018.
10. Borjas 2002.
11. Finn 2003.
12. Finn and Pennington 2018; Zweig, Chung, and Vanhonacker 2006.
13. Gaillard and Gaillard 1997; Johnson and Regets 1998.
14. Wallerstein 2011.
15. Zakaria 2008.
16. Zweig, Chung, and Vanhonacker 2006; Chen 2008.
17. Alberts and Hazen 2005.
18. For more on Haiwei Career, see http://zhiye.xdf.cn/en/.
19. Chinese Ministry of Education 2017, www.eol.cn/html/lx/report2017/wu.shtml.
20. Saxenian 2005.
21. Shen 2008.
22. The return and stay rate as analyzed in this chapter all refer to intentions.
23. Hira 2010; Hossain and Robinson 2012.
24. Yeung 2013.
25. See chapter 2.
26. Hyun 2005.
27. Zhou 2009; Zhou and Gatewood 2007.
28. Wank 1996; Wederman 2004.
29. *The Economist* 2012.
30. Wedeman 2012; Zhang and Li 2012.
31. Thomas 2017.
32. Xiang 2007.

10. WHAT AMERICAN HIGHER EDUCATION NEEDS TO KNOW ABOUT CHINESE UNDERGRADUATES

1. China has announced a plan to overhaul the Gaokao in the next few years. See Fu 2018.
2. Karabel 2006.

3. Perry 1970; Perry 1981.

4. Perez et al. 2009; Duckworth 2016.

5. Cameron et al. 2013.

6. Chapter 4 provides the discussions about ability- and effort-based learning; Stevenson and Stigler 1994; Dweck 2006.

7. Lee and Rice 2007.

8. Lockie 2018.

9. Louie 2017

10. Tinto 1987; Astin 1993.

11. Hofstede, Hofstede, and Minkov 2010; Hofstede 2001.

12. Abelmann 2009.

13. Hossler and Gallagher 1987; Perna 2006.

14. Stevens 2009.

15. Altbach 2006; Marginson and Van der Wende 2007.

16. Kipnis 2011.

17. Davies and Guppy 1997; Ma 2009.

18. Bourdieu and Passeron 1977; Lamont and Lareau 1988.

19. Chambliss 2014.

20. Lee and Rice 2007; Armstrong and Hamilton 2013.

21. Armstrong and Hamilton 2013.

22. Hofstede, Hofstede, and Minkov 2010; Bellah et al. 2007.

23. Borjas 2002.

24. Finn 2003; Finn and Pennington 2018.

25. Fong 2011.

26. Nye 2005a; Xuetong 2006.

27. Wang 2016.

28. Semotiuk 2018.

29. Wong 2018.

30. For China's emerging middle class and its social implications, please see Li ed. 2010; Babones 2018; Lu 2010; Hung 2015; Guthrie 2012.

APPENDIX

1. Wright 2005.

2. Sax, Gilmartin, and Bryant 2003.

References

Abelmann, Nancy. 2009. *The Intimate University: Korean American Students and the Problems of Segregation*. Durham, NC: Duke University Press.

Abelmann, Nancy, and Jiyeon Kang. 2014. "A Fraught Exchange? US Media on Chinese International Undergraduates and the American University." *Journal of Studies in International Education* 18, no. 4: 382–97.

Aik-Kwang, Ng. 2001. *Why Asians Are Less Creative than Westerners*. Singapore: Prentice Hall.

Aik-Kwang, Ng, and Ian Smith. 2004. "Why Is There a Paradox in Promoting Creativity in the Asian Classroom?" In *Creativity: When East Meets West*, ed. Sing Lau, Anna N. N. Hui, and Grace Y. C. Ng, 87–112. Singapore: World Scientific Publishing.

Alba, Richard, and Victor Nee. 1997. "Rethinking Assimilation Theory for a New Era of Immigration." *International Migration Review* 31, no. 4: 826–74.

Alberts, Heike C., and Helen D. Hazen. 2005. "'There Are Always Two Voices . . .': International Students' Intentions to Stay in the United States or Return to their Home Countries." *International Migration* 43, no. 3: 131–54.

Al-Sharideh, Khalid A., and W. Richard Goe. 1998. "Ethnic Communities Within the University: An Examination of Factors Influencing the Personal Adjustment of International Students." *Research in Higher Education* 39, no. 6: 699–725.

Altbach, Philip G. 2006. "The Dilemmas of Ranking." *International Higher Education*, no. 42: 2–4.

Altbach, Philip G., and Jane Knight. 2007. "The Internationalization of Higher Education: Motivations and Realities." *Journal of Studies in International Education* 11, no. 3–4: 290–305.

Ames, Roger T., and Henry Rosemont Jr. 2010. *The Analects of Confucius: A Philosophical Translation*. New York: Ballantine.

Amir, Yehuda. 1976. "The Role of Intergroup Contact in Change of Prejudice and Ethnic Relations." In *Toward the Elimination of Racism*, ed. Phyllis A. Katz, 245–308. Elmsford, NY: Pergamon.

Anderson, Benedict. 2006. *Imagined Communities: Reflections on the Origin and Spread of Nationalism*. London: Verso.

Andreas, Joel. 2009. *Rise of the Red Engineers: The Cultural Revolution and the Origins of China's New Class*. Stanford, CA: Stanford University Press.

Ang, Yuen Yuen. 2016. *How China Escaped the Poverty Trap*. Ithaca, NY: Cornell University Press.

Aristotle. 1992. *The Art of Rhetoric*. New York: Penguin.

Armstrong, Chris. 2006. "Global Civil Society and the Question of Global Citizenship." *Voluntas* 17: 349–57.

Armstrong, Elizabeth A., and Laura T. Hamilton. 2013. *Paying for the Party: How College Maintains Inequality*. Cambridge, MA: Harvard University Press.

Arthur, Nancy, and Sarah Nunes. 2014. "Should I Stay or Should I Go Home? Career Guidance with International Students." In *Handbook of Career Development*, ed. Gideon Arulmani, Anuradha J. Bakshi, Frederick T. L. Leong, and A. G. Watts, 587–606. New York: Springer.

Associated Press. 2015. "U.S. Prosecutors Allege Chinese Citizens in College Exam Scheme." *Wall Street Journal*, May 28, 2015.

Astin, Alexander W. 1993. *What Matters in College: Four Critical Years Revisited*. San Francisco: Jossey-Bass.

Babones, Salvatore. 2018. "China's Middle Class Is Pulling Up the Ladder Behind Itself." *Foreign Policy*, February 1, 2018. https://foreignpolicy.com/2018/02/01/chinas-middle-class-is-pulling-up-the-ladder-behind-itself/.

Banks, James A. 2004. *Diversity and Citizenship Education: Global Perspectives*. San Francisco: Jossey-Bass.

Bastedo, Michael N., Nicholas A. Bowman, Kristen M. Glasener, and Jandi L. Kelly. 2018. "What Are We Talking About When We Talk About Holistic Review? Selective College Admissions and Its Effects on Low-SES Students." *Journal of Higher Education* 89, no. 5: 782–805.

Baxter Magolda, Marcia B. 2004. *Making Their Own Way: Narratives for Transforming Higher Education to Promote Self-Development*. Sterling, VA: Stylus.

Baxter Magolda, Marcia B. 2009. "Promoting Self-Authorship to Promote Liberal Education." *Journal of College and Character* 10, no. 3: 1–6.

BBC News. 2016. "China Tops US in Numbers of Billionaires." October 13, 2016.

Bellah, Robert N., Richard Madsen, William M. Sullivan, Ann Swidler, and Steven M. Tipton. 2007. *Habits of the Heart: Individualism and Commitment in American Life*. Berkeley: University of California Press.

Beoku-Betts, Josephine A. 2004. "African Women Pursuing Graduate Studies in the Sciences: Racism, Gender Bias, and Third World Marginality." *NWSA Journal* 16, no. 1: 116–35.

Bevis, Teresa Brawner, and Christopher J. Lucas. 2007. *International Students in American Colleges and Universities: A History*. New York: Palgrave Macmillan.

Bian, Yanjie. 1997. "Bringing Strong Ties Back In: Indirect Ties, Network Bridges, and Job Searches In China." *American Sociological Review* 62, no. 3: 366–85.

Black, Sandra E., Kalena E. Cortes, and Jane Arnold Lincove. 2015. "Academic Undermatching of High-Achieving Minority Students: Evidence from Race-Neutral And Holistic Admissions Policies." *American Economic Review* 105, no. 5 (2015): 604–10.

Bodycott, Peter. 2009. "Choosing a Higher Education Study Abroad Destination: What Mainland Chinese Parents and Students Rate as Important." *Journal of Research in International Education* 8, no. 3: 349–73.

Borjas, George J. 2002. "Rethinking Foreign Students: A Question of the National Interest." *National Review*, June 17, 2002.

Bound, John, Breno Braga, Gaurav Khanna, and Sarah Turner. 2016. "A Passage to America: University Funding and International Students." National Bureau of Economic Research. Working paper no. 22981. https://www.nber.org/papers/w22981.

Bourdieu, Pierre. 1998. *The State Nobility: Elite Schools in the Field of Power*. Stanford, CA: Stanford University Press.

Bourdieu, Pierre, and Jean-Claude Passeron. 1977. *Reproduction in Education, Society, and Culture*. Thousand Oaks, CA: Sage.

Bradsher, Keith. 2017. "China Hastens the World Toward an Electric-Car Future." *New York Times*, October 9, 2017. https://www.nytimes.com/2017/10/09/business/china-hastens-the-world-toward-an-electric-car-future.html.

Briggs, Peter. 2017. "Responding to Campus Change, Rising Numbers of Chinese Undergraduates and Michigan State University's Response." In *Understanding International Students from Asia in American Universities: Learning and Living Globalization*, ed. Yingyi Ma and Martha A. Garcia-Murillo, 195–213. Cham, Switzerland: Springer International.

Brooks, David. 2011. "It Is Not About You." *New York Times*, May 30, 2011. http://www.nytimes.com/2011/05/31/opinion/31brooks.html.

Brooks, Rachel. 2008. "Accessing Higher Education: The Influence of Cultural and Social Capital on University Choice." *Sociology Compass* 2, no. 4, 1355–71.

Brooks, Rachel, and Johanna Waters. 2011. *Student Mobilities, Migration, and the Internationalization of Higher Education*. London: Palgrave-Macmillan.

Bunnell, Tristan. 2009. "The International Baccalaureate in the USA and the Emerging 'Culture War.' " *Discourse: Studies in the Cultural Politics of Education* 30, no. 1: 61–72.

Burton, Bollag. 2007. "Coalition of Exchange, Trade, and Research Groups Calls for a More Open Visa Policy." *Chronicle of Higher Education*, January 31, 2007. https://www.chronicle.com/article/Coalition-of-Exchange-Trade/122836.

Cain, Susan. 2013. *Quiet: The Power of Introverts in a World That Can't Stop Talking*. New York: Broadway.

Cameron, Lisa, Nisvan Erkal, Lata Gangadharan, and Xin Meng. 2013. "Little Emperors: Behavioral Impacts of China's One-Child Policy." *Science* 339, no. 6122: 953–57.

Cebolla-Boado, Héctor, Yang Hu, and Yasemin Nuhoğlu Soysal. 2018. "Why Study Abroad? Sorting of Chinese Students Across British Universities." *British Journal of Sociology of Education* 39, no. 3: 365–80.

Chambliss, Daniel F, and Christopher G. Takacs. 2014. *How College Works*. Cambridge, MA: Harvard University Press.

Chang, Hui-Ching. 1999. "The 'Well-Defined' Is 'Ambiguous': Indeterminacy in Chinese Conversation." *Journal of Pragmatics* 31, no. 4: 535–56.

Chao, Ruth K. 1994. "Beyond Parental Control and Authoritarian Parenting Style: Understanding Chinese Parenting Through the Cultural Notion of Training." *Child Development* 65, no. 4: 1111–19.

Charles, Maria, and Karen Bradley. 2009. "Indulging Our Gendered Selves: Sex Segregation by Field of Study in 44 Countries." *American Journal of Sociology* 114, no. 4: 924–76.

Chen, Liang-Hsuan. 2007. "Choosing Canadian Graduate Schools from Afar: East Asian Students' Perspectives." *Higher Education* 54, no. 5: 759–80.

Chen, Yun-Chung. 2008. "The Limits of Brain Circulation: Chinese Returnees and Technological Development in Beijing." *Pacific Affairs* 81, no. 2:195–215.

Cheng, Baoyan, and Po Yang. 2019. "Chinese Students Studying in American High Schools: International Sojourning as a Pathway to Global Citizenship." *Cambridge Journal of Education*. doi:10.1080/0305764X.2019.1571560.

Cheng, Rui, and Antony Erben. 2012. "Language Anxiety: Experiences of Chinese Graduate Students at US Higher Institutions." *Journal of Studies in International Education* 16, no. 5: 477–97.

Chiang, Yi-Lin. 2018. "When Things Don't Go as Planned: Contingencies, Cultural Capital, and Parental Involvement for Elite University Admission in China." *Comparative Education Review* 62, no. 4: 503–21.

Chinese Ministry of Education. 2017. *Chinese Students Study Abroad Report*. www.eol. cn/html/lx/report2017/wu.shtml.

Chiswick, Barry R. 1978. "The Effect of Americanization on the Earnings of Foreign-Born Men." *Journal of Political Economy* 86, no. 5: 897–921.

Chua, Ryan. 2017. "Agencies Helping Chinese Students Study Abroad Cash in on Lucrative Business." *CGTN America*, December 20, 2017. america.cgtn.com/2017/12/20 /agencies-helping-chinese-students-study-abroad-cash-in-on-lucrative-business.

Chu, Lenora. 2017. *Little Soldiers: An American Boy, a Chinese School and the Global Race to Achieve*. London: Hachette.

Chung, Angie Y. 2016. *Saving Face: The Emotional Costs of the Asian Immigrant Family Myth*. New Brunswick, NJ: Rutgers University Press.

Cortazzi, Martin, and Lixian Jin. 1996. "Cultures of Learning: Language Classrooms in China." In *Society and the Language Classroom*, ed. E. H. Coleman, 169–206. Cambridge: Cambridge University Press.

Costa, Daniel, and Ron Hira. 2015. "The Department of Homeland Security's Proposed STEM OPT Extension Fails to Protect Foreign Students and American Workers." Economic Policy Institute, December 1, 2015. https://www.epi.org /blog/the-department-of-homeland-securitys-proposed-stem-opt-extension -fails-to-protect-foreign-students-and-american-workers/.

Danni, Fu. 2018. "China Announces Radical Overhaul of College Entrance Exam." Sixth Tone, April 24, 2018. https://www.sixthtone.com/news/1001031/china -announces-radical-overhaul-of-college-entrance-exam.

Datta, Jashodeep, and Bonnie M. Miller. 2012. "International Students in United States' Medical Schools: Does the Medical Community Know They Exist?" *Medical Education Online* 17, no. 1: 10.3402/meo.v17i0.15748. http://doi.org/10.3402/meo .v17i0.15748.

Davies, Lynn. 2006. "Global Citizenship: Abstraction or Framework for Action?" *Educational Review* 58, no. 1: 5–25.

Davies, Scott, and Neil Guppy. 1997. "Fields of Study, College Selectivity, and Student Inequalities in Higher Education." *Social Forces* 75, no. 4: 1417–38.

Del Rossi, Alison F., and Joni Hersch. 2008. "Double Your Major, Double Your Return?" *Economics of Education Review* 27, no. 4: 375–86.

Deresiewicz, William. 2015. *Excellent Sheep: The Miseducation of the American Elite and the Way to a Meaningful Life*. New York: Simon and Schuster.

Deschamps, Eric, and Jenny J. Lee. 2015. "Internationalization as Mergers and Acquisitions: Senior International Officers' Entrepreneurial Strategies and Activities in Public Universities." *Journal of Studies in International Education* 19, no. 2. https:// doi.org/10.1177/1028315314538284.

Diamond, Jeremy. 2014. "New Visa Policy Elevates U.S.-China Relations." *CNN*, November 10, 2014. https://www.cnn.com/2014/11/10/politics/visa-10-years -obama-announces/index.html.

Dickson, Bruce J., Pierre F. Landry, Mingming Shen, and Jie Yan. 2016. "Public Goods and Regime Support in Urban China." *China Quarterly* 228: 859–80.

Dill, Jeffrey S. 2013. *The Longings and Limits of Global Citizenship Education: The Moral Pedagogy of Schooling in a Cosmopolitan Age*. New York: Routledge.

DiMaggio, Paul. 1982. "Cultural Capital and School Success: The Impact of Status Culture Participation on the Grades of US High School Students." *American Sociological Review* 47, no. 2: 189–201.

DiPrete, Thomas A., and Claudia Buchmann. 2013. *The Rise of Women: The Growing Gender Gap in Education and What It Means for American Schools*. New York: Russell Sage Foundation.

Dolby, Nadine, and Aliya Rahman. 2008. "Research in International Education." *Review of Educational Research* 78, no. 3: 676–726.

Drash, Wayne. 2015. "Culture Clash in Iowa: The Town Where Bubble Tea Shops Outnumber Starbucks." *CNN News*. https://www.cnn.com/interactive/2015/07 /us/culture-clash-american-story/.

Du Bois, W. E. B. [1903] 1982. *The Souls of Black Folk*. New York: Penguin.

Duckworth, Angela. 2016. *Grit: The Power of Passion and Perseverance*. New York: Simon and Schuster.

Dweck, Carol S. 2006. *Mindset: The New Psychology of Success*. New York: Random House.

Eagan, Kevin, Ellen Bara Stolzenberg, Joseph J. Ramirez, Melissa C. Aragon, Maria Ramirez Suchard, and Sylvia Hurtado. 2014. "The American Freshman: National Norms, Fall 2014." Los Angeles: Higher Education Research Institute, UCLA.

Eccles, Jacquelynne. 1994. "Understanding Women's Educational and Occupational-Choices: Applying the Eccles et al. Model of Achievement-Related Choices." *Psychology of Women Quarterly* 18, no. 4: 585–609.

The Economist. 2012. "Heartless Attacks." July 21, 2012. https://www.economist .com/china/2012/07/21/heartless-attacks.

The Economist. 2015. "Why Girls Do Better at School than Boys." May 6, 2015. www .economist.com/the-economist-explains/2015/03/06/why-girls-do-better-at -school-than-boys.

Espeland, Wendy Nelson, and Michael Sauder. 2007. "Rankings and Reactivity: How Public Measures Recreate Social Worlds." *American Journal of Sociology* 113, no. 1: 1–40.

Espenshade, Thomas J., and Alexandria Walton Radford. 2009. *No Longer Separate, Not Yet Equal: Race and Class in Elite College Admission and Campus Life*. Princeton, NJ: Princeton University Press.

Falcon, M. Sylvianna. 2008. "Mestiza Double Consciousness: The Voices of Afro-Peruvian Women on Gendered Racism." *Gender & Society* 22, no. 5.

Fan, Jiayang. 2016. "China's Rich Kids Head West." *New Yorker*, February 22, 2016. https://www.newyorker.com/magazine/2016/02/22/chinas-rich-kids-head-west.

Farrugia, Christine. 2017a. "Globally Mobile Youth: Trends in International Secondary Students in the United States, 2013–2016." *IIE: The Power of International Education*.

Farrugia, Christine. 2017b. "More International Students Seeking U.S. High School Diplomas." *IIE: The Power of International Education*.

Feng, Wang, Baochang Gu, and Yong Cai. 2016. "The End of China's One-Child Policy." *Studies in Family Planning* 47, no. 1: 83–86.

Finn, Michael G. 2003. *Stay Rates of Foreign Doctorate Recipients from US Universities, 2001*. Oak Ridge, TN: Oak Ridge Institute for Science and Education Oak Ridge.

Finn, Michael G., and Leigh Ann Pennington. 2018. *Stay Rates of Foreign Doctorate Recipients from US Universities*. No. 18-SAWD-0103. Oak Ridge, TN: Oak Ridge Institute for Science and Education Oak Ridge.

Fischer, Karin. 2019. "How International Education's Golden Age Lost Its Sheen." *Chronicle of Higher Education*, March 28, 2019. https://www.chronicle.com /interactives/2019-03-28-golden-age?cid=wsinglestory_hp_1.

Fong, Vanessa L. 2004. *Only Hope: Coming of Age Under China's One-Child Policy*. Stanford, CA: Stanford University Press.

Fong, Vanessa. 2011. *Paradise Redefined: Transnational Chinese Students and the Quest for Flexible Citizenship in the Developed World*. Stanford, CA: Stanford University Press.

Friedman, Thomas L. 2005. *The World Is Flat: A Brief History of the Twenty-First Century.* New York: Macmillan.

Fu, Danni. 2017. "China Announces Radical Overhaul of College Entrance Exam" Oct. 20, 2017. Six Tone https://www.sixthtone.com/news/1001031/china-announces -radical-overhaul-of-college-entrance-exam

Fuligni, Andrew J., and Wenxin Zhang. 2004. "Attitudes Toward Family Obligation Among Adolescents in Contemporary Urban and Rural China." *Child Development* 75, no. 1: 180–92.

Gacel-Ávila, Jocelyne. 2005. "The Internationalization of Higher Education: A Paradigm for Global Citizenry." *Journal of Studies in International Education* 9, no. 2: 121–36.

Gaillard, Jacques, and Anne Marie Gaillard. 1997. "Introduction: The International Mobility of Brains: Exodus or Circulation?" *Science Technology & Society* 2, no. 2: 195–228.

Gao, Ge. 1998. "Don't Take My Word for It': Understanding Chinese Speaking Practices." *International Journal of Intercultural Relations* 22, no. 2: 163–86.

Gareis, Elisabeth. 2012. "Intercultural Friendship: Effects of Home and Host Region." *Journal of International and Intercultural Communication* 5, no. 4: 309–28.

Gerber, Theodore P., and Sin Yi Cheung. 2008. "Horizontal Stratification in Postsecondary Education: Forms, Explanations, and Implications." *Annual Review of Sociology* 34: 299–318.

Gilley, Bruce. 2006. "The Meaning and Measure of State Legitimacy: Results for 72 Countries." *European Journal of Political Research* 45, no. 3: 499–525.

Glass, Chris R., Edwin Gómez, and Alfredo Urzua. 2014. "Recreation, Intercultural Friendship, and International Students' Adaptation to College by Region of Origin." *International Journal of Intercultural Relations* 42, no. 5: 104–17.

Gordon, Milton M. 1964. *Assimilation in American Life: The Role of Race, Religion, and National Origins.* Oxford: Oxford University Press on Demand.

Gordon, Virginia N. 1995. *The Undecided College Student: An Academic and Career Advising Challenge.* 2nd. ed. Springfield, IL: Charles C. Thomas.

Grigorenko, Elena L., Linda Jarvin, Weihua Niu, and David Preiss. 2008. "Is There a Standard for Standardized Testing? Four Sketches of the Applicability (Or Lack Thereof) of Standardized Testing in Different Educational Systems." In *Extending Intelligence: Enhancement and New Constructs*, ed. Patrick C. Kyllonen, Richard D. Roberts, and Lazar Stankov, 135–57. New York: Lawrence Erlbaum Associates.

Gu, Yan. 2008. "Chinese Learner: My Lived Experiences of Studying in Mainland China and Australia." *Critical Perspectives on Accounting* 19, no. 2: 217–21. doi: 10.1016/j.cpa.2006.09.006.

Guo, Steve, and Guangchao Feng. 2012. "Understanding Support for Internet Censorship in China: An Elaboration of the Theory of Reasoned Action." *Journal of Chinese Political Science* 17, no. 1: 33–52.

Guthrie, Doug. 2012. *China and Globalization: The Social, Economic, and Political Transformation of Chinese Society.* New York: Routledge.

Hail, Henry Chiu. 2015. "Patriotism Abroad: Overseas Chinese Students' Encounters With Criticisms of China." *Journal of Studies in International Education* 19, no. 4: 311–26.

Hao, Weiqian, Long Zhengzhong, and Zhang Jinfeng. 2011. *The History of Higher Education in the People's Republic of China* (in Chinese). Beijing: New World Press.

Hao, Xue, Kun Yan, Shibao Guo, and Meiling Wang. 2017. "Chinese returnees' motivation, post-return status and impact of return: A systematic review." *Asian and Pacific Migration Journal* 26, no. 1: 143–57.

Haugh, Michael. 2016. "Complaints and Troubles Talk About the English Language Skills of International Students in Australian Universities." *Higher Education Research & Development* 35, no. 4: 727–40.

Hedrick-Wong, Yuwa. 2018. "The Reality of China's Economic Slowdown." *Forbes*, August 23, 2018.

Heng, Tang Tang. 2016. "Different is Not Deficient: Contradicting Stereotypes Around Chinese International Students in U.S. Higher Education." *Studies in Higher Education* 43, no. 1: 1–15.

Heng, Tang Tang. 2017. "Voices of Chinese International Students in USA Colleges: 'I Want to Tell Them That . . .' " *Studies in Higher Education* 42, no. 5, 833–50.

Hira, Ron, 2010. "US Policy and the STEM Workforce System." *American Behavioral Scientist* 53, no. 7: 949–61.

Hofstede, Geert. 2001. *Culture's Consequences: Comparing Values, Behaviors, Institutions, and Organizations Across Nations.* Thousand Oaks, CA: Sage.

Hofstede, Geert, and Gert Jan Hofstede. 1991. *Cultures and Organizations: Software of the Mind.* New York: McGraw-Hill.

Hofstede, Geert, Gert J. Hofstede, and Michael Minkov. 2010. *Cultures and Organizations: Software of the Mind: Intercultural Cooperation and Its Importance for Survival.* New York: McGraw-Hill.

Hong, Miyoung, and Nam-Hwa Kang. 2010. "South Korean and the U.S. Secondary School Science Teachers' Conceptions of Creativity and Teaching for Creativity." *International Journal of Science and Mathematics Education* 8, no. 5: 821–43.

Hong, Ying-yi, Chi-yue Chiu, Carol S. Dweck, Derrick M.-S. Lin, and Wendy Wan. 1999. "Implicit Theories, Attributions, and Coping: A Meaning System Approach." *Journal of Personality and Social Psychology* 77, no. 3: 588.

Hoover-Dempsey, Kathleen, and Howard M. Sandler. 1997. "Why Do Parents Become Involved in Their Children's Education?" *Review of Educational Research* 67, no. 1: 2–42.

Hossain, Mokter, and Michael G. Robinson. 2012. "How to Motivate US Students to Pursue STEM (Science, Technology, Engineering and Mathematics) Careers." *US-China Education Review* 4: 442–51.

Hossler, Don, Emily Chung, Jihye Kwon, Jerry Lucido, Nicholas Bowman, and Michael Bastedo. 2019. "A Study of the Use of Nonacademic Factors in Holistic Undergraduate Admissions Reviews." *Journal of Higher Education* 89, no. 5: 1–27.

Hossler, Don, and Karen S. Gallagher. 1987. "Studying Student College Choice: A Three-Phase Model and the Implications for Policymakers." *College and University* 62, no. 3: 207–21.

Hout, Michael, Adrian E. Raftery, and Eleanor O. Bell. 1993. "Making the Grade: Educational Stratification in the United States, 1925–1989." In *Persistent Inequality: Changing Educational Attainment in Thirteen Countries*, ed. Yossi Shavit and Hans-Peter Blossfeld, 25–50. Boulder, CO: Westview Press.

Hu, Anning, and Xiaogang Wu. 2017. "Science or Liberal Arts? Cultural Capital and College Major Choice in China." *British Journal of Sociology* 70, no. 1: 190–213.

Huang, Shirlena, and Brenda S. A. Yeoh. 2005. "Transnational Families and Their Children's Education: China's 'Study Mothers' in Singapore." *Global Networks* 5, no. 4: 379–400.

Humanities Indicators. 2017. "Bachelor's Degrees in the Humanities." https://humanities indicators.org/content/indicatordoc.aspx?i=34.

Hung, Ho-fung. 2015. *The China Boom: Why China Will Not Rule the World*. New York: Columbia University Press.

Hyun, Jane. 2005. *Breaking the Bamboo Ceiling: Career Strategies for Asians*. New York: Harper Business.

Ibrahim, Tasneem. 2005. "Global Citizenship Education: Mainstreaming the Curriculum?" *Cambridge Journal of Education* 35, no. 2: 177–94.

Institute of Internal Education. 2017. "Economic Impact of International Students." IIE. Accessed July 18, 2019. https://www.iie.org/Research-and-Insights/Open-Doors/Data/Economic-Impact-of-International-Students.

Johanson, Mark. 2016. "Capital—A Lust For Speed: Young, Rich And Chinese In Rural America." *BBC News*, June 8, 2016.

Johnson, Jean M., and Mark C. Regets. 1998. "International Mobility of Scientists and Engineers to the United States: Brain Drain or Brain Circulation?" *SRS Issue Brief*. NSF 98–316. https://www.nsf.gov/statistics/issuebrf/sib98316.htm.

Jorgenson, Shelane, and Lynette Shultz. 2012. "Global Citizenship Education (GCE) in Post-Secondary Institutions: What Is Protected and What Is Hidden Under the Umbrella of GCE." *Journal of Global Citizenship & Equity Education* 2, no. 1: 1–22.

Joseph, Rebecca. 2013. "A Plea to Those Helping Students with College Application Essays: Let the 17-Year-Old Voice Take Center Stage." *Huffington Post*, December 15, 2013. www.huffingtonpost.com/rebecca-joseph/editing-college-application-essays _b_4105569.html.

Karabel, Jerome. 2006. *The Chosen: The Hidden History of Admission and Exclusion at Harvard, Yale, and Princeton*. Boston: Houghton Mifflin Harcourt.

Kariuki, Nick. 2016. "The New Language of American College Sports Is Chinese." *VICE*, March 4, 2016. https://www.vice.com/en_au/article/4xzd7d /the-new-language-of-american-college-sports-is-chinese.

Kaufman, Jason, and Jay Gabler. 2004. "Cultural Capital and the Extracurricular Activities of Girls and Boys in the College Attainment Process." *Poetics* 32, no. 2: 145–68. doi: 10.1016/j.poetic.2004.02.001.

Kim, Hyun J. 1991. "Influence of Language and Similarity on Initial Intercultural Attraction." In *Cross-Cultural Interpersonal Communication*, ed. Stella Tin-Toomey and Felipe Korzenny, 213–29. Newbury Park, CA: Sage.

Kim, Kyung Hee. 2005. "Learning from Each Other: Creativity in East Asian and American Education." *Creativity Research Journal* 17, no. 4: 337–47.

King, Gary, Jennifer Pan, and Margaret E. Roberts. 2013. "How Censorship in China Allows Government Criticism But Silences Collective Expression." *American Political Science Review* 107, no. 2: 326–43.

King, Gary, Jennifer Pan, and Margaret E. Roberts. 2014. "Reverse-Engineering Censorship in China: Randomized Experimentation and Participant Observation." *Science* 345, no. 6199: 1–10.

Kipnis, Andrew B. 2011. *Governing Educational Desire: Culture, Politics, and Schooling in China*. Chicago: University of Chicago Press.

Kudo, Kazuhiro, and Keith A. Simkin. 2003. "Intercultural Friendship Formation: The Case of Japanese Students at an Australian University." *Journal of Intercultural Studies* 24, no. 2: 91–114.

Kuhn, Thomas S. 2012. *The Structure of Scientific Revolutions*. Chicago: University of Chicago Press.

Kujawa, Anthony. 2006. "U.S. Eager to Attract More Foreign Students, Rice Says." Washington File, U.S. Department of State, January 6, 2006. https://wfile.ait.org. tw/wf-archive/2006/060106/epf505.htm.

Kweon, Yesola, and ByeongHwa Choi. 2019. "What Money Can Buy: Perceived Economic Security in China." *Journal of Contemporary China* 28, no. 119: 1–16.

Lamont, Michele, and Annette Lareau. 1988. "Cultural Capital: Allusions, Gaps, and Glissandos in Recent Theoretical Developments." *Sociological Theory* 6, no. 2: 153–68.

Lan, Shanshan. 2019. "State-Mediated Brokerage System in China's Self-Funded Study Abroad Market." *International Migration* 57, no. 3: 266–79.

Lareau, Annette. 2011. *Unequal Childhoods: Class, Race, and Family Life*. Berkeley: University of California Press.

Lee, Jennifer, and Min Zhou. 2015. *The Asian American Achievement Paradox*. New York: Russell Sage Foundation.

Lee, Jenny. J. 2010. "International Students' Experiences and Attitudes at a US Host Institution: Self-Reports and Future Recommendations." *Journal of Research in International Education* 9, no. 1: 66–84.

Lee, Jenny. J. and Charles Rice. 2007. "Welcome to America? Perceptions of Neo-Racism and Discrimination Among International Students." *Higher Education* 53: 381–409.

Lee, Meery, and Reed Larson. 2000. "The Korean 'Examination Hell': Long Hours of Studying, Distress, and Depression." *Journal of Youth and Adolescence* 29, no. 2: 249–71.

LeTendre, Gerald K. 1999. "The Problem of Japan: Qualitative Studies and International Educational Comparisons." *Educational Researcher* 28, no. 2: 38–45.

Levin, Ross, ed. 2009. *The Handbook of Practice and Research in Study Abroad: Higher Education and the Quest for Global Citizenship*. New York: Routledge.

Li, Cheng. 2001. *China's Leaders: The New Generation*. Lanham, MD: Rowman & Littlefield.

Li, Cheng, ed. 2010. *China's Emerging Middle Class: Beyond Economic Transformation.* Washington, DC: Brookings Institution Press.

Li, Fengliang, W. John Morgan, and Xiaohao Ding. 2008. "The Expansion of Higher Education, Employment and Over-Education in China." *International Journal of Educational Development* 28, no. 6: 687–97.

Li, Haizheng Z. 2010. "Higher Education in China: Complement or Competition to US Universities." In *American Universities in a Global Market,* ed. Charles T. Clotfelter, 269–304. Chicago: University of Chicago Press.

Li, Jin. 2012. *Cultural Foundations of Learning: East and West.* Cambridge: Cambridge University Press.

Li, Yao Amber, John Whalley, Shunming Zhang, and Xiliang Zhao. 2012. "The Higher Educational Transformation of China and Its Global Implications." In *The Globalization of Higher Education,* ed. Christine Ennew and David Greenaway, 135–62. London: Palgrave Macmillan.

Liberman, Kenneth. 1994. "Asian Student Perspectives on American University Instruction." *International Journal of Intercultural Relations* 18, no. 2: 173–92.

Lin, Chin-Yau Cindy, and Victoria R. Fu. 1990. "A Comparison of Child-Rearing Practices Among Chinese, Immigrant Chinese, and Caucasian-American Parents." *Child Development* 61, no. 2: 429–33.

Lin, Yu-Sien. 2011. "Fostering Creativity Through Education–a Conceptual Framework of Creative Pedagogy." *Creative Education* 2, no. 3: 149.

Ling, Minhua. 2015. " 'Bad Students Go to Vocational Schools!': Education, Social Reproduction and Migrant Youth in Urban China." *China Journal* 73: 108–31.

Liu, Eric. 1998. *The Accidental Asian: Notes of a Native Speaker.* New York: Vintage.

Liu, Jun. 2002. "Negotiating Silence in American Classrooms: Three Chinese Cases." *Language and Intercultural Communication* 2, no. 1: 37–54.

Liu, Meihua. 2006. "Anxiety in Chinese EFL Students at Different Proficiency Levels." *System* 34, no. 3: 301–16.

Liu, Meihua, and Jane Jackson. 2008. "An Exploration of Chinese EFL Learners' Unwillingness to Communicate and Foreign Language Anxiety." *Modern Language Journal* 92, no. 1: 71–86.

Liu, Ye. 2013. "Meritocracy and the Gaokao: A Survey Study of Higher Education Selection and Socio-Economic Participation in East China." *British Journal of Sociology of Education* 34, nos. 5–6: 868–87.

Liu, Ye. 2016. *Higher Education, Meritocracy, and Inequality in China.* New York: Springer.

Liu, Ye. 2018. When Choices Become Chances: Extending Boudon's Positional Theory to Understand University Choices in Contemporary China. *Comparative Education Review* 62, no. 1: 125–46.

Liu, Yi-Ling. 2015. "China's Nouveau Riche Have Landed on America's Campuses." *Foreign Policy,* September 1, 2015. https://foreignpolicy.com/2015/09/01/chinas-nouveau-riche-have-landed-on-americas-campuses/.

Lockie, Alex. 2018. "Trump Reportedly Considered Banning Chinese Student Visas to Keep Out Spies." *Business Insider,* October 2, 2018.

Loo, Bryce K. 2017. "Community Colleges: An Unexpected On-Ramp for International Students." *World Education News + Reviews*, November 8, 2016.

Louie, Vivian. 2017. "The One-Way Street of Learning and Living Globalization: Chinese MBA Students in American Universities." In *International Students from Asia: Learning and Living Globalization*, ed. Martha A Garcia-Murrilo and Yingyi Ma, 149–71. New York: Springer.

Loveless, Tom. 2006. *The 2006 Brown Center Report on American Education: How Well Are American Students Learning? With Special Sections on the Nation's Achievement, the Happiness Factor in Learning, and Honesty in State Test Scores*. Vol. 2, no. 1. Brookings Institution.

Lowell, B. Lindsay. 2010. "A Long View of America's Immigration Policy and the Supply of Foreign-Born STEM Workers in the United States." *American Behavioral Scientist* 53, no. 7: 1029–44.

Loyalka, P. K. 2009. *Three Essays on Chinese Higher Education After Expansion and Reform: Sorting, Financial Aid and College Selectivity*. PhD thesis. Stanford, CA: Stanford University.

Lu, Chunlei, and Wenchun Han. 2010. "Why Don't They Participate? A Self-Study of Chinese Graduate Students' Classroom Involvement in North America." *Brock Education Journal* 20, no. 1: 80–96.

Lu, Xueyi. 2010. *Research Report on Contemporary China's Social Stratification*. Beijing: Shehui kexue wenxian chubanshe.

Lucas, Samuel R. 2001. "Effectively Maintained Inequality: Education Transitions, Track Mobility, and Social Background Effects." *American Journal of Sociology* 106, no. 6: 1642–90.

Lyman, Stanford M. 2000. "The 'Yellow Peril' Mystique: Origins and Vicissitudes of a Racist Discourse." *International Journal of Politics, Culture, and Society* 13, no. 4: 683–747.

Lyon, Arabella. 2004. "Confucian Silence and Remonstration: A Basis for Deliberation?" In *Rhetoric Before and Beyond the Greeks*, ed. Carol S. Lipton and Robert A. Binkley, 131–45. Albany: State University of New York Press.

Ma, Yingyi. 2009. "Family Socioeconomic Status, Parental Involvement, and College Major Choices: Gender, Race/Ethnic, and Nativity Patterns." *Sociological Perspectives* 52, no. 2: 211–34.

Ma, Yingyi. 2010. "Model Minority, Model for Whom? An Investigation of Asian American Students in Science/Engineering." *AAPI Nexus: Policy, Practice and Community* 8, no. 1: 43–74.

Ma, Yingyi. 2011a. "Chinese Rural Women in Agriculture and Urban Work." *American Review of China Studies* 12, no. 1: 1–12.

Ma, Yingyi. 2011b. "College Major Choice, Occupational Structure, and Demographic Patterning by Gender, Race and Nativity." *Social Science Journal* 48, no. 1: 112–29.

Ma, Yingyi. 2011c. "Gender Differences in the Paths Leading to a STEM Baccalaureate." *Social Sciences Quarterly* 92, no. 5: 1169–90.

Ma, Yingyi. 2014. "Being Chinese Away from China." *China Daily*, August 23, 2014. http://europe.chinadaily.com.cn/opinion/2014-08/23/content_18474098.htm.

Ma, Yingyi. 2015. "Is the Grass Greener on the Other Side of the Pacific?" *Contexts* 14, no. 2: 34–39.

Ma, Yingyi, and Martha A. Garcia-Murillo, eds. 2017. *Understanding International Students from Asia in American Universities: Learning and Living Globalization.* Cham, Switzerland: Springer International.

Ma, Yingyi, and Yan Liu. 2015. "Race and STEM Degree Attainment." *Sociology Compass* 9, no. 7: 609–18.

Ma, Yingyi, and Amy Lutz. 2018. "Jumping on the STEM Train: Differences in Key Milestones in the STEM Pipeline between Children of Immigrants and Natives in the United States." In *Research in the Sociology of Education*, ed. Hyunjoon Park and Grace Kao, 129–54. Bingley, UK: Emerald Publishing.

Ma, Yingyi, and Lifang Wang. 2016. "Fairness in Admission: Voices from Rural Chinese Female Students in Selective Universities in Chinese Mainland." *Frontiers of Education in China* 11, no. 1: 44–73. doi:10.3868/s110-005-016-0003-1.

Marginson, Simon. 2014. "Student Self-Formation in International Education." *Journal of Studies in International Education* 18, no. 1: 6–22.

Marginson, Simon. 2016. "High Participation Systems of Higher Education." *Journal of Higher Education* 87, no. 2: 243–71.

Marginson, Simon, Chris Nyland, Erlenawati Sawir, and Helen Forbes-Mewett. 2010. *International Student Security.* Cambridge: Cambridge University Press.

Marginson, Simon, and Marijk Van der Wende. 2007. "To Rank or to Be Ranked: The Impact of Global Rankings in Higher Education." *Journal of Studies in International Education* 11, nos. 3–4: 306–29.

Matheson, Kathy. 2016 "Basketball Broadcasts at Temple Have an International Flavor." *USA Today*, February 22, 2016. www.usatoday.com/story/sports/ncaab/2016/02/22 /basketball-broadcasts-at-temple-have-an-international-flavor/80727064/.

Maxwell, Claire, and Peter Aggleton. 2016. "Creating Cosmopolitan Subjects: The Role of Families and Private Schools in England." *Sociology* 50, no. 4: 780–95.

McPherson, Miller, Lynn Smith-Lovin, and James M. Cook. 2001. "Birds of a Feather: Homophily in Social Networks." *Annual Review of Sociology* 27, no. 1: 415–44.

Miyazaki, Ichisada. 1981. *China's Examination Hell: The Civil Service Examinations of Imperial China.* New Haven, CT: Yale University Press.

Mooney, Paul. 2006. "Unable to Find Work, 20,000 College Graduates Refuse to Move Out of Dormitories in China." *Chronicle of Higher Education* 52, no. 46: A33.

Morris, Michael W., and Kwok Leung. 2010. "Creativity East and West: Perspectives and Parallels." *Management and Organization Review* 6, no. 3: 313–27.

Niu, Weihua. 2007. "Western Influence on Chinese Educational Testing System." *Comparative Education* 43, no. 1: 71–91. doi: 10.1080/03050060601162412.

Noddings, Nel. 2005. "What Does It Mean to Educate the Whole Child?" *Educational Leadership* 63, no. 1: 8–13.

Nussbaum, Martha C. 1997. "Kant and Stoic Cosmopolitanism." *Journal of Political Philosophy* 5, no. 1: 1–25.

Nussbaum, Martha. 2002. "Education for Citizenship in an Era of Global Connection." *Studies in Philosophy and Education* 21, no. 4–5: 289–303.

Nye, Joseph S. 2005a. "The Rise of China's Soft Power." *Wall Street Journal*, December 29, 2005.

Nye, Joseph. 2005b. "Soft Power and Higher Education." *Forum for the Future of Higher Education.* Accessed July 18, 2019. http://forum.mit.edu/articles/soft-power -and-higher-education/.

Oakes, Jeannie. 2005. *Keeping Track: How Schools Structure Inequality*. New Haven, CT: Yale University Press.

Oakes, Jeannie, and Gretchen Guiton. 1995. "Matchmaking: The Dynamics of High School Tracking Decisions." *American Educational Research Journal* 32, no. 1: 3–33.

Ogbu, John U. and Herbert D. Simons. 1998. "Voluntary and Involuntary Minorities: A Cultural-Ecological Theory of School Performance with Some Implications for Education." *Anthropology & Education Quarterly* 29, no. 2: 155–88.

Ong, Aihwa. 1999. *Flexible Citizenship: The Cultural Logics of Transnationality*. Durham, NC: Duke University Press.

Osburg, John. 2013. *Anxious Wealth: Money and Morality among China's New Rich*. Palo Alto, CA: Stanford University Press.

Osnos, Evan. 2014. *Age of Ambition: Chasing Fortune, Truth, and Faith in the New China*. New York: Farrar, Straus, and Giroux.

Ostrove, Joan M. 2003. "Belonging and Wanting: Meanings of Social Class Background for Women's Constructions of Their College Experiences." *Journal of Social Issues* 59, no. 4: 771–84.

Oxfam. 1997. *A Curriculum for Global Citizenship*. Oxford: Author.

Oxley, Laura, and Paul Morris. 2013. "Global Citizenship: A Typology for Distinguishing Its Multiple Conceptions." *British Journal of Educational Studies* 61, no. 3: 301–25.

Park, Hyunjoon. 2013. *Re-Evaluating Education in Japan and Korea: Demystifying Stereotypes*. London: Routledge.

Paulhus, Delroy L., Jacqueline H. Duncan, and Michelle S. M. Yik. 2002. "Patterns of Shyness in East-Asian and European-Heritage Students." *Journal of Research in Personality* 36, no. 5: 442–62.

Peck, Kaitlin. 2014. "The Impact of Academic Exchange between China and the U.S., 1979–2010." *Psi Sigma Siren* 8, no 1: article 4.

Perez, William, Roberta Espinoza, Karina Ramos, Heidi M. Coronado, and Richard Cortes. 2009. "Academic Resilience Among Undocumented Latino Students." *Hispanic Journal of Behavioral Sciences* 31, no. 2: 149–81.

Perna, Laura W. 2006. "Studying College Access and Choice: A Proposed Conceptual Model." In *Higher Education: Handbook of Theory and Research*, vol. 21, ed. John C. Smart, 99–157. Dordrecht, The Netherlands: Springer.

Perry, William G. 1970. *Forms of Intellectual and Ethical Development in the College Years: A Scheme*. New York: Holt, Rinehart and Winston.

Perry, William G. 1981. "Cognitive and Ethical Growth: The Making of Meaning." In *The Modern American College*, ed. Arthur W. Chickering, 76–116. San Francisco: Jossey-Bass.

Pitt, Richard N., and Steven A. Tepper. 2012. "Double Majors: Influences, Identities, and Impacts." Prepared for the Teagle Foundation, Curb Center, Vanderbilt University.

Pokorney, Therese. 2018. "Chinese Student Enrollment Declines." *Daily Illini*, September 17, 2018.

Porter, Christian, Craig Hart, Chongming Yang, Clyde Robinson, Susanne Frost Olsen, and Qing Zeng. 2005. "A Comparative Study of Child Temperament and Parenting in Beijing, China, and the Western United States." *International Journal of Behavioral Development* 29, no. 6: 541–51.

Purdue Center on Religion and Chinese Society. 2018. Purdue Survey of Chinese Students and Scholars in the United States: A General Report. https://www.purdue.edu/crcs/wp-content/uploads/2018/10/2018-Purdue-Survey-Report_Rev.pdf

Qing, Koh Gui, Alexandra Harney, Steve Stecklow, and James Pomfret. 2016. "How an Industry Helps Chinese Students Cheat Their Way Into and Through US Colleges." *Reuters*, May 25, 2016. https://www.reuters.com/investigates/special-report/college-cheating-iowa/.

Redden, Elizabeth. 2015. "In China, No Choice But to Cheat." *Inside Higher Ed* https://www.insidehighered.com/news/2015/07/09/admissions-process-broken-chinese-students.

Redden, Elizabeth. 2018a. "International Student Numbers Decline." *Inside Higher Ed*, January 22, 2018. https://www.insidehighered.com/news/2018/01/22/nsf-report-documents-declines-international-enrollments-after-years-growth.

Redden, Elizabeth. 2018b. "New International Enrollments Decline Again." *Inside Higher Ed*, November 13, 2018. https://www.insidehighered.com/news/2018/11/13/new-international-student-enrollments-continue-decline-us-universities.

Reginfo.gov. 2018. "Practical Training Reform." U.S. General Services Administration, Spring 2018. https://www.reginfo.gov/public/do/eAgendaViewRule?pubId=201804&RIN=1653-AA76.

Resnik, Julia. 2012. "The Denationalization of Education and the Expansion of the International Baccalaureate." *Comparative Education Review* 56, no. 2: 248–69.

Richardson, R., ed. 1979. *Learning for Change in World Society*. London: World Studies Project.

Riegle-Crumb, Catherine, and Barbara King. 2010. "Questioning a White Male Advantage in STEM: Examining Disparities in College Major by Gender and Race/Ethnicity." *Educational Researcher* 39, no. 9: 656–64.

Rimer, Sara. 2008. "Math Skills Suffer in U.S., Study Finds." *New York Times*, October 10, 2008. https://www.nytimes.com/2008/10/10/education/10math.html.

Rose-Redwood, CindyAnn R., and Reuben S. Rose-Redwood. 2013. "Self-segregation or Global Mixing?: Social Interactions and the International Student Experience." *Journal of College Student Development* 54, no. 4: 413–29.

Ruble, Racheal A., and Yan Bing Zhang. 2013. "Stereotypes of Chinese International Students Held by Americans." *International Journal of Intercultural Relations* 37, no. 2: 202–11.

Rui, Yang. 2014. "China's Removal of English from Gaokao." *International Higher Education* 75: 12–13.

Ruiz, Neil G. 2016. *The Geography of Foreign Students in U.S. Higher Education: Origins and Destinations*. Washington, DC: Brookings.

Russikof, Karen, Liliane Fucaloro, and Dalia Salkauskiene. 2013. "Plagiarism as a Cross-cultural Phenomenon." *The CAL Poly Pomona Journal of Interdisciplinary Studies* 16: 109–20.

Salisbury, Mark H., Brian P. An, and Ernest T. Pascarella. 2013. "The Effect of Study Abroad on Intercultural Competence Among Undergraduate College Students." *Journal of Student Affairs Research and Practice* 50, no. 1: 1–20.

Sauder, Michael, and Wendy Nelson Espeland. 2009. "The Discipline of Rankings: Tight Coupling and Organizational Change." *American Sociological Review* 74, no. 1: 63–82.

Sawir, Erlenawati, Simon Marginson, Ana Deumert, Chris Nyland, and Gaby Ramia. 2008. "Loneliness and International Students: An Australian Study." *Journal of Studies in International Education* 12, no. 2: 148–80.

Sax, Linda J., Shannon K. Gilmartin, and Alyssa N. Bryant. 2003. "Assessing Response Rates and Nonresponse Bias in Web and Paper Surveys." *Research in Higher Education* 44, no. 4: 409–32.

Saxenian, AnnaLee. 2005. "From Brain Drain to Brain Circulation: Transnational Communities and Regional Upgrading in India and China." *Comparative International Development* 40, no. 2: 35–61.

Schulte, Barbara. 2017. "Private Schools in the People's Republic of China: Development, Modalities and Contradictions." In *Private Schools and School Choice in Compulsory Education: Global Change and National Challenge*, ed. Thomas Koinzer, Rita Nikolai, and Florian Waldow, 115–31. Wiesbaden: Springer.

Scott-Clayton, Judith, Peter M. Crosta, and Clive R. Belfield. 2012. "Improving and Targeting of Treatment: Evidence from College Remediation." National Bureau of Economic Research, working paper no. 18457 (October). https://www.nber.org/papers/w18457.

Searle, Wendy, and Colleen Ward. 1990. "The Prediction of Psychological and Socio-cultural Adjustment During Cross-Cultural Transitions." *International Journal of Intercultural Relations* 14, no. 4: 449–64. doi:10.1016/0147-1767(90)90030-Z.

Semotiuk, Andy. 2018. "International Students Pour into Canada While the U.S. And Others Lag Behind." *Forbes*, November 16, 2018.

Semotiuk, Andy. 2019. "Recent Changes to the H1B Visa Program and What Is Coming in 2019." *Forbes*, January 2, 2019. https://www.forbes.com/sites/andyj semotiuk/2019/01/02/recent-changes-to-the-h1b-visa-program-and-what-is -coming-in-2019/#7b36e7e44a81.

Seymour, Elaine. 2000. *Talking About Leaving: Why Undergraduates Leave the Sciences*. Boulder, CO: Westview Press.

Shavit, Yossi, and Hans-Peter Blossfeld. 1993. *Persistent Inequality: Changing Educational Attainment in Thirteen Countries*. Boulder, CO: Westview Press.

Shen, Wei. 2008. "International Student Migration: The Case of Chinese 'Sea-Turtles.'" In *World Yearbook of Education 2008*, ed. Debbie Epstein, Rebecca Boden, Rosemary Deem, Fazal Rizvi, and Susan Wright, 211–31. New York: Routledge.

Shen, Xiaoxiao, and Kellee S. Tsai. 2016. "Institutional Adaptability in China: Local Developmental Models Under Changing Economic Conditions." *World Development* 87: 107–27.

Soong, Hannah. 2016. *Transnational Students and Mobility: Lived Experiences of Migration*. London: Routledge.

Soong, Hannah, Garth Stahl, and Hongxia Shan. 2018. "Transnational Mobility Through Education: A Bourdieusian Insight on Life as Middle Transnationals in Australia and Canada." *Globalisation, Societies, and Education* 16, no. 2: 241–53.

Steele, Liza G., and Scott M. Lynch. 2013. "The Pursuit of Happiness in China: Individualism, Collectivism, and Subjective Well-Being During China's Economic and Social Transformation." *Social Indicators Research* 114, no. 2: 441–51.

Stevens, Mitchell L. 2009. *Creating a Class: College Admissions and the Education of Elites*. Cambridge, MA: Harvard University Press.

Stevenson, Harold, and James W. Stigler. 1994. *Learning Gap: Why Our Schools Are Failing and What We Can Learn from Japanese and Chinese Education*. New York: Simon and Schuster.

Storer, Norman W. 1967. "The Hard Sciences and the Soft: Some Sociological Observations." *Bulletin of the Medical Library Association* 55: 75–84.

Storer, Norman W. 1972. "Relations Among Scientific Disciplines." In *The Social Contexts of Research*, ed. Saad Z. Nagi and Ronald G. Corwin, 229–68. New York: Wiley Interscience.

Sue, David., Sue M. Diane, and Steve Ino. 1990. "Assertiveness and Social Anxiety in Chinese-American Women." *Journal of Psychology* 124, no. 2: 155–63.

Suen, Hoi K., and Lan Yu. 2006. "Chronic Consequences of High Stakes Testing? Lessons from the Chinese Civil Service Exam." *Comparative Education Review* 50, no. 1: 46–65. doi: 10.1086/498328.

Tang, Joyce. 2000. *Doing Engineering: The Career Attainment and Mobility of Caucasian, Black, and Asian-American Engineers*. Lanham, MD: Rowman & Littlefield.

Taylor, Keeanga-Yamahtta. 2016. *From #BlackLivesMatter to Black Liberation*. Chicago: Haymarket.

Thomas, Susan. 2017. "The Precarious Path of Student Migrants: Education, Debt, and Transnational Migration Among Indian Youth." *Journal of Ethnic and Migration Studies* 43, no. 11: 1873–89.

Thornton, Arland, and Thomas E. Fricke. 1987. "Social Change and the Family: Comparative Perspectives from the West, China, and South Asia." *Sociological Forum* 2, no. 4: 746–79.

Times Higher Education. 2018. "World University Rankings." Accessed April 9, 2018. https://www.timeshighereducation.com/world-university-rankings/2018/world-ranking#!/page/0/length/25/sort_by/rank/sort_order/asc/cols/stats.

Ting-Toomey, Stella. 1989. "Identity and Interpersonal Bonding." In *Handbook of International and Intercultural Communication*, ed. Molefi Kete Asante and William B. Gudykunst, 351–73. Newbury Park, CA: Sage.

Tinto, Vincent. 1987. *Leaving College: Rethinking the Causes and Cures of Student Attrition*. Chicago: University of Chicago Press.

Tong, Yanqi. 2011. "Morality, Benevolence, and Responsibility: Regime Legitimacy in China from Past to the Present." *Journal of Chinese Political Science* 16, no. 2: 141–59.

Trice, Andrea G. 2004. "Mixing It Up: International Graduate Students' Social Interactions with American Students." *Journal of College Student Development* 45, no. 6: 671–87.

Trice, Andrea G. 2007. "Faculty Perspectives Regarding Graduate International Students' Isolation from Host National Students." *International Education Journal* 8, no. 1: 108–17.

Trow, Martin A. 1973. *Problems in the Transition from Elite to Mass Higher Education*. Berkeley, CA: Carnegie Commission on Higher Education.

Tsui, Amy B. M. 1996. "Reticence and Anxiety in Second Language Learning." In *Voices from the Language Classroom*, ed. Kathleen M. Bailey and David Nunan, 145–67. Cambridge: Cambridge University Press.

Tuan, Mia. 1998. *Forever Foreigners or Honorary Whites?: the Asian Ethnic Experience Today*. Rutgers University Press.

Tucker, Marc S. 2011. *Surpassing Shanghai: An Agenda for American Education Built on the World's Leading Systems*. Cambridge, MA: Harvard Education Press.

Turner, Yvonne. 2006. "Students from Mainland China and Critical Thinking in Postgraduate Business and Management Degrees: Teasing Out Tensions of Culture, Style, and Substance." *International Journal of Management Education* 5, no. 1: 3–11.

Tyre, Peg. 2016. "How Sophisticated Test Scams From China Are Making Their Way into the U.S." *Atlantic*, March 21, 2016. https://www.theatlantic.com/education/archive/2016/03/how-sophisticated-test-scams-from-china-are-making-their-way-into-the-us/474474/.

U.S. Citizenship and Immigration Services. 2017. "Buy American and Hire American." https://www.uscis.gov/legal-resources/buy-american-hire-american-putting-american-workers-first.

U.S. Citizenship and Immigration Services. 2019. "H-1B Fiscal Year (FY) 2019 Cap Season." https://www.uscis.gov/working-united-states/temporary-workers/h-1b-specialty-occupations-and-fashion-models/h-1b-fiscal-year-fy-2018-cap-season.

U.S. Department of State. 2005. "U.S. Extends Visa Validity for Chinese Students and Exchange Visitors." June 15, 2005. https://2001-2009.state.gov/r/pa/prs/ps/2005/47974.htm.

Wacker, Gudrun. 2003. "The Internet and Censorship in China: Gudrun Wacker." In *China and the Internet*, ed. Christopher R. Hughes and Gudrun Wacker, 70–94. London: Routledge.

Wallerstein, Immanuel. 2011. *The Modern World-System I: Capitalist Agriculture and the Origins of the European World-Economy in the Sixteenth Century, with a New Prologue.* Vol. 1. Berkeley: University of California Press.

Wang, Feng. 2008. *Boundaries and Categories: Rising Inequality in Post-Socialist Urban China.* Stanford, CA: Stanford University Press.

Wang, Feng. 2016. "China's Population Destiny: The Looming Crisis." *Brookings,* July 28, 2016.

Wang, Xiang. 2016. "Why a Trump Crackdown on Visa Programs Would Benefit Foreign Students." *Forbes,* December 1, 2016. https://www.forbes.com/sites/xiangwang/2016/12/01/why-a-trump-crackdown-on-visa-programs-could-benefit-foreign-students/#7dd3ac49e0ac.

Wank, David L. 1996. "The Institutional Process of Market Clientelism: Guanxi and Private Business in a South China City." *China Quarterly* 147: 820–38.

Waters, Johanna L. 2005. "Transnational Family Strategies and Education in the Contemporary Chinese Diaspora." *Global Networks* 5, no. 4: 359–377.

Waters, Johanna L. 2007. " 'Roundabout Routes and Sanctuary Schools': the Role of Situated Educational Practices and Habitus in the Creation of Transnational Professionals." *Global Networks* 7, no. 4: 477–97.

Wederman, Andrew. 2004. "The Intensification of Corruption in China." *China Quarterly* 180: 895–921.

Wedeman, Andrew. 2012. *Double Paradox: Rapid Growth and Rising Corruption in China.* Ithaca, NY: Cornell University Press.

Weenink, Don. 2008. "Cosmopolitanism as a Form of Capital: Parents Preparing their Children for a Globalizing World." *Sociology* 42, no. 6: 1089–106.

Wei, Meifen, Puncky P. Heppner, Michael J. Mallen, Tsun-Yao Ku, Kelly Yu-Hsin Liao, and Tsui-Feng Wu. 2007. "Acculturative Stress, Perfectionism, Years in the United States, and Depression Among Chinese International Students." *Journal of Counseling Psychology* 54, no. 4: 385.

Weisberg, Robert W. 1993. *Creativity: Beyond the Myth of Genius.* New York: W. H. Freeman.

Whyte, Martin King, ed. 2010. *One Country, Two Societies: Rural-Urban Inequality in Contemporary China.* Cambridge, MA: Harvard University Press.

Will, Nancy Li. 2016. "From Isolation to Inclusion: Learning of the Experiences of Chinese International Students in US." *Journal of International Students* 6, no. 4: 1069–75.

Wong, Alia. 2018. "Should America's Universities Stop Taking So Many International Students?" *Atlantic,* June 28, 2018. https://www.theatlantic.com/education/archive/2018/06/international-students/563942/.

Wright, Kevin B. 2005. "Researching Internet-Based Populations: Advantages and Disadvantages of Online Survey Research, Online Questionnaire Authoring Software Packages, and Web Survey Services." *Journal of Computer-Mediated Communication* 10, no. 3: JCMC1034.

Wu, Cary, and Rima Wilkes. 2017. "International Students' Post-Graduation Migration Plans and the Search for Home." *Geoforum* 80: 123–32.

Wu, Qi. 2015. "Re-Examining the 'Chinese Learner': A Case Study of Mainland Chinese Students' Learning Experiences at British Universities." *Higher Education* 70, no. 4: 753–66. doi:10.1007/s10734-015-9865-y.

Wu, Wendy. 2018. "US Voids 10-Year Multiple-Entry Visas for Some Chinese Researchers." *South China Morning Post*, November 22, 2018.

Wu, Xiaogang, and Zhuoni Zhang. 2010. "Changes in Educational Inequality in China, 1990–2005: Evidence from the Population Census Data." In *Globalization, Changing Demographics, and Educational Challenges in East Asia*, ed. Emily Hannum, Hyunjoon Park, and Yuko Goto Butler, 123–152. Bingley, UK: Emerald Group Publishing.

Wu, Xiaogang. 2010. "Economic Transition, School Expansion and Educational Inequality in China, 1990–2000." *Research in Social Stratification and Mobility* 28, no. 1: 91–108.

Wu, Xiaoxin. 2012. "School Choice with Chinese Characteristics." *Comparative Education* 48, no. 3: 347–66.

Xiang, Biao. 2007. *Global "Body Shopping": An Indian Labor System in the Information Technology Industry*. Princeton, NJ: Princeton University Press.

Xu, Xiaoqiu. 2006. "The Dilemma of Chinese Students in America: To Return or Stay?" Unpublished MA thesis, University of Southern California.

Xu Xinchen. 2018. "What Does It Take to Get into China's Top Unversities?" *China Global Television Network* (CGTN), June 9, 2018. https://news.cgtn.com/news/3d 3d674e7841444d78457a6333566d54/share_p.html

Xu, Xueyang, Zhuoqing Morley Mao, and John A. Halderman. 2011. "Internet Censorship in China: Where Does the Filtering Occur?" In *International Conference on Passive and Active Network Measurement*, 133–42. Berlin: Springer.

Xuetong, Yan. 2006. "The Rise of China and Its Power Status." *Chinese Journal of International Politics* 1, no. 1: 5–33.

Yan, Kun, and David C. Berliner. 2011. "Chinese International Students in the United States: Demographic Trends, Motivations, Acculturation Features, and Adjustment Challenges." *Asia Pacific Education Review* 12, no. 2: 173–84.

Yan, Min. 2010. *The History of Sociology in China* [in Chinese]. Tsinghua University Press. Beijing, China.

Yeung, Wei-Jun Jean. 2013. "Higher Education Expansion and Social Stratification in China." *Chinese Sociological Review* 45, no. 4: 54–80.

Young, Natalie A. E. 2017. "Departing from the Beaten Path: International Schools in China as a Response to Discrimination and Academic Failure in the Chinese Educational System." *Comparative Education* 54, no. 2: 159–80. doi:10.1080/03050 068.2017.1360566.

Yu, Xie, and Alexandra A. Killewald. 2012. *Is American Science in Decline?* Cambridge, MA: Harvard University Press.

Yuan, Wenli. 2011 "Academic and Cultural Experiences of Chinese Students at an American University: A Qualitative Study." *Intercultural Communication Studies* 20, no. 1, 141–57.

Yum, June Ock. 1988 "The Impact of Confucianism on Interpersonal Relationships and Communication Patterns in East Asia." *Communications Monographs* 55, no. 4: 374–88.

Zakaria, Fareed. 2008. *The Post-American World*. New York: Norton.

Zane, Nolan W., Stanley Sue, Li-tze Hu, and Jung-hye Kwon. 1991. "Asian-American Assertion: A Social Learning Analysis of Cultural Differences." *Journal of Counseling Psychology* 38, no. 1: 63–70.

Zanten, Agnès van. 2015. "Introduction: Educating Elites: The Changing Dynamics and Meanings of Privilege and Power." In *World Yearbook of Education 2015: Elites, Privilege and Excellence: The National and Global Redefinition of Educational Advantage*, ed. Agnès van Zanten, Stephen J. Ball, and Brigitte Darchy-Koechlin, 3–12. London: Routledge.

Zemach-Bersin, Talya. 2007. "Global Citizenship and Study Abroad: It's All About US." *Critical Literacy: Theories and Practices* 1, no. 2: 16–28.

Zhang, Gaoming, Yong Zhao, and Jing Lei. 2012. "Between a Rock and a Hard Place: Higher Education Reform and Innovation in China." *On the Horizon* 20, no. 4: 263–73.

Zhang, Hongliang, and Haifeng Li. 2012. "Ways Out of the Crisis Behind Bribegate for Chinese Doctors." *Lancet*, January 21, 2012.

Zhao, Chun-Mei, George D. Kuh, and Robert M. Carini. 2005. "A Comparison of International Student and American Student Engagement in Effective Educational Practices." *Journal of Higher Education* 76, no. 2: 209–231.

Zhao, Tianshu, and Jill Bourne. 2011. "Intercultural Adaptation—It Is a Two-Way Process: Examples from a British MBA Programme." In *Researching Chinese Learners: Skills, Perceptions, and Intercultural Adaptations*, ed. Lixian Jin and Martin Cortazzi, 250–73. New York: Palgrave MacMillan.

Zhao, Yong. 2007. "Education in the Flat World: Implications of Globalization on Education." *Edge Magazine (Phi Delta Kappa International)* 2, no. 4: 1–19.

Zhao, Yong. 2009. *Catching Up or Leading the Way: American Education in the Age of Globalization*. Alexandria, VA: ASCD.

Zhou, Min. 2009. *Contemporary Chinese America: Immigration, Ethnicity, and Community Transformation*. Philadelphia PA: Temple University Press.

Zhou, Min, and James V. Gatewood, eds. 2007. *Contemporary Asian America: A Multidisciplinary Reader*. New York: NYU Press.

Zuckerman, Harriet, and Robert K. Merton. 1971. "Patterns of Evaluation in Science: Institutionalization, Structure, and Function of the Referee System." *Minerva* 9: 66–100.

Zweig, David, Siu Fung Chung, and Wilfried Vanhonacker. 2006. "Rewards of Technology: Explaining China's Reverse Migration." *Journal of International Migration and Integration* 7, no. 4: 449–71.

Index

Page numbers in *italics* represent figures or tables.

college major choices: American
contrasted with Chinese students,
137–42, *138*, 159; change in,
experience with, 157–58; in China,
11, 137–40, *138*; creativity and, 82–84;
cultural capital role in, 140–42,
145, 233, 238; double majoring
in, 155–57, 159; family networks
influence on, 154; for first-generation
college students, 146, *147*, 152, 159;
future plans to return or stay and,
146, *148*, 148–50, *149*, 159, 210–11,
211, 212, *213*; Gaokao role in, 137;
gender role in, 145–46, *146*, 148,
149, 159; idealism fueling, 151–52;
institutional type role in, 146, *147*,
148, *149*, 159, *159*, 235; parental
education and, 146, *147*, 152, 159;
parental influence on, 152–54, 159;
for politicians in China and U.S.
compared, 139; practical and financial
impetus for, 149–51, 159, 233;
pragmatic collectivism contrasted
with expressive individualism in, 7,
24, 142–45, 233, 237; ROI and debt
to parents influencing, 145, 150–51,
238; SES and privilege role in,
135–37, 140–42, 159, 237–38; social
contexts for, 137–42; theoretical
implications on, 237–38; U.S. labor
market role in, 148, 155. *See also*
business major; humanities major;
science, technology, engineering, and
mathematics
Colorado State University, 47
Columbia University, 217
Confucianism: on authority questioning,
168–69; in speech anxieties, role of,
167–69, 173
corruption, Chinese, 13, 25, 174, 219,
220, 221–22
cosmopolitan capital: cultural capital
and, 36, 42, 233; defining, 42; global

citizenship and, 186; in study abroad
reasons, 36–37, 42–45, 52
cramming/cram lessons, 75, 181, 231
creativity: American education system
promotion of, 80–84; Chinese
education system approach to, 79, 83;
college major choices and, 82–84;
multiple perspective and, 81–82;
student reflections on, 24, 81–84, 232
critical thinking: American education
promotion of, 84–89, 108, 197,
203, 232; dualist to multiplistic to
relativistic thinking with, 85–86, 232;
process over outcome emphasis in,
87–89; student reflections on, 24,
79, 84–89, 232; truth-seeking and
challenging authority aspects of,
86–87
cultural barriers: in admissions/
application process, 7, 9, 60–61,
62, 174; neoracism and, 115; social
integration issues with, 7, 113–14,
119–21, 133; in speech/speaking up
anxieties, 5–6, 7, 167–72, 180, 181,
232; in U.S. labor market, 217–18.
See also language barriers
cultural capital: Chinese international
divisions in public schools selectivity
on, 58; Chinese international
students loss of, 141–42, 233, 238,
243–44; in college major choices,
role of, 140–42, 145, 233, 238;
cosmopolitan capital and, 36, 42,
233; defining, 58; social reproduction
and, 6–7; STEM majors and, 140–42;
transnational mobility and loss of,
243–44
Cultural Foundations of Learning (Li), 167
Cultures and Organizations (Hofstede and
Hofstede), 79, 120

debt to parents, financial and
emotional, 6, 219; college major

race: achievement gap and, 196; race
relations and, 188
racism, 164, 188–89. *See also* neoracism
rankings: American universities and, 36;
Chinese universities and, 4, 29–30;
college choice influenced by, 5, 7,
21, 24, 28, 45–49, *46*, 51, 61, 216–17,
235, 236, 237; cultural rationales
behind adherence to, 48–49; family
networks influence over, 50, 51;
hyper-focus on, impact of, 61, 71,
76–77, 237; student reflections
on, 47; student transfers based on,
47–48; test-oriented education and
preoccupation with, 49
Reevaluating Education in Japan and Korea
(Park), 80–81
research universities. *See* institutional type
return on investment (ROI): college
major choice influenced by, 145,
150–51, 238; in future plans to stay or
return, 222–24
rural America, disillusionment with, 111,
118–19, 133, 220, 233, 238
rural China: socioeconomic divide
between urban and, 13–14, 21, 38,
118; study population from, 21

San Diego State University, 47
SAT: Chinese private schools
negotiations on, 75; Chinese public
school international divisions
negotiations on, 47; Gaokao
opportunities compared with, 32–33;
Gaokao scores in lieu of, 252n1;
preparation and anxiety with taking,
59, 60; requirements, 54, 252n1
Sauder, Michael, 45
Saxenian, AnnaLee, 209
school rankings. *See* rankings
Schulte, Barbara, 73
science, technology, engineering, and
mathematics (STEM): change from

major in, 157–58; Chinese culture
promotion and strengths in, 7, 24,
83–84, 99–102, 137–40, *138*; Chinese
international students in, 100–102,
101, 138–42, *141*, 146, *147*, *148*, 148–50,
153–54, 157, 159, 210–11, *211*, *212*, *213*,
233; cultural capital and choice of,
140–42; effort-based learning impact
for, 91, *92*, 97–101, 108, 233–34; future
plans factors for choice of, 146, *148*,
148, 210–11, *211*, *212*, *213*; gender and
choice of, 139, 146, *146*, 148, 156–58;
global statistics on enrollment in,
97, *98*; immigrant children choosing,
139; Obama on importance of, 97;
U.S. enrollment in, 97, *98*, 135–36,
138, 159; visa policies for students of,
205, 223, 226
selective institutions. *See* institutional
type
SES. *See* socioeconomic status
Smith College, 104
social change in China, transformative:
Chinese students understood in
light of, 10, 12–13; class divisions
increasing with, 38; future plans
and rationales impacted by, 227–28,
230; history and statistics of, 11–12;
middle class expansion and impacts
with, 6–7, 12–14, 38–39, 41, 51, 229–30,
244; study abroad culture and, 12–13,
229–30, 244
social class. *See* middle class expansion
in China; privilege; socioeconomic
status
social inequalities: intergenerational
transmission of, 37–42; transnational
mobility impact on, 13–14; urban-
rural divide in China, 13–14, 21,
38, 118
social integration: American high
school and, 122, *123*, 125, *125*, 127–29;
American "imagined community"

urban-rural divide: American
  disillusionment and, 111, 118–19,
  133, 220, 233, 238; social inequalities
  with, 13–14, 21, 38, 118; survey data
  indications of, *20*, 21, 118

Vanderbilt University, 32, 116, 172, 189
visa policies, U.S.: under Bush, 14, 205;
  future plans to stay or return and,
  2, 205–7, 209, 213–14, 223–24, 226,
  239; H-1B, 205–6, 213–14, 223; under
  Obama, 15, 205–6; OPT, 205–6, 209,
  223–24, 226; for STEM students,
  205, 223, 226; transnational mobility
  under, 206–7, 226; under Trump,
  15, 206, 213–14; after World Trade
  Center attacks, 14–15

Wallenstein, Immanuel, 207–8
Washington University, 214
Waters, Johanna, 7
Weenink, Don, 42
well-rounded education, 27, 40
Wharton School of Business, 217,
  225–26
working class, 12, 38, 41, 51, 223
World-System Theory, 207–8
World Trade Center attacks, 14–15
Wu, Xiaogang, 140

Yu Xie, 97–98

Zhao, Yong, 83
Zhejiang University, 36, 44
Zhou, Min, 89